Date Loaned

INTERGROUP RELATIONS
IN TEACHER EDUCATION

COUNCIL ON COOPERATION IN TEACHER EDUCATION

AMERICAN ASSOCIATION OF COLLEGES FOR TEACHER EDUCATION

AMERICAN ASSOCIATION OF SCHOOL ADMINISTRATORS

ASSOCIATION FOR CHILDHOOD EDUCATION

ASSOCIATION FOR STUDENT TEACHING

ASSOCIATION FOR SUPERVISION AND CURRICULUM DEVELOPMENT

ASSOCIATION OF AMERICAN COLLEGES

DEPARTMENT OF CLASSROOM TEACHERS OF THE
NATIONAL EDUCATION ASSOCIATION

DEPARTMENT OF ELEMENTARY SCHOOL PRINCIPALS OF THE
NATIONAL EDUCATION ASSOCIATION

EASTERN STATES ASSOCIATION OF PROFESSIONAL
SCHOOLS FOR TEACHERS

NATIONAL ASSOCIATION OF BUSINESS TEACHER-TRAINING INSTITUTIONS

NATIONAL ASSOCIATION OF SCHOOLS OF MUSIC

NATIONAL ASSOCIATION OF SECONDARY-SCHOOL PRINCIPALS

NATIONAL ASSOCIATION OF STATE DIRECTORS OF
TEACHER EDUCATION AND CERTIFICATION

NATIONAL COMMISSION ON TEACHER EDUCATION AND PROFESSIONAL
STANDARDS OF THE NATIONAL EDUCATION ASSOCIATION

NATIONAL COUNCIL OF CHIEF STATE SCHOOL OFFICERS

NATIONAL INSTITUTIONAL TEACHER PLACEMENT ASSOCIATION

NATIONAL LEAGUE OF TEACHERS ASSOCIATION

NATIONAL SOCIETY OF COLLEGE TEACHERS OF EDUCATION

NORTH CENTRAL ASSOCIATION OF COLLEGES AND SECONDARY SCHOOLS

STUDENT PERSONNEL ASSOCIATION FOR TEACHER EDUCATION

Executive Committee

KARL W. BIGELOW, *Chairman*, Delegate-at-Large
WILLIS E. DUGAN, Student Personnel Association for Teacher Education
EDGAR FULLER, National Council of Chief State School Officers
CHARLES W. HUNT, American Association of Colleges for Teacher Education
MARGARET LINDSEY, Association for Student Teaching
CHARLES D. LUTZ, American Association of School Administrators
WILLIAM W. WHITEHOUSE, Association of American Colleges

Intergroup Relations in Teacher Education

An Analytical Study of Intergroup Education in Colleges and Schools in the United States: Functions, Current Expressions, and Improvements

LLOYD ALLEN COOK

Director, College Study in Intergroup Relations and Chairman, Department of Educational Sociology Wayne University

AMERICAN COUNCIL ON EDUCATION

98502

Intergroup Relations in Teacher Education is the second volume in a two-volume report on the College Study in Intergroup Relations. The present book, unlike Volume I, *College Programs in Intergroup Relations* (descriptive of concrete programs), uses data from the College Study but is not confined to this source. The Study was a project of the Council on Cooperation in Teacher Education of the American Council on Education. It was financed during the four years of field work and the year of writing by a grant from the National Conference of Christians and Jews, 381 Fourth Avenue, New York, N.Y.

Foreword

This book has grown out of the first comparative effort in the United States to improve teacher education in respect to intergroup relations. It is the second volume of a two-volume report. The first, *College Programs in Intergroup Relations,* was published by the American Council on Education in 1950. It provided an account by twenty-four college committees of concrete studies, projects, and activities, plus some orientation and analysis by the editor, Lloyd Allen Cook. In the present book Dr. Cook, who served as the national director of the College Study in Intergroup Relations, has undertaken a systematic treatment of problems of intergroup relations with special reference to teacher education. The two volumes are complementary and should be read and studied together.

The College Study in Intergroup Relations was sponsored by the Council on Cooperation in Teacher Education of the American Council on Education, and supported by a grant of funds from the National Conference of Christians and Jews. It was actively participated in by the twenty-four colleges already referred to, institutions widely spread geographically and varying in many ways but all deeply concerned with the education of teachers. The project was fortunate in having as its national director Dr. Cook, an educational sociologist of repute and a skillful organizer and coordinator of field activities. It benefited from the interest of the educational associations that make up the membership of the Council on Cooperation and of the officers of the American Council on Education.

To all who were associated in the enterprise, the C.C.T.E. gratefully expresses its appreciation. Particular acknowledgment is made to the National Conference of Christians and Jews whose officers gave the participants and leaders in the Study every encouragement and assistance. Those participants—scores of college administrators, faculty members, and students—also merit special thanks. But most of all tribute must be paid to Dr. Cook and the staff associates whom he selected. To their scholarship, skill, and devotion the success of the College Study is significantly attributable.

It is therefore most satisfying to be able, through this book, to make generally available the matured views of its author. Dr. Cook has, of course, not been subject to any censorship on the part of the Council on Cooperation in Teacher Education, the American Council on Education, or the National Conference of Christians and Jews. Officers and members of those organizations must not, therefore, be presumed necessarily to agree with every statement that has been made.

KARL W. BIGELOW, *Chairman*
Council on Cooperation in Teacher Education

April 2, 1951

Preface

This book is a final report on a four-year field project in teacher education, the College Study in Intergroup Relations. The first report, *College Programs in Intergroup Relations,* described concrete study-action-training programs for the reduction of prejudice, the teaching of cooperative attitudes and behaviors. The present volume is analytical and interpretative, using College Study experiences but not limited to this source. Its focus is on majority-minority relations in the nation, especially on the deep clefts of "race," creed, and national origin, which put such fearful strains on so many people. The basic aim is to combine theory and practice for the improvement of intergroup education in colleges and schools.

From one standpoint, the story to be told can be called a study in school and community relations. Everywhere today, as one moves about among school people, he can observe signs of a new social realism in education, a gradual turning to sociological data. What has happened is that the community has come rushing into the school and has spread its problems in social living over the curriculum. At a slower tempo schools have moved out into the community and are inspecting the ideologies of people, their human relations, handicaps, and aspirations. It is out of this new partnership of school and community that intergroup education, as understood in this volume, has been shaped. It was born when, to the look-see and feel ideas of teachers, the concept of *doing*—the ideal of actual experimental change—was added.

Intergroup educators, in the College Study and outside, must do their work in high tensional areas, areas where fears run deep, tempers are short, and risks of failure are very great. Under such circumstances no realist will expect a startling success story, but rather a batting average of hits, runs, and errors. Our report is, then, a record of field work, subject to all the limitations this im-

vii

plies. No instructor in the Study's participating institutions, no school-teacher, agency worker, or civic official, was freed for College Study activity. All had other full-time, or near full-time, duties. It would be immodest to add, were it not read as a tribute to these many persons, that we have never seen so much done at so little cost in overhead expense, so much undertaken on a voluntary, cooperative basis.

In Part I, the intent is to set a framework, to point an orientation. The approach to intergroup relations is by way of status, the high-to-low ratings given individuals within their groups; thus, in the full development of this idea a basis is given for the consideration of whole segments of our population in "majority" and "minority" terms. Part II focuses on prejudice in general and then on teachers in particular, and concludes with chapters on change induction through education. Here, as elsewhere in the volume, liberal use is made of case material, the assumption being that these concrete data may show insights and procedures which teachers will find of use.

Part III turns back upon the College Study, analyzing it as a project in in-service education, a kind of self-induced crisis to which each college had to respond. This part also deals with off-the-job training as it goes on in experimental centers of human relations and workshops, and with the developing field of strategy and tactics in community work. If teachers and school heads are to bridge gaps between conflicting civic groups, if colleges are to do more than reflect the confusions in our culture, a great deal of attention will have to be paid to group-management techniques. These are, we believe, the center of *group-process education,* a point of stress throughout the volume. Part IV concludes the book, reviewing some theoretical and practical issues which, in the hurry of College Study years, were tossed into a so-called "confusion corner."

At no time in this writing is education regarded as a panacea for the nation's disunity problems. On the contrary, the need is for widely united action to end undemocratic behaviors, *a total push effort on all fronts.* What can be expected of school and college people is, first of all, that they will get their own house in order, clean up their ways of handling youngsters, their classroom teaching, their community relations. Until every common school, every college and university, can show in its way of life what it would teach to learners, fine sentiments can make little difference in the habit patterns of people.

Next, it can be expected that teachers will look anew at area life about them, the culture of which they are a part, the prejudices imposed on children, the curtains dropped about to blind out light. These teachers, we venture, will take action to end such mangling of young people, such distortion of every youngster's birthright. They will support civic movements, perhaps organize them, to stop the waste of talent, to insure freedom under the law in the exercise of human rights. They will know their many educational allies, the good-will and fair-play agencies of the community and the nation, and they will work with these groups in whatever ways they can be professionally useful. Out of this process, we expect in time a new kind of teacher to emerge, a *teacher-leader*, treated all too briefly in the present study.

On occasion, we find ourselves thinking that prejudiced people are happy people, happier than the unprejudiced. We do not mean the poor neurotic souls, living on their need to hate, but rather normal persons, *the gentle people of prejudice* who fasten this evil on the land. These are decent, kindly people, top-level in every community, on whom we as teachers pattern and from whom, in a sense, we draw our pay. And so to ask that educators, with good sense and firmness, cause these persons to inspect their values, to review the history which is ours, is indeed to ask a great deal. Yet we can see no escape from this, for surely we live today in a glass house. All the world looks in at our intergroup relations, our race riots and court cases, housing covenants and job discriminations, social snobbery, and segregated education. It is a sobering thought to realize that over two-thirds of the world's people are nonwhite.

In the *College Programs* volume we gave credit to a number of persons for their assistance in College Study work. One cannot reflect on those years of rather hectic effort, of travel and contacts and friendships, without feeling a desire to extend the list, to thank by name many individuals to whom we have become indebted. To our colleges, their school and community groups, in particular to general committee chairmen, we can only say that this Study was their burden to carry, their contribution to the profession. To the executive committee of the Council on Co-operation in Teacher Education, especially to its ever-helpful chairman, Karl W. Bigelow, we are sincerely grateful for the opportunity to do College Study work. The Study was financed by a grant from the National Conference of Christians and Jews, and to this great unity of faith groups, notably to Herbert L. Seamans of its Commission on Educational Organizations, we are happy to acknowledge both financial and advisory assistance. For obvious reasons, we owe a great deal to Dean Waldo E. Lessenger and the administration of Wayne University, more than a simple acknowledgment can indicate.

On a more personal basis, we want to thank our office staff for its genuine enthusiasm and untiring work efforts. To work with Paul K. Hatt, Raymond P. Harris, and Richard H. Williams, each of whom was associate director of the College Study for one year, was an educative experience in itself. To Mrs. Eleanor Janutol, secretary and typist, we are indebted for handling the main load of office business, for typing manuscripts, and the like. To College Study consultants, each employed for a special job, especially to Elaine Forsyth Cook for work on tests, we are deeply appreciative.

On every page, almost, we have had to discuss controversial questions, questions on which scholarly persons differ honestly. We have tried to deal fairly with issues, to lessen differences, to close ranks. We have sought the advice of respected colleagues, a score of whom have read large sections of the book in manuscript form, but the final responsibility for ideas and phrasings has been ours. In 1932, Donald Young, sociologist, published the first realistic, integrated college text on majority-minority group relations. Like this author, we dedicate the present volume to our friends "across the line," whatever that line may be, *in the hope that they will remain friends,* that the issues we have undertaken to discuss are, indeed, discussable.

June 1950   LLOYD ALLEN COOK

Contents

PART I: A GENERAL ORIENTATION

CHAPTER

Criticisms and Confusions; College Study: Background Data; Need for a Frame of Reference; Status as a Center of Concern; The Focus on Social Tensions; Minority-Majority Viewpoint; Bases of Minority Groupings; Prejudice and Discrimination; Science and Normative Values; In Conclusion

PART II: PREJUDICE AND ITS REDUCTION

Current Theories of Prejudice; Prejudice, An Interpretation; Prejudice in Child Life; Some Studies of Religious Feelings; Philadelphia Early Childhood Project; Importance of Mass Media; Prejudice in Youth and Adults; Minority Reactions to Prejudice; In Conclusion

Nature of College Study Data; School Anecdotal and Survey Data; Student Experiences and Life Histories; Some Findings from Formal Tests; Projective Data and Other Test Scores; Inter-test Correlations; Variations in Ethnic Attitudes; Some Community Study Data; Group Description and Sociographic Study; The Need to Know

Range of Study-Action Projects; Change Experiments; Conclusions from Change Projects; Nature of Academic Education; Course Work in Intergroup Relations; Changes Wanted in Learners; A Critique of Test Knowledge; Science, Consistency, and Reality

Grade and High School Cases; College Group-Process Cases; Some Foundational Elements; Functions of Groups in Life; The Problem of Group Building; Group Structure and Processes; The Teacher-Leader

List of Tables

List of Figures

Part I

A GENERAL ORIENTATION

1. Nature of Intergroup Education

An impressive fact of the times is the growth of college and school interest in intergroup relations, a trend that is recent, sizable, and significant. We speak of it as growth, although a concern for people—how people treat people—is as old as the nation. It has deepened in recent years, become more genuine and inclusive. Its prime foci have been equal rights and opportunities for all citizens, common duties and freedoms, civic health and well-being. At the international level the basic views of democratic nations have been translated into a *Universal Declaration of Human Rights,*[1] a twentieth-century Magna Carta, a potential conscience of mankind.

In this *Declaration* one will find the freedoms about which Americans have dreamed since the nation's origins—the rights to life, liberty, and security, to full protection under the law of person and property, to free choice of an occupation, to personal health and public welfare, to freedom of thought, conscience, and religion, to participation in community life and civic action, all without restrictions as to race, creed, language, or national origin. Article 26 deals specifically with education.

> 1. Everyone has the right to education. Education shall be free at least in the elementary and fundamental stages. Elementary education shall be compulsory. Technical and professional education shall be made generally available and higher education shall be equally accessible to all on the basis of merit.
>
> 2. Education shall be directed to the full development of the human personality and to the strengthening of respect for human rights and fundamental freedoms. It shall promote understanding, tolerance and friendship among all nations, racial or religious groups, and shall further the activities of the United Nations for the maintenance of peace.

[1] Passed by the General Assembly of the United Nations in December, 1948. For copies of text in quantities at 1¢ each, order from Department of Public Information, United Nations, Lake Success, N.Y.

Public schooling has many aims, many functions, but none of greater worth than these—the development of personality, the strengthening of human freedoms, the promotion of social unity, world peace, and progress. These are minimal prerequisites for decent living everywhere, the kind of life all people have a right to expect. If these basic aspirations are applied to the American scene, to areas of greatest groupwise cleavage and danger, they define correctly the general field of intergroup education.

The present volume is the second of two reports growing out of the College Study in Intergroup Relations, a four-year field program in pre- and in-service teacher education. The first book,[2] written largely by college committee chairmen, was descriptive in nature, detailing concrete projects and procedures in intergroup work. In this concluding volume the writing is critical, with the College Study viewed as an experience to be analyzed. The book is, therefore, *an inquiry,* not a propaganda piece, although it does state values and reason from them. It is, in the main, a social science study of college, school, and community contributions to the developing field of intergroup education, especially in the high tensional areas of race, creed, and national origin.

CRITICISMS AND CONFUSIONS

The literature on "intergroup education" "intercultural education," "educating for human relations," etc., will suggest the mental climate in which the Study operated. Impressions are of a sizable volume of writing, recent in origins, growing rapidly, moralistic and promotional. It is, for the most part, a good-will offering, urging everyone to be *fair,* to act *right,* to act *now.* Beneath the world of words, one senses a considerable vitality, the desire of educators to play a more active part in helping the nation realize fully its democratic goals.

Critical reviews,[3] in contrast to popularized writing, allege that

[2] Lloyd Allen Cook (ed.), *College Programs in Intergroup Relations* (Washington: American Council on Education, 1950), 365 pp., $3.75.

[3] Critical samples are Don Hager, in *Journal of Educational Sociology,* XXIII (1950), 278–90; William W. Brickman, in *School and Society,* LXX (1949), 341–46; Leo Shapiro (ed.), *Journal of Educational Sociology,* XXI (1947), 64 pp.; Lloyd Allen Cook, in *Review of Educational Research,* XVII (1947), 266–78; and in *Encyclopedia of Educational Research* (rev. ed.; New York: Macmillan Co., 1949).

intergroup education is not in a healthy state. It is said that its aims are unclear, its methods unscientific, its assumptions naïve, and its claims of results far in excess of the data and/or logic of its studies and projects in change-making. After sampling these studies, Hager concludes that:

> It would seem reasonably clear . . . that the "lettered" and "unlettered" are guilty of producing a type of literature that, with few exceptions, contains little to attract the serious student of human affairs. . . . One could, perhaps, dismiss the evangelism . . . of contemporary writings in intergroup education as but a magnificent display of naïveté. On the other hand, it is more likely the result of a failure to comprehend not only the scientific method, but the contribution that it can make to an understanding of human behavior. Furthermore, authors proceed with complete disregard for knowledge about the structure of American society and of groups within that society, and with no recognition of the meaning and utility of the concepts they do employ.[4]

While these views may run to extremes, they contain enough truth to give an educator pause. It is, of course, unfair to assess an emphasis in education by its low level expressions, to ignore the work of such persons as the late Kurt Lewin, Gordon Allport, Else Frenkel-Brunswick, Bruno Bettelheim, Arnold Rose, and a score of others. Secondly, critics are academicians, few of whom are known for their contacts with schools, their interest in a teacher's everyday work tasks, so that it is easy to misjudge what is possible of achievement. And finally, while criticism is to be encouraged, it has always seemed easier to tear down houses than to build them, to show what is wrong rather than what should be done to make it right.

What criticisms show, we believe, is a strong but still unchanneled impetus in education, a trend having various origins yet pointed toward a more scientific work-level. For college educators, its center is change-making, the problem of *re-educating youth and adults in democratic values and behaviors.* Our viewpoint is in part that of an academic researcher who adds his little bit to a nascent science of human relations, but mostly that of a social engineer, using scientific knowledge so far as it exists in bridging the gap between ideals and practices in everyday life.

[4] Hager, *op. cit.,* pp. 283, 289.

COLLEGE STUDY: BACKGROUND DATA

It was in this sort of climate that the College Study had its origin and did its four years (1945–49) of field work. Since this project is an object of considerable attention in the volume, we shall describe its nature before continuing with a discussion of intergroup education. What is said is not a summary of *College Programs in Intergroup Relations,* a volume that merits reading in its own right.

Applications for admission to the College Study were always more numerous than could be accepted, so that some choice was possible. In general, the aim was not to select the best colleges or the worst but rather a widely varied sample.

BASES FOR SELECTING APPLICANT COLLEGES

1. Colleges selected must be representative of the nation's various types of teacher education, notably state colleges and universities (large and small), urban institutions, liberal arts colleges, private and church-related schools.

2. These colleges must also be representative of the nation's major ethnic areas, creedal views, immigrant cultures, rural-urban and class-level differences.

3. Intergroup tensionality, as well as cooperative relations, must be evidenced, though not to a degree which would prevent student-teacher inquiry and potential change projects.

4. Staff members must give evidence of sensitivity to intergroup problems, willingness to work toward improving human relations, plus administrative support of their efforts.

5. Colleges must have well-channeled contacts with public schools in their service area and with the community agencies, involving these organizations in a cooperative program.

6. The situation must be favorable to the achievement of College Study goals in that the work is not conceived as an added assignment to faculty members, or as extra to, or separate from, the main-line teacher-training program of the college.

7. Colleges will be admitted to the project for a period of one year, with the responsibility of making a report at the end of that year. Reapplication year by year, while strongly favored, will be judged on the basis of the past year's work.[5]

When these points were elaborated on the initial visit to an applicant college, a tentative theory of intergroup education was

[5] For discussion, see *College Programs* volume, pp. 10 ff.

outlined. Of prime importance here is a general statement of College Study goals.

COLLEGE STUDY GOALS

1. To study and appraise in child and adult life the role of race, creed, immigrant cultures, in light of time, place, and class-level differences.

2. To create in colleges and schools a total environment in which all persons are viewed, valued, and treated in terms of their personal worth.

3. To teach prospective teachers a deeper concern for, and a fuller understanding of, human relations in the school and outside, and to increase their group study-action skills.

4. To make basic improvements in teacher-educating programs in respect to their emphasis on intergroup relations, and to diffuse these changes within the profession.

5. To work directly, and to cooperate actively, with local groups and state and national agencies for the progressive democratization of our common life.

All these criteria for admission were purposely left rather vague, for it was not assumed that a central office staff, or its advisory committee, could know the study-action potentials of any college, school, or community group. Moreover, the conditions of the experiment called for local planning and involvement; in fact, the success of the project depended on these factors more than upon any others. At no time did the writer, or any staff member, play other than a consultant role, an advisory part in program building.

Inspection of Table 1 will show the colleges admitted to the Study, a list that meets fairly well the criteria specified. One notable exception was our failure to get into the far Northwest, a time-cost limitation, and another was the inability to enlist the participation of any Catholic teacher-educating institution. In several cases where a Catholic college drew up an application, it was not cleared finally to our executive committee for acceptance. Whatever the reason, it was not because of Catholic faculty disinterest. On the contrary, several of the colleges visited were actively engaged in intergroup work and became regular users of our materials.

Aside from a few general agreements, as we have said, each college in the Study was free to plan its specific program. Each was

TABLE I

COLLEGES IN THE COLLEGE STUDY, 1945–49*

COLLEGE OR UNIVERSITY	YEAR OF PARTICIPATION†				TOTAL YEARS OF PARTICIPATION†			
	1945	1946	1947	1948	1 Yr.	2 Yrs.	3 Yrs.	4 Yrs.
Atlanta University		√			√			
Arizona State College, Tempe		√			√			
Central Michigan College of Education, Mt. Pleasant		√	√			√		
Central Missouri State College, Warrensburg		√		√		√		
City College, New York City		√	√	√			√	
Colorado State College of Education, Greeley		√	√	√			√	
University of Denver		√			√			
Lynchburg College, Virginia		√		√		√		
Marshall College, Huntington, W.Va.	√	√	√				√	
New Jersey State Teachers College, Trenton	√	√	√	√				√
New York State College for Teachers, Albany	√	√				√		
Ohio State University, Columbus		√			√			
Roosevelt College, Chicago		√			√			
San Francisco State Teachers College			√	√		√		
Southwest Texas State Teachers College, San Marcos		√			√			
Springfield College, Massachusetts			√	√		√		
State Teachers College, Eau Claire, Wis.	√	√				√		
State Teachers College, Milwaukee, Wis.		√			√			
Moorhead State Teachers College, Minnesota			√	√		√		
Talladega College, Alabama		√			√			
University of Florida, Gainesville	√	√				√		
University of Pittsburgh	√	√				√		
Wayne University, Detroit, Mich.	√	√	√	√				√
West Virginia State College, Institute	√	√	√	√				√
Total	8	21	10	10	8	10	3	3

* Taken from *College Programs in Intergroup Relations*, p. 7.
† Does not include the eight colleges continuing in the Study, after one or more years of participation, on a "limited service" basis.

encouraged to study its teacher education needs, its intergroup situation, and do what its general committee believed should be done. Activities were coordinated at both local and national levels in the usual ways. Workshops were conducted from time to time— in all, over a hundred during the four years. All colleges received a number of services from the College Study office, chiefly a grant of funds for specific projects, regular consultant visits, study forms, reading materials, and program suggestions. Whatever seemed to work in one place was passed along for inspection at other places.

One consequence of freedom was that college programs became very different. They differed in areas of concern, in tenacity of purpose, in skill levels of work, in community involvement. This was, to an extent, as Study sponsors intended, the idea being to see what a selected top-to-bottom run of institutions could do with limited help. Colleges could discontinue participation at will, a request that was never made, and each drew up a new application at the end of the academic year when projects were reported. In two cases, colleges were dropped because of inaction, and in a few instances it was necessary, because of College Study staff shortage, to place colleges on a partial service basis.

To summarize briefly, college programs were conducted some what as follows. A committee of the faculty, or the whole faculty in smaller institutions, laid out a series of problems which seemed important. Often this general committee contained school heads, social agency and community representatives. Each project was worked on by a fairly small team, and all of these groups were co- ordinated by the local director of the intergroup program. College Study staff members served as consultants, with decision-making lodged in campus committees.

A word should be said here about staff backgrounds and biases, viewpoints which entered directly or otherwise into field work and writing. College Study staff members consisted of the director (the present writer), successive associate directors (each on leave for a year from his college), consultants requested by colleges for special work, and technicians on a per diem basis for such service as sta- tistical tabulation. Unless the context calls for specificity, all these persons will be referred to as staff members, consultants, or ad- visers.

Full-time staff members were Northern, native white, middle class, and Protestant. They were college teachers on leave, and trained chiefly in sociology, psychology, and education. All had taught at some time in public schools and/or held an administrative post, and all were concerned with the advancement of professional teacher education. All were strongly biased in favor of democratic unity and welfare values, the use of science to solve practical problems, and the worth of cooperative intergroup effort. In respect to human relations it was felt that nothing granted one citizen should be denied another because of race, creed, national origin, or the like, and that the failure to realize this principle within our country should be the concern of every thoughtful person.

Need for a Frame of Reference

In retrospect, we are inclined to view the College Study as a four-year search for meaning, a quest for a rationale within which to do intergroup work. Not that the project had this origin, or that it ever completed this task. On the contrary, the Study was committed to practical activities, the "improvement of teacher education," a service function which it never lost.[6] And yet changes in emphasis did occur, mostly when our mistakes became evident, when the effects desired did not turn out, thus making new plans necessary.

In 1945 there was a tendency for committees to run off in various directions, to search about in a great hurry, to do the things at hand. With time, the usual discovery was made, *that good doing is hard to do,* and this brought two quite opposite effects. On some campuses it reduced morale, which led a few committees to abandon intergroup work. In other cases the problem of re-educating people in attitudes and behaviors was given a new measure of critical thought, deeper thought than heretofore. Thinking was not fragmental but college-wide, ideas being shared at faculty meetings and student assemblies, and debated far beyond allotted time. Out of these exchanges a body of principles began to emerge,

---

[6] See "Getting the College Study Started," *Twenty-fourth Yearbook of American Association of Teachers Colleges* (Oneonta, N.Y.: The Association, Charles W. Hunt, Secretary, 1945), pp. 42-51.

and faculties tried in several colleges to draw up a statement to which everyone could subscribe.

We enter upon the theory part of these discussions with misgivings, for our preferred work has been of another kind. Moreover, we know the distaste of many educators[7] for sociological theory, their conviction that it can be put to no practical use. And yet it is most unlikely that intergroup education will amount to much, or that it will find a permanent place in teacher training, unless current theory problems can be solved. Without a general frame of reference, specific undertakings would seem to make little sense, to lay no foundations for continuing work. Where, in colleges and schools, a basic orientation has come into being, old projects have evolved new ones, the intergroup work gathering strength as it has moved along.

STATUS AS A CENTER OF CONCERN

Our first task in developing a mental map to guide us in group-process work was to find a center of concern, a pivotal point around which other interests could be clustered. Since discussion of society in abstract terms was ineffective, consultants began to look for concrete school problems about which to build language and ideas. Usually these were found in routine classroom or community situations, as an example will illustrate.

POOR JOHNNY! NOBODY LIKES HIM BECAUSE—

"Poor Johnny!" some elementary teacher had said, "nobody likes him because. . . ." In school and college classrooms, we asked actual and prospective teachers to complete the sentence, to write down reasons why children would not like Johnny. Assuming that these reasons might not be the true causes of dislike, we asked next that "the real reasons" be listed, and received in all over a thousand papers.

Little time need be spent now on this exercise. Johnny was said to be dirty, selfish, rough, loud, different, a tattletale, always right, bad, good (teacher's pet), to fight, not to fight, etc. In only a few cases did writers see that these ratings were functions of social situations, that behavior which brought prestige in one group, such as the classroom, might bring disrepute in another, say at the gym or on the street. It

[7] To avoid cumbersome phrasing, we shall use "educator" to mean a teacher engaged in professional teacher education, whether in colleges or in schools. "Teacher training" is used only where it is necessary to escape undue repetition of "teacher education," which is much the preferred term.

was clear to teachers, however, that ratings were an index of a child's role in a group, his participation, and the status accorded him.

In their "real reasons," teachers tended to repeat the ratings attributed to children, showing their own level of insight. Well over three-fourths of all answers were in moral and psychological terms, indicating the strength of traditional modes of thought. Child groups, in class and outside, were presumably a massing of individuals, each person being different, each with unlike needs. Each learner was, in teacher viewpoints, a closed behavioral system, a "whole child" who operated as a kind of law unto himself. There was, in sum, no perception of groupness as a sharing of concern, an integrated pattern of common meanings.

Using the interest created by this assignment, a language was developed in which to begin the study of personality in its group relations. What one is or is said to be—dirty, kind, selfish, etc.— was defined as his *status* in that group, the group's indication of his nature and worth. What he does, how he behaves, was his *role*, for instance, good learner, funny boy, bully, sissy, teacher's pet, and so on. By reason of role and status, chiefly the latter, each individual comes to have a *position* in his groups, a location in group structure. Persons positioned at much the same level form a rank order or class; in society at large a *social class*, a hierarchical level indicating general prestige in the community. To each position in any class structure, *authority* and *responsibility* are attached, which define the rights, duties, and freedoms assigned, not to the person, but to the position he occupies. No social group could exist, nor could individual "needs" be met, without some such analysis of groupness.

THE FOCUS ON SOCIAL TENSIONS

Once the idea of status was clear enough for use, we began to build a feel for social tensions in and about the school. The root meaning of "tension" is a kind of physical tightening, applied, say, in biology to the contraction of muscles. This suggests a readiness to act, for instance to strike out, to release pressure and regain equilibrium. At the human level the term may indicate the difficulty tensed persons have in restraining themselves from explosive action, the tendency to aggress in nonconventional ways such as violence against a disliked person or group.

A social tension, in ordinary parlance, implies two things: first, a relation between persons or groups that is taut, that threatens to rupture; and, second, attitudes on the part of the persons or groups related that are hostile. That this constellation of meaning has become fixed in a single term is probably no accident. It derives from the nature of social relationships. A break of an established relationship is usually a deprivation for one or both parties, hence its threat arouses hostility.[8]

Angell, from whom the quotation is taken, makes an additional point as underlying the UNESCO Tensions Project. Negative feelings, ranging from mild dislike to extreme hostility, may be displaced on persons other than those at the taut end of a polar relation, for example, the "taking-out" of frustrations on some convenient scapegoat.

Thus, social tensions are latent conflict, a cold war which always threatens to grow hot. In theory, tensions are disruptive of group unity and order, whether in a classroom, a community, or the world at large. Again, in theory, they can be relaxed in three ways. One way is to promote conflict, a test of might that may appear to offer relief. Another is to lessen the differences between groups by increasing common rights and understandings. The third way is really a version of the one just stated, yet it may lead to a widening of group differences. It is the idea of extending intergroup tolerances, of winning acceptance for the right to be one's self.

While these ideas carry various implications, one point seems especially relevant. Teachers are problem conscious, which means that they spend much time on the behaviors of deviant children. These problems may show no intergroup content, but rather may center on subject mastery, classroom order, and so on. Moreover, teachers are heavily loaded with work tasks, in themselves a distracting influence. By focusing on tensions, scatteration activities were curtailed and real intergroup relations came to the fore. To guard against a teacher's finding problems when none existed, every college in the Study collected all the examples of good will and cooperation which it could find, cases that were then used to describe the kinds of friendly relations which should prevail.

[8] Robert C. Angell, "UNESCO and Social Science Research," *American Sociological Review*, XV (1950), 283.

Minority-Majority Viewpoint

Teachers with whom we worked knew that they wanted to deal with disadvantaged persons, improve status in tensional relations. They knew, too, that the College Study was not to be another project in special education to deal with low IQ cases or the physically handicapped, as needful as this work is. Our program, by contrast, was to be social in nature, to center on groupwise differences that limited participation, that gave low-rated youth a tremendous load of strain and worry to carry.

On occasion, for instance at Greeley, Colorado, the Mexicans outside the city's rim were named as these low status people. Where, in College Study institutions, a fact-finding approach was made, pre- and in-service teachers might be asked to consider a list of some sixty terms, all names of racial, creedal, or other groupings, and to mark those most in need of understanding and assistance. Marks were concentrated the country over on such terms as "nigger," "wop," "hunkie," "kike," "Chink," "Mex," with pronounced local and regional variations. Where this survey was followed by interviews, deep-lying doubts, tensions, and conflicts were uncovered, matters too controversial to admit on a signed survey form.

From such data we derived a *majority-minority* viewpoint, an orientation preferred in most College Study institutions. While this orientation has limitations, critics do not seem to appreciate the difficulty of finding an adequate language in which to discuss group relations. Admitting that we are "one people, many cultures," how is one to refer to different peoples? What will he call them in order to distinguish one from another? "Cultural diversity or uniformity," "differences in unity," etc., do not designate flesh-and-blood persons in their interactions, and hence seem inept if one wishes to talk about everyday realities back and forth across racial, creedal, or other lines.

Minorities are, by definition, lower status groupings. Having less prestige than majority-group members, they tend to have less power to maintain themselves and advance their interests. To a variable degree, they are disadvantaged and underprivileged, though one must admit great differences among the nation's outstanding minority groups. In general, a minority is a disliked people,[9] a fact that helps to create their in-group consciousness and unity. They tend to view themselves as somewhat separate and apart, usually as subjected to prejudice and discrimination. Each minority is united in various ways but chiefly in a commonality of feeling. It forms a dispersed but identifiable community of interests, a fact most clearly demonstrated when its members face a common crisis.

BASES OF MINORITY GROUPINGS

Obviously, the majority-minority viewpoint takes into account only certain aspects of human relations. It comprises those contacts of people where such factors as race, creed, and national origin are made a basis of social superordinate and subordinate divisions. While we believe the factors named would likely appear in any comprehensive listing, colleges in the Study were constantly finding new areas of concern. Rural-urban differences were regarded as important in a number of places, as were labor-management relations and democracy-communism. While each of these areas may well be included in the content of intergroup education, colleges studied here have somewhat arbitrarily focused on traditional domestic conflict situations as already defined. Since 1945–49, the educational situation has changed somewhat, because of war and the unpredictable international situation.

By "race" is not meant a biological stock, a breed of people, but an identifiable color grouping defined in popular views as a "race," for example, the white race, the colored (Negro) race, and others. "Ethnic" is the preferred scientific term in that the human differences of concern are ethnocentric cultural viewpoints. By "creed" is meant religious groups, notably Protestants, Catholics, and Jews. Jews are admittedly more than a creedal body, and even

---

[9] "The mere fact of being generally hated because of religious, racial, or nationality background is what defines a minority group," write Arnold and Caroline Rose, *America Divided* (New York: Knopf, 1948), p. 3. While we have a high opinion of these straight-thinking writers, the term "hated" may be too strong. Moreover, insofar as hatred does exist, it is probably reciprocal—whites hating Negroes, Negroes hating whites, and so on—so that the definition of a minority group lacks any fixed point of reference. This is not to deny, however, that hatred is an element in intergroup relations, nor would we underrate its importance.

on creed they vary widely in their views. They are best thought of, perhaps, as a dispersed but interactive community, a belongingness based to an extent on what Lewin[10] calls "an interdependence of fate." A strong assimilative tendency has characterized Jewish people in this nation, with great numbers passing over into the general population.

"Nationality" brings to mind the many immigrant peoples who have come to this country, plus their native-born children. School teachers know this area better in terms of cultural heritages—the ways of living that children bring to school, the differential values placed on customs, and the consequent conditions of cultural conflict and social isolation.

Closer inspection of these traditional concepts will leave no doubt as to their complexity. Race is regarded in popular thought as summing up all kinds of personality differences—physical, mental, and moral—with these differences felt to be inborn and immutable. Color is made the basis for classifying people, with whites assigning to nonwhites a lower status rating. That there are no human races in an exact biological sense does not prevent the spread of these erroneous beliefs and practices.

Creed, like race, is widely viewed as lifelong, in spite of the fact that the U.N. *Declaration* specified freedom to change one's religion as a universal right. While each of the non-Protestant faith groups in the nation is a minority, they are en masse unlike other minority groupings in various ways. For instance, they differ among themselves and with the Protestant majority almost wholly on ideological matters, rather than in disparate conditions of life, the struggle for food, housing, jobs, and so on.

National heritages, like class level and rural backgrounds, are seen by average Americans as subject to change, provided they are not linked to race and/or creed. An Old World immigrant, an Irishman, Czech, or Pole, will become a citizen, in time a full citizen, and, if not this foreign-born adult, then his native-born children. With all such persons improvement in status is felt to be a question of time, though we know that time alone is not a determinant of group identification and adjustment. Assimilation is a two-way process, a desire to become an American and to obtain acceptance by Americans into intimate contact. Intermarriage is

[10] Kurt Lewin, *Resolving Social Conflicts* (New York: Harper & Bros., 1948), p. 184.

often taken as a crucial test, *de facto* evidence that equals accept equals as equal.

In all these cases, but in varying degree, minorities are accorded inferior ratings and are limited in social participation. Their general prestige, i.e., their caste-class position in society, is below that of majority-group members, although within a specific locality this relation may be reversed. In the abstract the majority group comprises people who are white, of native birth, old family, Protestant, and urban. In the concrete, a majority should always be defined in reference to a specific minority, for example, white-Negro, Gentile-Jew, Protestant-Catholic. Neither grouping has any meaning except in relation to the other, and each pair forms a social system which can be isolated for study. The majority group is *the great power-holding body of people,* a fact that should never be lost to sight in realistic intergroup education.

PREJUDICE AND DISCRIMINATION

Intergroup education, to restate the main point we have tried to make, centers on the differential treatment of people defined as belonging to an ethnic or other minority. "Treatment" is a sponge word, absorbing several unlike but related ideas. One is "prejudice," a way of feeling, and another is "discrimination," a way of acting. Both rest upon perceptions, the manner in which people come to see human relations, and upon motivations toward them (meanings). It would be in error to assume that any of these terms has a clear connotation, that general usage of a symbol guarantees common understanding.

Prejudice is a difficult concept to define, so slippery yet so pivotal in intergroup learning that a chapter has been given to it. For the present, it can mean a *feeling of "againstness" not based on valid perceptions,* a negativism directed toward all members of an out-group. Discrimination, by contrast, is an unfair action, a *behavior that is detrimental to out-group members.* It handicaps them in competing for whatever rewards a social situation offers, for jobs, justice, education, and less tangible values such as self-respect. Both prejudice and discrimination subvert the "free enterprise system," the equal life-chances ideal, on which the nation is founded, hence become matters of grave concern in public education.

Prejudice and discrimination take various forms, show different intensities, and exist in different combinations. On the latter point, consider their common paradigmatic relations.[11] All four possible P-D patterns can be illustrated by almost any reader. There is the prejudiced person who discriminates, and the unprejudiced-undiscriminating individual, and both are consistent character structures. While the first contains some pathological types, it is composed mostly of so-called normal people. The second, the "all-weather liberal," is oriented in terms of democratic ideals. If he can be harnessed for action, he is a potential force for ending group inequities.

Educational interest is greater, possibly, in the two remaining types. One, the unprejudiced discriminator, can be illustrated by a property owner who signs a restrictive housing convenant in which he does not believe. The other, the prejudiced nondiscriminator, may be a person who holds that "undesirables" should be kept out of a residential area, yet refuses to take action against them. Both kinds of characters are expedient adjusters to the turn of events, "do-gooders" if it promises to pay off. Judging from College Study data, these persons are found everywhere. They perceive their inconsistency to an extent, or so we have come to believe, and may even have a guilt complex. All things considered, they are prime targets for an educational change of heart.

We have touched briefly on prejudice and discrimination because of a noticeable tendency in intergroup education to talk about grand abstractions. "Cooperation" is a good example, a word with which we have no quarrel, in fact will use often. But cooperation with whom and under what conditions of fair play? So with brotherhood, unity, good-will, all meaningful terms provided their referents are made explicit. If this is done, account must be taken of prejudice and discrimination, for they are dynamic elements in human relations. It would not be too strong, we hope, to say that *the central purpose of realistic intergroup education is to end these ways of treating people.*

[11] For an insightful analysis see Robert K. Merton, "Discrimination and the American Creed," in R. M. MacIver (ed.), *Discrimination and National Welfare* (New York: Harper, 1949), pp. 99-126.

SCIENCE AND NORMATIVE VALUES

It is time to clarify a point assumed in past pages, the relation of science to values in intergroup education. It has been said many times that the prime function of education is cultural transmission, that society counts on schools to pass along the vast body of ideals and practices called the social heritage. If this is meant to be taken literally, the task appears neither possible nor desirable. Some selection must be made: some heritages lost, some enriched and preserved. Put even more clearly, colleges and schools have three change-making functions—to support certain trends in our culture, to oppose other trends, and to initiate some that are new altogether.

It is in relation to deliberate change efforts that values become of crucial importance. They mesh in countless ways with social science, both in knowledge and in method, and with the teaching art, the practical engineering of behavioral modifications. While the entire volume deals with these triadic variables, their relevance to intergroup education is so central that some present comment seems desirable.

A science of human relations, as it is likely to emerge, will be an organized and calculated effort to understand personal-social living. It will be an integration, no doubt, of present social and psychological sciences, a systematic body of knowledge that will permit prediction of behavior in life situations. With prediction there is the possibility of control, of shaping events to human purposes, and it is in this faith that intergroup educators are inclined to act. Their science is *an applied science,* mostly an experimental effort to secure measured changes in attitudes and behaviors along racial, creedal, and other lines.

In writing about these matters, Dewey[12] envisions a "science of ethics" which would tell us how to transform human nature from within so that, in time, individuals would come to hold the ideals essential to cooperative community living. These ideals, goals, purposes, would not be imposed by authority, however benevolent or malign, but be arrived at through reasoning about the common good. On these grounds Dewey pleads for the application of science

---

[12] John Dewey, *The Problems of Men* (New York: Philosophical Library, 1946).

to human affairs, deploring what he views as a slacking-off of effort. All of this sounds very fine; yet it seems anything but certain that science would be used in the only way envisioned, namely, to determine and secure the public good. On the contrary, the chances are better that science would be used as it now is, for private as well as public purposes. Scientists would be arrayed on every side of every large issue, much as in the continuing struggle for the control of nuclear weapons.

Lundberg's solution of this means-ends dilemma, as we understand it, is not wholly clear.[13] To find which values social science should implement, scientists must go to the masses of men. By polling them on their wants, a picture will emerge of "the better society we all want," a society based presumably for us on democratic ideals.[14] While this proposal seems instrumental, rational, and humanitarian, it apparently ignores a very stubborn fact. Men want incompatible things. They continue to want incompatibles even after learning, and relearning, that one want must be sacrificed for another—things for ideals, ideals for things, ideals for ideals. *Values cost values,* the hardest doctrine that a realistic educator must face, and science cannot resolve these value clashes. It can make known the consequences of choice, yes, forecast choices, but it cannot determine their direction.

In rejecting science as a determiner of values, we do not, of course, depreciate its importance and its uses. What is meant is that other forces are operating to influence human action. Inertia is one, indifference is another, personal gain is a third, religion a fourth, and so on. The one of most concern to us is *the human rights values* with which the chapter opened, the application of democratic ideals to areas of human relations where prejudice and discrimination have been conspicuously evident.

Our general view of education is that both colleges and schools must do more than transmit a culture, more than perpetuate local mores and clamorous vested interests. They have leadership functions, much as expressed by Dean Redfield in his address to college heads on the college "quota system."

[13] George A. Lundberg, *Can Science Save Us?* (New York: Longmans Green, 1947).
[14] Lundberg regards this statement as contrary to his meaning and intent. For debate on the point, see Lundberg's exchange of letters with Jessie Bernard, *American Sociological Review*, XIV (1949), 796–801.

I reject the view that it is the simple duty of a university to bring together teachers and scholars, each separately teaching and studying what [he] wants to study or is hired to teach. A university is put there by society, not that each of its professors shall pursue his own interests, *but that there shall be a better society*. . . . Knowledge is to be sought and to be taught for the common good. The very privileges of academic people, the special opportunities which they enjoy, give the university a role of leadership in the common effort which it would be stupid to ignore and cowardly to refuse. The university, in this view, is not a mere agency of public opinion. It is an institution of moral leadership in the community, and *it is to lead toward justice*.[15]

If, now, our task were to make this value thinking more specific, we would suggest as *major goals in intergroup education:*

1. To teach the moral worth of all people, their equal citizenship rights, their various freedoms, their actual and potential contributions to our culture.

2. To equalize as far as possible in school and outside the conditions of free enterprise competition by reducing intergroup tensions, prejudices, and discriminations.

3. To promote positive cooperation across racial, creedal, and other barrier lines, involving where feasible all the educational forces in a community.

4. To apply these objectives primarily in the education of young people, studying the role of colleges and schools with the aim of improving their effectiveness as change agents.

5. To provide leadership in school and community coordination for educational and welfare purposes, making certain that minority representatives share in plan-making.

6. To use the techniques of the psychosocial sciences in experimental efforts to change behaviors, and to popularize scientific findings as to human nature and group relations.

These goals focus on people, rather than on culture, and on people in their everyday group-related modes of life. They center on deep fissures in community life, the clefts made by race, creed, national origin. They affirm without ambiguity the nation's democratic ideals of equal rights, and they cast teachers in the role of change makers. They conceive intergroup education, not as a sentimental impulse to do good, but as a cautious kind of social en-

[15] Robert Redfield, "Race and Religion in Selective Admission," *Journal of the American Association of Collegiate Registrars*, XXI (1946), 527–42.

gineering, *a sensible effort to do whatever is possible to further fair play and unity values.* They call upon educators, at all school levels, to guard against prejudice and discrimination, to search out individual talent, to promote positive cooperation on the part of all citizens. This is, we believe, the substance of intergroup education, a study-action-training program in better human relations.

In Conclusion

Aside from acquainting the reader with the College Study, a source of data throughout the present volume, the purpose of the chapter has been to begin an initial orientation to a field of study, action, and training in professional teacher education. By "study" is meant the collection of evidence to facilitate action, a process ranging from the simple sizing-up of a situation to complicated testing procedures. Action means change-making, changes in attitudes, perceptions, and behaviors, within and across racial, creedal, and other lines.

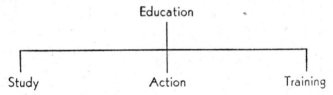

Fig. 1.—General conception of teacher education

We have used the term "training" with reluctance, knowing educational objections to it, and yet having no better word at hand. Pre- and in-service teachers need experience in study-making and in problem-solving, the kinds of experience that can come only in "suffering and undergoing," as Dewey uses these concepts. This is what is meant by the idea of *training.*

We cannot, in view of College Study experience, overstress the importance of the training concept. More than anything else, more even than ideas and values, teachers need *skill training in human relations,* experiences in trying to effect changes in people rather than in talking about them. They need methods, procedures, techniques, whatever language best conveys the thought of "learning by doing." Without this training in practical teaching arts, the search for better values can readily fail in its mission. "While saints engage in introspection," as Dewey once remarked, "burly sinners run the world."

Part II

PREJUDICE AND ITS REDUCTION

2. Prejudice: Nature and Development

If sight-saving work is to be undertaken in a school, one would need to know a lot about vision. The program's aims would be put in positive terms, yet the focus would be on handicapped children. So with any social "illness" such as prejudice. Unlike many organic defects, groupwise fears and hatreds are no simple matter. On the contrary, they are obscure and complex, so much so that experts disagree as to their nature and control. While ethnic and creedal prejudices are found in some sick persons, chiefly paranoiacs, they are not limited to the lunatic fringe. "Four-fifths of all Americans," writes Allport[1] in reviewing available data, "live mental lives in which feelings of group hostility play an appreciable role." Given our kind of society, intergroup antagonisms seem very normal.

What is proposed in Part II is to canvass current theories of prejudice, to analyze its development in child life, to study its expressions in teacher attitudes and experiences, and then to give successive chapters to various kinds of re-education. We speak of re-educating persons in democratic values and behaviors on assumption that pre- and in-service teachers are people, that all people already know a great deal about human relations, that the prime problem is one of personality change. The major approach to this problem in College Study work has been through *group-process education,* a viewpoint that will appear in some form or other in the remainder of the volume. We do not know enough about group-process learning to make extravagant claims for it, yet we do regard it as very promising. Its spread has already begun to make a difference in teacher education, a diffusion which the College Study staff has tried to further in the past four years of intensive field work.

[1] Gordon W. Allport and Bernard M. Kramer, "Some Roots of Prejudice," *Journal of Social Psychology,* XXII (1946), 6.

CURRENT THEORIES OF PREJUDICE

Group prejudice,[2] especially ethnic and creedal views, has long engaged the attention of social scientists. Systematic theories as to the nature of prejudice, its causes and consequences, fill the literature, as even a cursory survey will show, and each is a potential guide to educative efforts aimed at control. Theories which may appear different are, as a rule, not as different as they seem, owing to word choices and emphases. Most of the views would look to be complementary, rather than conflicting, each containing some part of the truth.

A common mode of thought about prejudice regards it as an *expression of ignorance*. Prejudiced persons do not know; they are uninformed or else misinformed from a reality point of view. Whether they lack contact with facts, or mismanage mental processes, they do poor cause-effect-cause reasoning, and hence fall victim to their own bad logic. From this standpoint prejudice can be dispelled by the spread of information, the use of sociological, anthropological, and psychological data. The more directly the truth is made known, the more vigorous its presentation, the more effective it will be.

While much of this makes sense, the idea of ignorance would seem to apply with greatest force to the pre-prejudiced, the immature whose outlooks are still fairly unstructured. It would apply also to reasoning persons, such as college students, who search for meanings, who want to know. The viewpoint appears of less worth in respect to persons whose ideas are firmly set, whose attitudes toward people are deeply ego-centered. In such cases discussion of race, creed, or nationality is likely to be interpreted as a personal attack, a psychological affront—a truth we have observed time and again in College Study work. In these individuals, one can readily sense a firming-up of enthnocentric views, a resort to defensive and/or aggressive action, as talk goes on and its pressure increases.

Since the prejudiced person is aware in part of his own illogic,

---

[2] Main focus of the chapter, in truth of the volume, is on prejudice, as to be expected in a book addressed to teachers. Discrimination, "the denial of equal access to public opportunities," is of concern in various places, chiefly in sections on community life.

his limited knowledge and experience, more facts simply add to his feeling of inadequacy. As his anxiety mounts, he must fight back, for his self-respect and group status are involved, or else he sits, a silent nonparticipant, feeling deeply that he is misunderstood, perhaps being picked on by some teacher whom he never liked anyhow. The end effect may be to stimulate the very emotions which led the individual to be prejudiced in the first place, to fix more firmly whatever biases he may have had.

The *unpleasant incident theory* is a favorite theme in student papers on prejudice, freely written accounts of "What I Believe and Why." Adults recall childhood experiences reaching back to preschool days. A little white girl is splashed by two Negro boys as she passes a mud puddle. A Negro boy is told, in pre-adolescence, that he is no longer to play with a white boy, to visit in his home, though these children have been boon companions for several years. A penny is lost, a little Jewish girl finds it and keeps it, fixing imagery of "the stingy Jew." On her first day at public school, a Catholic girl is called names which she finds painful to write about now, in her adulthood. A Mexican youth is beaten up in a street fight by a gang of white boys. Children from across the tracks remember the snobbery of the better-off youngsters in their hometowns.

Such stories are commonplace and can be had from any school or college class or any group of teachers. Mostly, unpleasant incidents are remembered, a trick of memory that is well documented. Aside from a very few cases of traumatic shock, one cannot regard these normal happenings as causes of deep-seated prejudices. Unless they are re-enforced by continuous experience, chances are against their being integrated into a general viewpoint. Moreover, any collection of incidents will show the force of adult admonitions and peer-level reactions, the two great prisms giving early childhood much of its color and content. Mother's knee, while rightly famous as a place of learning, may teach lessons that will handicap a child for years to come, perhaps for life itself.

"One drop of Negro blood thickens the lips, flattens the nose, kinks the hair, and dulls the intellect." I can still hear my mother reading this sentence, her voice trembling with emotion. I can still recall the effect it had on me. She believed it sincerely, and her fear that Negroes might ruin our Nordic race filled me with terror. I was aged about six, and I had never seen a Negro. . . . In the little town in southern Utah were I was born and had lived, there were none. For me, Negroes were in the same class as goblins, ghosts, witches, and devils—a superstition lasting for many years.[3]

Another theory of prejudice can be called the *"obnoxious traits theory."* In substance, this is a "contrast conception," the imputation to out-group members of the shortcomings, defects, and vices of one's own group. Other people not only look different, act different, but are made to seem much more different than they are. Jews are said to be "dishonest, selfish, domineering, too clever, too ambitious, clannish, vulgar, noisy, and inclined to radicalism." Negroes are "unrestrained, passionate, violent, immoral, animal-like, untrustworthy, and lazy." Native white Old Americans are . . ., but there is no need to go on with this mode of thought. Every in-group does its own stereotyping of out-group members, nurtures its own brand of enthnocentric blindness and mistrust.

One cannot doubt the existence of such distortions, their widespread diffusion and their influence on behavior. But what the obnoxious traits theory does not explain is why certain groups in our society are selected as scapegoats. Why not rural dwellers, city people, fat ones, tall ones, or redheads? Projection seems evident enough; yet other facts are needed to account for persistent, bitter hatreds of a whole people, concretely a minority's visibility, cultural history, and general defenselessness.

> In the past, fairy tales have dealt with sorcerers, witches, Jews, Jesuits, Masons, and so forth. Today, Jews are chosen from this list because they combine with the mysterious foreignness which makes them acceptable as scapegoats, a position of prominence in the community which makes attack apparently logical and fruitful. No one can make political capital now out of an attack on witches. No one can unite a nation rived by caste and economic cleavages by presenting it with an enemy which is obviously trivial.[4]

To suggest some reasons why the Jew is a prime target of Gentile hostility is not an effort to try to disclaim for Jews any responsi-

[3] Lewis I. Dublin, "Death and the American Negro," *American Mercury*, XII (1927), 42.
[4] David Riesman, "The Politics of Persecution," *Public Opinion Quarterly*, Spring Issue, 1942, p. 4. Used by permission.

bility in keeping anti-Semitic views alive. While far more sinned against than sinning, the Jewish people would make no claim to perfection. Like other people, whatever their creed, national origin, or color, Jewish Americans come in all shapes and sizes. At times one thinks that there is no idea so absurd, no stereotype so farfetched, that it does not approximate some bit of reality. The fault lies in making an individual the basis for a group valuation, in allowing one case or a few to freeze perceptions in an invariable mold.

In *symbolical theories* of prejudice, the above projections are not taken at their face value. "Prejudice," says Rose,[5] "is more than false belief; it is a structure of false beliefs with a purpose." Reasoning that these purposes represent "substitute satisfactions" of needs which cannot be openly met, or even admitted, this writer sees the Negro as a symbol of sex. Anti-Negro feeling is a revolt against rigorous sex repressions, an envy of the Negro's alleged sex freedom and prowess. The Jew is, for many anti-Semites, a symbol of the big city, with its sharp competition, commercialism, and radicalism. Prejudice is a hatred of the city, hence of Jews, the most urbanized of all people. To rid one's self of prejudice, or so Rose reasons, one "must first understand his repressions," see them as conflicts between personal and social (moral) values.

If symbolism is omitted, the above theory is much like the popular *frustration-aggression hypothesis*. From this standpoint all people are assumed to have a long list of postulated needs, wants, desires, for example to achieve, to belong, to be secure, and the like. Life is struggle, a struggle to meet needs, and in the process much thwarting, blocking, frustration, is inevitable. As aggression builds up, it seeks outlet, and is discharged to a degree on outgroup members. To the aggressor, prejudice and discrimination are ways of releasing tensions, also of squaring himself with himself, that is, compensatory behavior. Moreover, in these group-sanctioned actions, righteous people as well as vicious ones can build credit for themselves, provide a kind of social capital (status feelings) to fall back upon in any "squeeze" or thwarting.

[5] Arnold Rose, "Anti-Semitism's Root in City-Hatred," *Commentary*, VI (1948), 374–78.

Lest the frustration theory be streched further than it can reach, it should be stated that, so far as the evidence shows, not all prejudiced persons seem to have experienced any unusual kinds of blocking, and there are no uncontested data to prove that frustrated persons are any more prejudiced on the average than the nonfrustrated. The best case for the general theory is made by Frenkel-Brunswick[6] in studies of college students who adhere rigidly to middle-class values, then worry over the lapses in themselves.

By slight changes, the viewpoint just stated becomes the *social crisis concept* of some sociologists. Under conditions of accommodation as in American Negro slavery, intergroup relations tend to stabilize. Superior and inferior statuses are defined, rights and duties accepted, and there is apparent harmony. Prejudice emerges on threat of change, actual or imagined. It is a pragmatic attempt to hold a competitive advantage, to re-establish a disintegrating divisional line. Thus, prejudice is the product of crisis, of hard times and sudden changes. That such accommodation in our history, or in any given present locality, is always precarious, always incomplete, is seen by recurring minority revolts and covert aggressions, and by majority-group efforts to maintain by artifice or force a disintegrating status system.

The *disordered personality theory* explains chiefly the fantastic views of neurotic persons. While there is no simple relation between mental illness and group prejudice, clinicians report many cases where sadistic impulses, free-floating aggression, and delusions have been directed toward a whole people. Persons so afflicted are prime organizers of hate movements, leaders of lynching mobs, and popularizers of doctrinal views. They show common behaviors in extreme forms, differing only in degree from the mine-run of prejudiced people.

As an *in-group defense mechanism,* prejudice is an effort to keep an ethnic stock "pure," to buttress up its ways of life, to preserve its social status, its economic and other gains. Under a caste-class system, out-group members may be denied full citizen rights,

[6] E. Frenkel-Brunswick and R. N. Sanford, "Some Personality Factors in Anti-Semitism," *Journal of Psychology,* XX (1945), 271–91; also T. W. Adorno, *et al., The Authoritarian Personality* (New York: Harper & Bros., 1950).

limited as to jobs, excluded from various public places, kept in their "place," whatever that may be. To the prejudiced, such inhumanness needs no justification, or rather it is its own justi-fication. In-group ways are right ways, in-group values are best, in-group dominance is what counts. Out-groupers have few rights which must be respected, few claims to a common humanity. They can be stigmatized en masse and treated, gently or with violence, as beyond the pale. In-groupness can mean conformity to a way of life in which prejudice is an entrance ticket.

Among remaining theories, one seems of obvious worth, the old sociological idea of *differential associations*. If prejudices are learned, they must be taught. Some children get them; some do not. Some get certain views, others a different set, all varying in amount. Some children unlearn prejudices very young, others much later, and still others not at all. In them, distortion seems to feed upon distortion, to curtain off larger and larger segments of the social world. Why does this occur? Much evidence in the College Study points toward a recurring theme—the company a person keeps. In intergroup relations, learning is mostly from people, often the people one wants to be like. Learning prejudice is in part a matter of differential association.

Prejudice, an Interpretation

Before turning to empirical evidence on prejudice, we want to suggest a general interpretation. Obviously, prejudice is a complex behavioral pattern. It is no extrahuman force, like gravitation; no inborn function like the hunger urge. It is more like an appetite in that it is acquired, usually without conscious intent or thought. *It is a kind of situational orientation, a feeling of againstness to-ward out-group members.* Assuming that unfriendly-to-hostile views toward whole categories of people are resident in our cul-ture, the real problem at issue is why some persons get them and others do not.

On looking closely at prejudice, it will be seen to have at least a five-point character. There is, first of all, an *emotional element,* a negative feeling tone ranging from mild dislike to violent hatred. There is, next a *cognitive aspect,* a perception of meanings in environmental stimuli, an "understanding" of what people are like. That faulty vision and bad logic enter here does not invalidate the point, for the world to a prejudiced person is as he perceives it to be. Prejudicial action (or *discrimination*) is a third variable, running from simple avoidance of contact through discourtesy to organized exclusiveness, exploitation, and violence.

By inference one can judge that a prejudiced person has *values* to advance and protect, or personality needs to be met, whichever statement is preferred. These values range from material gain through status striving to subconscious impulses of which the actor is unaware. To the extent that he knows his actions to be in conflict with the broader ideals of his culture, an actor will tend to *rationalize* his behavior, to give good reasons rather than real ones for whatever he may do.

Assuming again the presence of prejudice in a given environment, for instance in a school district, these ideologies will have for individuals a different appeal. Their acceptance will depend, first, on exposure to them, and secondly, on personality needs. By the latter is meant, in part, the degree to which individual motives, impulses, wishes, and so forth, are being satisfied or thwarted, thus setting a "readiness" for learning. In theory, this susceptibility to prejudice can be gauged through study, although this also raises a complex problem.

Some prejudices are expressed openly in words or by overt actions, lying on the surface of personality. Other prejudices are deeper seated, so that one cannot judge their nature by what a person says. He may hold viewpoints which he cannot, or dare not, admit to a friend or to himself, much less to a teacher on direct inquiry. These are cases for the clinician, taking a "depth interview" (or some kind of projective test), as illustrated in the next chapter. In sum, what a person says about himself, what he knows but will not say, what he does not know and hence cannot say, all represent different levels of personality structure. Each of these levels may indicate a readiness for prejudicial action, a behavioral potential that depends upon situational pressures.

To repeat, intergroup prejudice is resident in our society and is acquired through *normal processes of acculturation*. It is built in through social learning, pointing one toward discriminatory action, rewarding him for conformity to in-group norms. In studying it, account should be taken of personality needs on the one hand, and of situational demands on the other, the two interacting to produce the prejudiced person. In short-time perspective, some prejudices seem rational, meaning that they are logical means-to-ends relations, apparently sensible from an actor's standpoint in achieving his goals. But from any broader viewpoint, prejudices are irrational, a way of saying that they are invalid generalizations, usually from the hearsay evidence of other persons. They come often from frustration, more often still from passive in-group conditioning, and in mass society they are spread by interest groups for their own advantages.

The presence of prejudice in American life is at once commonplace and significant. Prejudice, like all culture, precedes the individual, awaits his coming, so to speak. It offers him alternative response patterns—as discussed in the next section—and among them are anti-somebody feelings. While these vary in time and place, they are always the product of social processes, especially of hard times, mass propaganda, and sudden social changes. In one sense, democracy itself causes prejudice. It teaches all people the ideals of our society, the common human rights on which the nation is founded. When aspirations are blocked by unfair treatments, minorities become insistent upon their rights, as democratic theory encourages them to be. Prejudice, once latent, becomes kinetic, a dynamic element in the further shaping of society.

PREJUDICE IN CHILD LIFE

To understand more about prejudice, a teacher should have some general theory of child socialization, some idea that goes beyond the common-sense notion that children, somehow, come of age.[7] Born an animal, dynamic and out-reaching, incomplete and multipotential, without instincts but an amazingly able learner, any normal child if given the opportunity can acquire any culture, enter any form of group life. Many American children are heir to at least three cultural systems, each overlapping yet distinguishable. One centers about our national ideals, the worth and dignity of

---

[7] For systematic viewpoints, Kingsley Davis, "The Child in the Social Structure," *Journal of Educational Sociology*, XIV (1940), 218–30; Carson McGuire, "Child Socialization," in *Encyclopedia of Educational Research*, ed. Walter S. Monroe (rev. ed.; New York; Macmillan Co., 1950).

every person, his common human claims to equal opportunity and fair play. Another culture consists of local community practices, stratified on social-class levels and similar within geographic regions. In addition, minority children have a third culture—their racial, creedal, or alien heritages. For many this is their first culture, the in-group ways closest to them, thus most determinative of early experiences in acculturation.

From the standpoint of society, socialization is the process of fitting the young into the forms and norms of group living. It consists, in the main, of presenting children with approved modes of response, rewarding right choices, and punishing wrong ones. These ways of acting are, in technical language, the roles that young people play, roles based on age, sex, race, family status, class level, and so on. One type of role consists of *ascribed roles*, the things children are expected to do within their immediate culture, things enforced upon them; and another type comprises *achieved roles*, the ambitions youth hold for themselves. While no detailed analysis is needed, a student summary of an actual case will suggest the ways in which a teen-age Negro boy broke with area influences and defined a role for himself.

Chester is a self-made man, an example of talent mobility. In spite of low class origins, he has learned that he can get ahead by doing well the things his mother, his teachers and age-mates, value. He makes good grades at school, though grades are not his forte. By dint, chiefly, of hard work, he has become a star athlete. He has been taken up by the smart set, knows all the lingo, goes on parties, and dates within the crowd. What money he can make at odd jobs, he spends on clothes, dressing a bit beyond his means. He knows the value of a good line, good manners, and he avoids the hoodlums in his neighborhood. He takes an active part in youth groups in school and at church, and he wants to go to college after graduation. His heart is set on becoming a physician.[8]

In every society, both ascribed and achieved role-models are apparent. Ascribed roles give stability to a social order, a "like father, like son" continuity so that a community has assurance that its ways of life will go on. In our society, a democracy, achieved roles are the channels up and out for many people, the ambitious,

[8] Summarized from Allison Davis and John Dollard, *Children of Bondage* (Washington: American Council on Education, 1940), chap. 5, "Self-Made Man."

the talented, the lucky. They are escapes from poverty and deprivation, pathways to comfort levels of living, to wealth and power
and privilege.[9]

Of most interest in socialization is the idea of social learning,
the learning one does about people and culture. How does a
person map his social universe, determine his "life space," or
simply get notions about self and others? The query is more difficult than it seems, and we shall return to it in other connections.
To say that learning comes from learning is indisputable, for past
learnings push us on. To add that some learning comes to us hap-
hazard, a pickup from associates, whereas other learnings are
products of conscious, goal-seeking efforts, is a distinction worth
noting. Reflective learning is, apparently, a *continuous reorganiza-
tion of experiences to meet personality needs,* a perception of
barriers that obstruct or threaten habitual action and of new ways
toward goal achievement.

To get these ideas back to human relations, it is quite likely
that concepts of self and others are learned simultaneously and
within a group context. Asked who she was, a little four-year-old
said, "Papa is Greek, Mamma is English, and I am Greek, too."
Preschool children know many ways in which they differ from
other children, in which their family is unlike other families.
They know the customs of their street, the language used, the
conformities expected, the taboos enforced. They know which
children are nice or tough or snobbish. They have already met
barriers to free choice, compulsives of the culture; hence they
have moved far in their differentiation of stimuli and integration
of behaviors into approved social roles. One can see them playing
these roles in reference to in- and out-group members, practicing
the parts that for the time seem to preserve personal integrity and
make for group acceptance.

Some Studies of Religious Feelings

There is no doubt that religion is one of the most complex
facets of child life, hard to comprehend because youngsters can

[9] Autobiography and fiction provide rich sources of study, for example M. Ravage,
An American in the Making; Richard Wright, *Native Son;* C. Morley, *Kitty Foyle;*
and J. Marquand, *H. M. Pulham, Esq.* and *Point of No Return.*

frame so little of their feeling in word forms. Following a method developed by Harms,[10] we have gone far enough in College Study work to sense the value of an imaginative approach to inner religious experiences. Study projects have been small and carried on by graduate students who were teachers. After speaking about religion, its importance in one's life, teachers asked their children to "imagine how God would look to them," to draw a picture on paper of what came to their mind, and to tell in words what the picture meant. Older children, especially adolescents, might flatly refuse to make a drawing and were given permission to put their ideas in writing.

In analyzing several thousand drawings, Harms finds most uniformity of expression among children aged three to six years. Our cases here were so few that we shall confine comment to his thought. This is "the fairy-tale state" of religious conceptions, whether God is "a king," or "daddy of all children," or lives in "a golden house above the clouds," or floats in the form of "a polar bear" over the landscape. Children think in fairy-tale imagery, with no variations noted in creedal backgrounds. What distinguishes this thought from secular ideas, that is makes it religious, is the awe with which children approach the high and exalted, their unmistakable reverence and devotion.

The second stage is "the realistic period," the period of critical queries of a Tom Sawyer and Huck Finn, lasting for many children up to adolescence. Young people have come to see how seriously grownups take God and to learn details of a particular creedal doctrine. Children feel religion with a deep concern, adapting themselves more willingly than at any later time to the demands of institutionalized worship and teachings. Religious symbols seem to arouse great fascination, being used often to represent God. The crucifix appears frequently, also the Jewish star since this religion forbids creating "an image" of God. Next, in frequency, come pictures of priests, or priestlike figures, with comment to show that they are mediators and representatives of God. God is drawn in what might be judged a conventional style, and some few writings suggest the beginning of a viewpoint best seen in

[10] Ernest Harms, "The Development of Religious Experience in Children," *American Journal of Sociology*, L (1944), 112–22.

the next period. For example, appended to one drawing of a god-like head were the words: "He is a Jew and a Christian and both kinds love Him."

The final period studied, that of mid- and post-adolescence, was called "the individualistic stage." In Harms' data, as in our own, there was evidence of a "practical idealism," yet more impressive was the fact that cases seemed to fall into at least three large types. Group A, varying somewhat with creedal backgrounds, comprised individuals who appeared to have absorbed a specific church doctrine, to think pretty much within it, and to portray their experiences in formal symbols such as the Madonna, conventional angels, and biblical scenes. Group B showed little interest in the dogmatic content of religion, including the faith to which they belonged by reason of parental affiliation. Individuals felt themselves alone, felt the need to think for themselves about life and death, sin and virtue, joy and sorrow, hope and faith. Drawings revealed much originality and sensitivity—the sun breaking through a dark sky, Atlas holding up the world, shadows of death, paths to heaven, good Samaritan symbols, personal credos embellished with abstract designs.

Group C individuals were the most consistent of all the types Their religious attitudes crossed in-group creedal lines, transcending the usual boundaries set by the more exclusive religions. At times symbolism seemed to come from some ancient period in world history, say from Persian mythology, or from some esoteric cult, but mainly it was up-to-date, social, and earthy. For example, one adolescent drew a doctor, with a mass of people crowding about him, raising their arms for help. It was her deistic idea of medicine, a good man (doctor) watching over the world and administering to its well-being. "Life," she said, "was God's greatest gift to mankind," and people "were His greatest creation." It would be wrong, we believe, to call such attitudes irreligious, for they seem to imply a deeply spiritual view of the universe.

A fourth type of persons in our own cases was called simply "the non-cooperators." For one reason or another they failed to make responses which were complete and genuine, or else made no response at all. It is probable that this group contained persons who doubted, or disbelieved, in any religion, although one should go beneath verbal response to explore this guess. Harms did not list this classification, and we have made no particular study of it. At Lynchburg College, Virginia, some cases of this type were found in a general campus survey, though no detailed analysis was attempted.

Studies of religious experience belong in a chapter on prejudice because of some difficult problems which educators are obliged to face. In our country, by far the majority of children are processed in some religious faith, taught the doctrines of that faith. On a secular basis, this accords with the nation's principles of religious freedom, the right to follow conscience on faith matters. A major problem arises in connection with the in-group character of religious indoctrination, the learner's attitudes toward church groups other than his own.

Of particular relevance are the Studies in Prejudice by a group of psychologists and others at the University of California at Berkeley, research in progress since 1944. In one volume, *The Authoritarian Personality*,[11] several sections deal with religion and prejudice. While the central focus is on "the potential fascist" in American life, religion is given enough attention to make a review pertinent. Subjects studied were non-Jewish, white, native-born, middle-class Americans, including college students, schoolteachers, business and professional persons, day laborers, prison inmates, and so on. Although the sample numbered about 2,000, it was felt to be inadequate as a basis for conclusions applying to the nation at large. Questionnaires were used, followed by intensive depth interviews, within a framework of personality theory.

In brief summary, subjects who professed some religious affiliation expressed more prejudice toward Jewish and other minority groups than those who did not identify themselves with any church. Variability among these prejudiced subjects was almost as great as in the sample as a whole. Aside from Unitarians and a few small Protestant faiths, no denomination was outstanding in liberalism. While frequency of church-going was not very significant, it was found that persons who never attended church made lower prejudice scores than those who went to church, a conclu-

---

[11] T. W. Adorno, *et al., The Authoritarian Personality* (New York: Harper & Bros., 1950), pp. 208–21, 727–43, ff. All these studies were sponsored by the American Jewish Committee, New York.

sion believed to be "added evidence that people who reject organized religion are less prejudiced than those who accept it."

Subjects whose parents presented "a united front" on religious matters, perhaps insistent that their views be followed, were more prejudiced than those from homes were parental religious influences were "inconsistent, partial, or nonexistent." Subjects who considered their church important to them "were very considerably more anti-Semitic" than those who regarded the church as unimportant, or thought of religion in its more personal, or more ethical, or more rational, aspects. In general, it appeared that formal church membership, attendance, etc., were less significant in understanding the relation of religion to prejudice than were the subject's attitude toward religion and the content he imputed to religion.

In their interpretation of these findings, the authors express the view that religion plays "a relatively minor role" in the structuring of personality. It has declined steadily in influence and been somewhat "neutralized" as a cultural good, a common value. It moves people neither toward fanatical hatreds nor toward universal brotherhood and fellowship in the sight of God. While "emasculated" in its profoundest claims, religion persists in "noncommittal ideologies" which are apt to assume "an aspect of rigidity and intolerance such as we expect to find in the prejudiced person." The more dubious revealed truth becomes, "the more obstinately its authority is upheld and the more its hostile, destructive and negative features come to the fore."

A question of concern to educators is whether the great faiths in which the nation believes can be taught so that *no one undermines another,* no person is made weaker in his effort to build a spiritual foundation for his life.[12]

PHILADELPHIA EARLY CHILDHOOD PROJECT

The place was a border-state city, the school a white school in what looked like a middle-class area. A panel of upper-grade children had put on as a special program a general assembly, a discus-

[12] While this is the viewpoint taken, if we rightly understand its report, by a recent educational committee made up of members of the nation's three great faiths, all value-judgments implying the equal worth of religions should be labeled controversial. See *The Relation of Religion to Public Education* (Washington: American Council on Education, 1947).

sion of race relations in American society. Just before the bell, a chubby little boy arose from his front-row seat, turned and faced the audience. He grimaced and paused, asserting the weight of what he had to say. "Well, now," he began, "I don't care 'bout 'em," motioning at the panel, "but I just ain't gonna marry no ol' Negro, or Jew, or nothing." No doubt the boy had sat for a long time with this idea in his mind, although there had been no discussion whatsoever of intermarriage. His confession, for it had that feel, was greeted with pupil applause, after which the boy visibly relaxed and sank back into his seat. He paid no attention to a panel member who, with some feeling, redefined the human relations of concern to the panel.

Why did this grade-school youngster behave as he did? Were the answer fully known for various kinds of persons, we would be a long way ahead in understanding personality and group life. What do negative views really mean to those who hold them, what basic needs do they serve, how do they function in styles of living, and why are they so resistant to change?

A suggestive research lead, detailed here as one of several promising studies, is the Philadelphia Early Childhood Project, a continuing inquiry only now beginning to report.[13] The work of present interest was a projective test and interview study of a sample of two hundred and fifty children, aged five to eight years (kindergarten, first, and second grades), from six schools representing various racial and creedal groups in the city. Children were from lower-middle to lower income levels, with half their fathers in skilled trades and factory work.

In one part of the study a "social episodes test" was used, a series of photographs with racial and creedal actors in various situational combinations. One scene, to illustrate, showed Negro and white children at play, with one child looking on. Another scene was a schoolroom, with two pupils coming in late. As in the College Study PT-10 projective tests (see p. 69), subjects were asked

[13] Under general direction of Helen G. Trager, of the Bureau for Intercultural Education. Publications on which our account is based are Marian Radke, Helen G. Trager, and Hadassah Davis, "Social Perceptions and Attitudes of Children," *Genetic Psychology Monographs,* XL (1949), 327–447; Marian J. Radke and Helen G. Trager, "Children's Perceptions of the Social Roles of Negroes and Whites," *Journal of Psychology,* XXIX (1950), 3–33.

to tell what was happening in the picture, why someone was behaving as he did, what it means to be such and such a person. In another part of the study, cutout black and white dolls were used. Children were asked to dress these "persons" (adults, both sexes) from three sets of costumes: dress-up clothes, work clothes, and shabby clothes, and then to tell where the characters were going or what they were going to do, that is, work, play, and so forth. The idea was to see to what extent children made differential responses, that is, assigned roles advantaging or disadvantaging ethnic and creedal groups.

The nature of children's responses is illustrated by the case of a kindergarten girl, white, Protestant. Asked to tell about the playground picture, the girl said that the boys were "playing ball." Asked about the colored boy, standing nearby and looking on, the child replied, "He is coming to watch them." He was not playing, she said, "because he had just came down and saw them." The question: "Why don't they ask him to play?" brought the reply, "they have too much boys now," suggesting that exclusion was due, in the child's mind, to circumstances rather than to prejudice. Questioned further, the little girl felt that the Negro boy was not glad that he was colored, for "white children don't like coloreds because they fight too much," thus showing a common stereotype. Asked if the Negro boy would sometimes want to be a white boy, the child said yes, "because white boys do more things than coloreds. More gooder things."

When this same scene was given an intercreedal setting, children's viewpoints were much less clear. A little Catholic first-grader said the one boy, watching the others at play, was Protestant, which she defined as "when you go to a different kind of church than Catholic." She then identified herself as Protestant, which she was not, adding that the children at play "were Catholic, but sometimes they like to be Protestant too." Of another picture showing two boys coming out of a synagogue and other boys standing on the street corner, a second-grader said these latter boys "were going to beat them up because Catholics don't like Jewish people." Other children thought all these boys were friends, that they were "going off and do something for fun."

Findings from these projective tests leave no doubt that intergroup attitudes were evident in these city children at ages five to eight years. Whereas none of the subjects failed to identify Negro and white characters, many did not recognize, or else did not give content to, intercreedal differences. While friendly interracial feelings were not uncommon, both white and Negro children trended strongly toward expressions of aggression (exclusion, rejection) , a finding thought to correspond exactly with the state of adult life in the area. Among religious groups, Jewish children were the object of more hostility than either Catholics or Protestants, there being much less acceptance of them as intimates and equals. Similar attitudes were felt to come from similar childhood experiences, including both a child's family and peer cultures. While many boys and girls seemed to find security in belonging to a group which appeared most desired, the security principle was judged to be inadequate as a general explanation of negative projections.

Asked first if the dolls were different, almost every child identified them as Negro and white, with white children more explicit as to differences, a trend that increased with age. At each age level, white and Negro youngsters dressed the dolls differently, each favoring the doll of the child's own race. Colored children showed by far the stronger favoritism, assigning dress-up clothes to Negro dolls about three times as often as to white dolls. Asked what the man or woman would be doing wearing such clothes, about two-fifths of the white children created work roles for the white dolls which were distinctly more desirable than the roles they assigned Negro dolls. A fourth of these children ascribed leisure activities to the white men and women, and work pursuits to Negro characters. Concrete responses show the social meaning of race to these white children.

First-grader. (Negro doll given shabby costume; white doll, dress-up clothes.) "She [Negro] could be cleaning; all ladies colored are maids." "She [white] had a child and went out to buy shoes."

Second-grader. (Same costume assignments.) "She [Negro] a nigger working in the house." "She [white] out to buy food."

Second-grader. (Same costume assignments.) "He [Negro] is coming out of jail." "He [white] is taking a walk." "He [Negro] is black and is Chinese, but this one [white] is an American."

In only 9 percent of the cases did white children give Negro men and women, as represented by the dolls, the preferred activities and occupations. In these cases, the Negro doll was described as "going out," "going to a movie," or "walking on the street," while the white doll was seen as "washing dishes," "coming home from work," or "doing housework."

About half the Negro children projected similar activities for both types of dolls, 43 percent gave more desirable pursuits to the Negro doll, and 8 percent described work for the Negro doll and leisure for the white. Motivations seemed to show a desire to escape from the fact that whites have on the average better jobs than do Negroes, plus a good deal of wishful and compensatory thinking. Aggressions were evident in both racial groups. Many role assignments by Negro children to Negro dolls were in non-competitive social activities—for example, going to church—where no comparison of social status was likely to be implied.

In another part of the study, two good houses and two poor ones were shown the children, so that placement of any doll did not preclude an identical placement for any other. A good house was given predominately to the white doll, that is, by 77 percent of white children and 60 percent of colored. Four-fifths of the whites put the Negro doll in a poor house, with the remainder reversing this assignment. Negro children assigned a poor house to the Negro doll in 67 percent of the cases and to the white doll in 40 percent. Questioned as to their reasons, Negro boys and girls were vague in their answers. At times they rationalized, for example, "white ladies has got their houses cleaner," or "colored men is poorer." White children seem to perceive better the realities of area housing, with whites occupying better home units.

What these early childhood studies appear to show is that all the children studied tended to have a greater comprehension of intergroup relations than had been supposed from research studies to be the case. Negative attitudes and biased perceptions were felt to arise together in childhood experiences; thus, the need for further definitive study of their interrelations is suggested. Negro children, while predisposed to favor their own ethnic group, had caught enough of the prevalent white viewpoint or else enough of the life conditions about them, to be divided in their attitudes, and often conferred a preferred status on the white characters in the test. On the basis of their findings the investigators concluded that re-education along intergroup lines, if it was to be effective, *should be started at the time children enter school.*

IMPORTANCE OF MASS MEDIA

We have spoken about "environmental cues," the guides to meaning, hence to action, in the world about us. We see with our eyes, to be sure; yet what is seen are things we have learned to look for. Perception is not only an organic fact, it is also a social act, *a consequence of group membership.* To illustrate, in one eastern college a businessman addressed a class on "Human Relations." He was heard with due respect but did not fare well under questioning. One student in particular caused him trouble, probing into his facile views. Still smarting a bit, the speaker asked the professor in charge if he knew the student and was told his name. "Ah," he said, "Bernstein, huh, a damned Jew," settling back as if everything now was quite clear. To the professor, Bernstein had behaved as a graduate student should behave, seeking the truth. Bernstein, student and Jew, was what each man's past experiences had made him, i.e., quite a different object.

A significant point about perceptions is that they get patterned from experience, one kind of pattern being the tendency to stereotype. In this process, the prejudiced person looks for visible pegs (cues) on which to hang his biases, for sight, sound, smell, and touch stimuli. Just as the college speaker reacted to a surname, so many majority-group members react to skin color, shape of nose, slant eyes, manner of speech, gestures, type of dress, food, occupation, and so on. These are the differentiae by which they classify people, assign them moral worth, and govern contacts with them.

I learned about Negroes first, I guess, when I was about eight years old, on a visit to my grandfather in Virginia. On the farm, Johnny [white boy] and I played with three colored children about our age. One day they got the better of us in a corn-cob battle, until we charged in and they started to run. We chased one of the boys, caught him, and I was pummeling him proper when I felt a hand on my shirt collar, pulling me away. It was gramp and I expected a scolding, for he was a kindly old soul and wouldn't hurt a flea. "Now son," he said, "don't ever do that. Don't use your fists; take a club. Why, son, you could break your hands on *a nigger's thick skull!*"

Stereotyping is learned, of course, in the give-and-take of personal contact, learned from parents, playmates, schoolteachers, and others. It is learned also in less intimate face-to-face ways—happenings on the street, travel, and the like. Yet our society being as it is, ever more complex and impersonal, a prime source of learning will be missed unless attention is paid to *media of mass communication*. Stereotypes come from stereotypes, from vicarious experience where fact and fiction intertwine and make the same psychological assault.

In one analysis of short stories, more than 90 percent of the 889 characters were so-called Anglo-Saxons, the remaining 9.2 percent being ethnic menials, villains, touts, and deadbeats of some kind.[14] Story heroes were, by contrast, rich, powerful, moral, stylish, in short the type any dreamy adolescent might want to be like. In the movies in particular, every word, every character, becomes a fanciful projection of the American way of life, its human relations values, its inanities, absurdities, and contradictions. In a study of a hundred films involving Negro themes and characters, seventy-five were judged to stereotype the race, thirteen to be neutral, and twelve as favorable to Negro people.[15] All radio networks have a policy prohibiting offense to minorities; yet their flow of chatter makes ethnics the butt of many ludicrous happenings. Newspapers slant the news in line with dominant white values. Many still use a race label (Negro) in reporting crimes, even though the alleged lawbreaker has been apprehended. Many carry discriminating job and real estate advertisements.

While the situation is slowly changing in mass communications media, ethnic minorities generally figure in the dim backgrounds of the picture, playing roles that seldom lift their self-respect or reveal them as likeable, talented persons. The same cannot be said with equal force for either creedal or national minorities, the former being a particularly notable exception.

PREJUDICE IN YOUTH AND ADULTS

We have spoken about early childhood. It is a long jump through school years to adulthood, with important studies of prej-

[14] From David Kretch and Richard S. Crutchfield, *Theory and Problems of Social Psychology* (New York: McGraw-Hill Book Co., 1948), chap. 12, "Race Prejudice."
[15] *Ibid.*, p. 473.

udice marking each developmental period.[16] Adolescence is notably significant for then, with marriage somewhere in the offing, intimate intergroup contacts become suspect. The adolescent, too, is in process of cutting apron strings, of asserting his own maturity and independence. As we scan high school case material, much of it has a symbolical flavor. Associations between the sexes, wild escapades, and groupwise delinquencies might well be studied as a protest reaction, a deliberate attempt to right some wrong, real or imaginary, suffered at the hands of well-meaning parents.

At the college level, the Allport and Kramer[17] data are typical. In brief summary, anti-Semitic students identified more Jewish faces on a picture test than did fair-minded students, and thus displayed the greater importance of these perceptions in their life. On every kind of prejudice, there was a constant increase in negative memories with the increase of antagonism. Anti-Jewish memories were more common than anti-Negro, indicating either more experience or sharper imagery or both. While students showing most prejudice on an attitude scale tended most to mirror parental viewpoints without change, more than half the students who claimed not to have been influenced by their parents fell into the upper half (prejudiced) of the scale, leading the researchers to suggest a general lack of insight. In respect to school memories, the clearest conclusion was that there was an absence of vivid teaching in any phase of group relations, a judgment based on the vagueness of student replies.

So far as the data indicated, genuine friendly contacts of equals with equals tended to minimize hostile feelings, whereas either formal or intimate contacts of unequals (master, servant) had the reverse effect. More students in the prejudiced group than in the other half of the scale claimed that organized religion had been an influence in their upbringing, a finding interpreted as "the highly prejudiced person has been brought up to lean on external, institutionalized sanctions which imply hostility toward groups

[16] For a bibliography, see Kretch and Crutchfield, pp. 496–98.
[17] Gordon W. Allport and Bernard M. Kramer, "Some Roots of Prejudice," *Journal of Social Psychology*, XX (1946), 9–39. Conclusions drawn from this study of 437 college undergraduates have been confirmed in several later researches, for example Judy F. Rosenblith, "A Replication of 'Some Roots of Prejudice,'" *Journal of Abnormal and Social Psychology*, XLIV (1949), 470-89.

who do not subscribe to the same institutional patterns." Being
victimized as an object of prejudice might, apparently, lead either
to antipathy toward or to sympathy with an oppressor group, the
assumption being that a college student who reported such experiences in childhood would come to identify himself with either
unforgiving-rebellious or liberal-understanding campus groupings.

Students who regarded the world as a hazardous place to live,
a system of jungle ethics, were more prejudiced than their oppo-
sites, as were students who thought that there was too little discipline in our democratic way of life. Those who sympathized with
the underdog, or who suffered guilt feelings because of minority-
group treatment, were low in prejudice, much lower than students

TABLE 2

PUBLIC REACTIONS TO MINORITY GROUPS*

	PERCENT RESPONDING		
	Too Much Economic Power	Too Much Political Power	Should Be Getting a Better Break
Negroes	8	8	34
Protestants	2	4	8
Catholics	12	15	7
Jews	36	21	10
None of them	39	49	49
No response	11	12	9

* Courtesy of *Fortune* magazine, XXXVI (1947), 5–10.

who felt that they were unprejudiced or who viewed prejudice
as natural and normal. Students suspicious of being tricked in the
routine affairs of life made higher prejudice scores than the reverse,
as did those who disapproved of the FEPC or other government
efforts to control discrimination. When asked to rate themselves
as to prejudice, the most prejudiced students were furthest off in
their self-appraisals in comparison with test scores.

In respect to noncollege adults, or to adults in general, two
national *Fortune* opinion surveys are suggestive of the range of
prejudice. In response to three questions, a national sample of
Americans replied as shown in Table 2.

When the national sample was asked what should be done in
colleges about discussing racial and religious prejudices, replies
were as shown in Table 3.

From these tables, it might seem that our national house was in pretty good order. A third to a half of the people polled felt that no one group had too much economic or political power, or deserved better treatment than it was receiving. Unease on the power count was expressed in respect to Jews, and possibly a troubled conscience was reflected by a third of the sample in wanting Negroes to have a better break, more opportunity to get ahead. Fewer Catholics than Protestants approved a discussion of racial and religious prejudices in school classes or outside, and Jews were the

TABLE 3

DISCUSSION OF PREJUDICES IN COLLEGES*

	PERCENT FAVORING			
	Protestants	Catholics	Jews	Average
Have classes on these matters..........	38	34	56	38
Discuss only when students ask........	24	22	14	22
Have no discussion at all..............	22	28	22	23
Expressed no opinion	16	16	8	17

* Courtesy of *Fortune* magazine, Supplement for September 1949, p. 9.

most favorable of all to free and open discussion. Opinion polls, while generally accepted as a rough indicator of public attitudes, do not attempt to probe into underlying values.

Myrdal[18] has dug deeply into values in Negro-white relations, particularly in the South, arraying in rank order white expressions of anti-Negro feelings. Highest in this order and most inviolable is opposition to intermarriage, especially of Negro men to white women. Next come numerous barriers against so-called socializing activities, for example eating together, handshaking, use of common forms of address, and other symbols of social equality. In third position are public segregations and discriminations, for instance in schools, and fourth, are the various forms of political disfranchisement. Fifth are discriminations in courts, by police and other public servants, and sixth, barriers to securing jobs, housing, credit, public relief, and the like.

Two points are of special interest in respect to this value hierarchy. For white people it is quite likely to hold the country over

[18] Gunnar Myrdal, *et al., An American Dilemma* (New York: Harper & Bros., 1944), pp. 60–61.

with only slight changes.[19] Secondly, if the listing is reversed, it will show in a fairly exact way what many Negroes say their race most wants—jobs, housing, schooling, etc., with intermarriage a distant last on the list.

MINORITY REACTIONS TO PREJUDICE

How do minority-group members react to prejudice? Again, the problem is too complex for any brief answer. Some minority young people never seem to have met prejudice, at least to have recognized it; but in well over two-thirds of the cases on which College Study committees secured evidence, hostility and discrimination appeared to be basic factors in personality conditioning. Prejudice has functioned in ambivalent ways, for example setting handicaps, thwarting action, developing indifference, arousing counteraggression, challenging thought, stimulating ambition.

It should be stated, first of all, that prejudice tends to create prejudice; it may mold the very personality traits, the sullenness, bad manners, and brutality which the prejudiced person attributes to minorities. MacIver,[20] among others, has made clear this effect of hatred *as a vicious circle,* a turning wheel that is self-perpetuating. The idea is that the more severe the hatred and discrimination, the more minority members will show the kinds of traits and reactions used to justify their persecution. Stated abstractly, *a* sets *b* in motion, and *b* in turn keeps *a* going, a principle of circularity which one can frequently see in routine intergroup contacts.

Another important effect of prejudice on minorities is to stimulate *in-group unity and morale,* to lift these goals at times to the status of major motivations in what might otherwise have been an uneventful life. There is nothing in biology to integrate any group, to give it a sense of kinship and common lot, to weld it into a disciplined, self-respecting body. Admitting the operation of pull factors within the group, say unique cultural heritages or doctrinal views, there is still no reason to think these factors could unify a people as they do without the push of outer influences. One of

[19] For an empirical study, W. S. M. Banks, II, "The Rank Order of Sensitivity to Discriminations of Negroes in Columbus, Ohio," *American Sociological Review,* XL (1950), 529–34.
[20] R. M. MacIver, *The More Perfect Union* (New York: Macmillan Co., 1948), chap. 4, "Balances and Circles."

these, perhaps, the most important, is majority-group prejudice, though also in operation are such other factors as economic hard times and technological change.

Group morale is the level at which a group functions, its cohesiveness and aspirations, its will to push ahead no matter how tough the going. High morale in a minority people leads to organization, to protest movements, to strategic defensive and offensive action.[21] Pressures are put on group members to stay within the ranks, to conform to conduct standards, to fend off disintegrating forces, to compete for the rewards that the society offers. Such morale, too, bounces back upon the majority group, the prime cause of low status and frustration, turning what may have been covert minority unrest into an open, ongoing two-sided battle.

Low morale, as is plain to see, is a sorry matter, an invitation to insult and injury. One way to get chased is, of course, to run away, if there is no close-knit group in which to find shelter. Here Lewin[22] has made an observation which seems important. It is not the outer circumstances of Jewish life, or even its inner psychological hurts, that really demoralize Jewish children. It is their loss of strong in-group identification, the sudden or prolonged collapse of "the social ground" on which they stand. Though Jewish parents debate this point in the education of their children, many student life-histories support its validity.

Group self-hatred is another minority reaction to prejudice, the exact opposite of *group pride and participation*. It gets mixed with individualistic behaviors, for example, the self-blaming tendency; yet its group-wide expressions are fairly evident. Group self-hatred is found, first, in overt actions, any and all efforts to escape in-group identification, to pass as an out-group member, to break all ties with people among whom one's lot has been cast. It is found, secondly, in symbolical behaviors, for example, belittling the achievements of one's own racial, creedal, or other grouping, wishing one were not what he is, advocating an escapist point of view.

Regardless of the form group self-hatred may take, one of its

---

[21] Arnold and Caroline Rose, *America Divided* (New York: Knopf, 1948), chap. 7, "Group Identification and Morale." See also Arnold M. Rose, *The Negro's Morale: Group Identification and Protest* (Minneapolis: University of Minnesota Press, 1949).

[22] Kurt Lewin, *Resolving Social Conflicts* (New York: Harper & Bros., 1948), chap. 12, "Self-Hatred among Jews."

causes is the taking-over of majority views and values, the internalization of majority prejudices. "Negroes," writes Du Bois,[23] "are brought up like other Americans," in spite of segregation. They share in what he calls "average American culture," including group valuations. "It is quite impossible," he claims, "for any Negro boy in any white northern school or college to come out with any high idea of his own people, or any deep faith in what they can do." To add that Du Bois wrote a decade ago that conditions have changed, should not dull the point of his comment. Wherever such miseducation still exists, it is imperative to correct it, a task in which schools themselves should be expected to take initiative.

In Conclusion

However prejudice is viewed, it is in part a matter of custom, a traditional way of treating out-group members. In part, too, it is a deliberate effort by privileged people to preserve the position they occupy in social life, their advantages and gains. There is nothing in any type of group hatred that is inborn except the ability to acquire it. It is learned by children in their normal growth experiences, mostly from parental admonitions and peer mates. This learning appears to be an integrative process, a fitting together of perceptions into a whole. Under conditions of urban life, prejudices are learned at such early ages as to make the re-education of children in human relations a prime need at the elementary school level.

To assert that error often has more fascination than fact, that it meets better many personal-social needs, should not blind anyone to the long-run values of reality thinking. Organized ignorance has a long history in human affairs,[24] playing positive as well as negative roles. All things considered, its use as a device to teach group cleavages has nothing to recommend it to anyone interested in people. While the substitution of knowledge for ignorance can never perhaps be perfect, day-by-day stress in child and adult education of what is known about prejudice should go a long way toward developing the fair-minded attitudes idealized in our national history.

[23] W. E. B. Du Bois, *Dusk of Dawn* (New York: Harcourt, Brace, 1940), p. 191.
[24] See W. E. Moore and M. M. Tumin, "Some Social Functions of Ignorance," *American Sociological Review*, XIV (1949), 787–95.

3. Pre- and In-Service Teacher Views and Values

Anything as basic as prejudice in society, as much a prop to personality and culture, is a formidable enemy to attack. Its roots go deep into the fabric of national life—the social functions of ignorance, preservation of privilege, frustrations inherent in living, the force of democratic ideals. To end group antagonisms would require the concerted action of all the nation's good-will forces, coordinate with a law enforcement effort in which government would take the lead. Even then our knowledge might be too slight, or the public will too weak, or the cost too great—risks that every ameliorative program is obliged to take.

In any serious effort to end prejudice, schools are bound to play an important part. It was, of course, on this assumption that the College Study was undertaken, a four-year effort to appraise the situation and to get college action started. Part of the work task turned out to be the collection of data on pre- and in-service teachers, their experiences, attitudes, and information relating to intergroup relations. The aim of the chapter is to report so far as space permits a sampling of these study methods and findings.

NATURE OF COLLEGE STUDY DATA

It will be recalled that each college was free within broad limits to plan its own group study-action program. It could deal with some one cleavage in our society, or two or more as it liked. It could test for base-line data or not test, or test in any way it wished. Consultants paid regular visits to the campus, offering technical advice and study forms. So far as circumstances permitted, good use was made of this assistance.

Enough has been said to suggest the field-study character of the fact-finding to be reported, its imperfections from a rigorously scientific viewpoint. Some colleges were big and well staffed, whereas others were small and with a heavily loaded faculty. In these latter situations, as a faculty member said, "there is no time for research and no basic training for it." Everywhere, fortunately, students in training to become teachers were used in study designing, fact-finding, and interpretation.

SCHOOL ANECDOTAL AND SURVEY DATA

A simple way to study human relations is by means of "look-see" reports. In the first year of the College Study in particular, when more complex study forms were either unavailable or their use required considerable training, all colleges sent students into schools, community agencies, and the like. In most cases student reports took the form of *anecdotal records,* a practice which continued in many colleges even after better designs came into fairly general use.[1] With few exceptions anecdotal data-gathering was regarded as a student-learning (or teacher-training) experience; hence "findings" are neither exact nor complete.

Cursory inspection of chapters in Volume I will show an amazing range of student experiences with race, creed, and nationalities.[2] One anecdote which reports a street scene commonplace in many urban underprivileged areas, will suggest the form of the data.

A gang of Irish boys came down the street and stopped before the —— Temple. They began to chant in imitation of the cantor and then to toss pebbles at the windows. A man came out and asked that they leave, and they got smart, telling him to "go soak himself." At this point, some Jewish boys came around the corner, saw what was up and told the Irish kids to move along. When the latter continued to throw stones at the windows, two Jewish boys jumped on an Irish boy and threw him down. I walked toward the fight from a little ways up the street but, almost at once, a police cruiser came around the corner and both gangs disappeared.

In this type of study, weekly "logs" became the basis of student-teacher conferences at which materials were interpreted. Data

[1] At the close of field work in 1949, it had been decided to continue the circulation of College Study forms as a service to teachers, as announced in the *College Programs* volume. We regret to say that this has proved impossible, that the tests and forms reported here cannot be supplied by the author.

[2] For concrete materials, drawn in part from College Study schools, see *Improving Intergroup Relations in School and Community Life* (1946), a 48-page booklet by a committee of the North Central Association of Secondary Schools and Colleges. (Distributed by Paul W. Harnley, Secretary, Public Schools, Wichita, Kan., and by the present writer.)

suggest that children are color conscious long before they come to school, that some have picked up words and meanings which seem discriminatory, that groupwise viewpoints are clearly evident by the third or fourth grade, that prejudice is checked somewhat by the idealism of adolescence. Data also indicate the operation of various kinds of variables, notably propinquity, sex, family backgrounds, and success or failure at school. More important, perhaps, is what one learns from these records about pre- and in-service teachers—their initial sensitivities, value orientations, means-ends proposals, and changes over time. Teacher growth profiles, or their lack, are as firmly etched here as in more exact study procedures.

Another simple study form, yet one that can be turned into a complex approach, was known around the college circuit as a *school survey*. Students might spend a number of days in a given school, or visit several schools, or live for a period of time in a community of their own choice and work in the schools. In most cases they kept a log of observations, interviewed teachers and parents, worked in school activities, perhaps developed a teaching unit. Again, with conditions so variable, it would smooth down data too much to do anything more than to indicate impressions.

In some instances, school surveys were kept informal in nature, much as suggested by the writer in helping to instruct a group of students who were to begin practice teaching assignments in urban elementary schools.

SURVEYING FOR HUMAN RELATIONS DATA

Your first job, as has been said, is to do a good teaching job, to let nothing whatsoever interfere with that; but beyond that we want you to begin to see what a school is like as a system of human relations. . . . Now, the outline put on the board has opened up this problem, opened up your eyes to things to look for. But remember, the things of most importance are things that have no faces—shades of meaning, subtle gestures, obscure behaviors, things you have to watch for, to smell out, or else try to make happen in situations of your own contriving.

If this is a bit puzzling, remember that human relations may be like that—puzzling, unclear. A scholar is a searcher after truth, the repetitive truth of how and why things happen, and the answer may not lie on the surface. It may be buried deep beneath formal events, for on these occasions people do what is expected of them. They make a good appearance, or say the right words, or treat people in ways other than they would if they were not on guard. It is a scholar's business to learn what people are like, for otherwise it would be quite impossible ever to re-educate them. So, we have not set you on any easy task, but then you didn't ask for something easy.

Now this is what I am coming to do, the part I want you to hear, so that you can make notes on whatever questions you want to ask. Insofar as your teaching duties permit, put yourself in the way of happenings. . . . Write up what happens each day in your log, then digest and rewrite the events of the week, so that your survey will read like these paragraphs from a student paper. As I read, remember that a student teacher is speaking and that these incidents are taken from her report.

"When we got around to talking about my special interest, the principal told me that there was no prejudice in the school, that the school was a big and happy family. She said I might visit classes when my own work permitted, and I have been doing this. . . . What I found out was like what the principal said. In mixed classes (white, Negro, Mexican), all children seemed to be given a fair chance to recite, to take leadership and to do things. . . , I would say that there is no prejudice in this school, or if there is I have not observed it. . . .

"One day I decided, quite by accident, to see some nonacademic work, although my field is an academic one. I went to the gym and found a group of little tots playing games. The teacher asked me if there was anything special I wanted to see, and I asked to see some children's plays, the kind they improvise as they go along. I sat at the front of the class, facing both the children and the stage. What happened was this: the teacher asked who wanted to give a play and hands went up. The teacher selected a little white girl. She climbed the steps to the stage, faced the class, paused for quite a while and then said she would give The White Rabbit. Who would be the rabbit? Hands went up all over and she chose a white girl. Who would be the rock? Again, almost everybody wanted in and she named a white boy. So on for two more parts in the play, which was given after much whispered planning. Except for the choice of one Negro boy, the same thing happened in the second play—the teacher naming a white pupil, and the pupil naming white boys and girls.

"Since the next play would be our last one, I asked to pick the play giver and selected a little Mexican girl. Imagine my surprise when, after announcing her play and getting the usual show of hands, she chose all white participants except one, a Negro boy. She did not choose a single Mexican child, as I had expected, and I am at loss to explain this. There were six Mexican children in the class, fourteen Negro pupils, and twenty-two whites. In all, eleven characters were chosen, of whom only two were nonwhite. Is there race prejudice in this school? I would like to have this question answered at our next group conference."

While there is no easy definition of prejudice, it probably did exist in this school. Aside from what some teachers may have done to create or express it, negative feelings had seeped in from the community, guiding children in their choice patterns. Do not prejudge any classroom: observe it and see what it is like. But remember that these teachers are *gatekeepers,* so to speak. They can keep wrong ideas out of classrooms and teach right ones. Study also the freer contacts of children in the gym, hallways, playground, clubs, hangouts. In fact, it is in these areas that we want most of your survey to fall. If you find these informal contacts kind and fair, you may feel certain that there is no prejudice in the school.

After scanning several hundred of these teacher-training surveys, we have been most impressed with six kinds of facts: the broad

TABLE 4

WISHES EXPRESSED BY 618 NEGRO CHILDREN IN GRADES THROUGH 12 IN THREE SAMPLE WEST VIRGINIA COMMUNITIES*

COMMUNITY	BELONG-ING	ACHIEVE-MENT	ECONOMIC SECURITY	FEAR WORRY	LOVE AND AF-FECTION	TO BE WHITE	TO SHARE	PARTICI-PATION
	Average Number of Wishes per Child							
A.......	2.2	5.3	3.4	2.3	3.0	1.3	3.5	5.1
B.......	2.2	5.4	3.4	3.4	3.2	0.8	3.8	5.9
C.......	3.3	5.9	4.3	3.7	4.3	1.1	4.3	5.4
	Percentage of Total Response							
A......	8.5	20.2	13.2	8.9	11.5	4.9	13.2	19.6
B.......	7.7	19.1	12.0	12.1	11.5	2.9	13.3	20.8
C.......	10.2	18.2	13.3	11.6	13.2	3.3	13.3	16.8

* From *College Programs in Intergroup Relations,* p. 64.

geographic variations in intergroup attitudes, the rise in hostile feelings in schools where minority-group children were increasing, the strengthening of in-group lines as youngsters approached adolescence, the lack of interest of many subject-centered teachers in the human relations of the school, and the good work done by some teachers in almost every school. The sixth conclusion is that fair-mindedness has a positive relation to a teacher's ability to envision *the whole school as a school,* rather than to react to it in terms of some personal work function, some specific teaching field.

Formal school surveys, in contrast to the observational ones just discussed, were numerous, with most committees using their own forms. At West Virginia State College, for example, the Ohio State Wishing Well Test was adapted to the kinds of conditions under which Negro children lived. Table 4 shows grade school responses in three communities selected as typical of the state.

Table 4 suggests the strong desire of Negro children for achievement and participation, a finding usually true of minority-group children everywhere. Since percent responses show no great variation from place to place, it can be concluded that the wishes expressed are basic in child life and that young children are predisposed toward positive intergroup relations. On the other hand, in these West Virginia communities a survey of the experiences teen-age youngsters had had with white people showed that contacts were predominantly of a public, impersonal sort, rather than of a personal, friendly type. Negro high school students (chiefly southern) turned in over five hundred cases of alleged community discrimination against them.

In one hundred four schools, the use made of a College Study inventory form was exact enough to warrant statistical summary. This blank was filled in for each school by a committee of teachers in two-thirds of the cases and by a graduate student, in conference with the principal or a teachers committee and after several school visits, in the remainder of the sample. All the schools were urban junior and senior high schools, and almost all were located in the East and Middle West. Schools varied in size from a few hundred students to more than four thousand.

Group cleavages were most common along racial lines; next in respect to income levels; third, national cultures; and fourth, creedal differences, notably Protestant children versus Jewish and Catholic. Bad feelings seldom led to gang fights or other violence, being expressed most often in name calling, chronic teasing, clique actions, and choice of friends. Teacher favoritism toward majority-group members, for example white Protestant children, was reported in only 12 percent of the schools, a fact that may understate the general situation. Friendly contacts were the rule in almost all classrooms, in teacher conferences with pupils, and in formal school affairs, with exceptions worth noting in after-game dances

and on occasions when students competed for class or team positions and school honorary awards. Unfriendly relations were most
prevalent in informal student contacts, especially in corridors and
hallways, loafing places about the school, locker rooms, lunchrooms,
playgrounds, and on the way to and from home.

When a check was made on general minority-group behavior,
Jewish students were reported as overly aggressive, that is, "more
than normal," in about half the schools where they formed a third
or more of the student body, a conclusion that was less true of
other minorities under similar circumstances. Where numbers
were less, especially under 10 percent of school enrollment, withdrawing behaviors were listed as common. Jewish students held
far more than a proportionate share of student offices in various
kinds of nonathletic activities, second generation whites about their
average, Negroes and Mexicans far less. In athletics, Negro students
were outstanding relative to numbers, but they had on the average
very low scholarship ratings. Jewish students were high in grade
marks, with other groupings falling at or near the median.

In three-fourths of the schools, the parents reported as "giving
most trouble" were those of lowest social-class status. Racial and
creedal organizations were most likely "to interfere in school
policy," though far less so than were other community pressure
groups. Less than a tenth of the schools showed any "special and
serious effort," in the rater's judgment, to solve intergroup problems, and in most cases where such effort had been made, it was
by administrative request. Most teachers in every school expressed
interest in intergroup study and action, although cases were few
in number (8 percent) where this had led to any specific program.
Most school action to solve intergroup problems took the form of
special assembly or auditorium programs, departmental club meetings, unit teaching, use of resource persons, community visits, and
field trips.

STUDENT EXPERIENCES AND LIFE HISTORIES

While much more could be said about anecdotal and survey
findings, we shall pass on to a somewhat similar kind of data,
student autobiographical papers. While college practices varied,
the usual thing was to request "experience papers" as a class assignment, or to obtain them from student-faculty committees. Spontane-

ous, unguided accounts were collected over the four years in some colleges, whereas in other places a suggested College Study outline came into use.[3] In some manner or other, a great number of education majors and experienced teachers—and there is no accurate count—have turned in papers from 10 to 140 pages in length. Coming from every part of the country, every walk of life, these "biograms" give a fascinating picture of group-related experiences.[4] Some, to be sure, are of little worth, but others are naturals, that is, a good reporting job, freely written, involving feelings, and showing a time trend.

The kind of sample we would like to cite, a single complete case, might well fill the chapter. Having to settle for less than this, in fact for much less, we shall go to the other extreme. The case given consists of three excerpts from a 110-page typescript, a voluntary, unpaid-for piece of writing and much above the average. The document was written by a white college teacher, male, age thirty-eight, with teaching experience in two small colleges. Born in Ohio, educated in northern schools, the writer is no hothead on race matters; yet his interest in their improvement is very evident. The incidents cited prove nothing about race relations in the South. They do suggest the tenseness found at times, a fact that needs no particular documentation.

I LOSE MY FIRST COLLEGE TEACHING JOB

I took this job after graduate school with many misgivings. The pay was low, the college a Negro school located not far from a large city in the South. . . . Experiences combined that first year in one, two, three, four order, to get me fired, and I shall tell about them in their natural sequence.

Shortly after settling down at the college, I thought of a good friend living in the city, a Negro professor teaching at a college there, and I wrote him a letter. He set a date two weeks later and met us, my wife and me, at the bus station. We set out to find a place to eat and were lucky, or so we thought, on the second try.

Midway in the meal, two police officers entered the restaurant and came straight to our table. They took our names, addresses, etc., and then said that "we must be strangers to the South, that white and

---

[3] Patterned on a form prepared by Gordon W. Allport, Harvard University, entitled "A Guided Life History Outline" (unpublished).

[4] See Theodore Abel, "The Nature and Use of Biograms," *American Journal of Sociology*, LIII (1947), 111–18.

colored did not eat together." When they asked that we get up and leave, I took a pretty firm stand on my citizen rights. One thing led to another and an argument was on. They got mad and we got mad, with my wife trying to keep peace among us. The upshot was that we were arrested on a double count, first for "loitering" and second for "resisting arrest," and hauled to a downtown station, booked and put in separate cells.

Maybe this was my first lesson in Jim Crowism south of the M-D line, though I had traveled this country several times. At any rate, my second lesson came after I had phoned the president of the college and he had posted bail for us. He had driven in, arriving about 4:00 A.M., and all the way home he lectured us on race relations. It was a "peculiar situation," he said, "a cross the Negro must bear," and the college was dependent on white good will and financial support. We had learned about race the hard way and, while his teachers had "full academic freedom," any more trouble might be "the little straw that breaks the camel's back."

While this warning had been clear, I drifted into the third affair without the slightest foresight. It was toward the end of December and I planned to attend the annual meeting of a professional society. To get to Chicago, I had to take a 5:10 A.M. plane, so I came to the city early that evening and stayed overnight with my friend. To catch the plane, I had to make a 4:30 airport pickup at a downtown hotel, and this was where the trouble came. White taxicabs would not come to the Negro section of town for passengers, so that my friend arranged for a colored cab to take me, with the understanding on my part that this was against a city ordinance and that I would help the driver if he were challenged.

Everything went fine until we reached the downtown hotel. It was still pretty dark and I was fumbling with some change. The cab door was thrown open and two white cab drivers peered in. Both were burly men and plenty mad, and my driver and I sat still. "Are you nigger or are you white," one asked. Thinking that this was trouble, I began to stall. "Well, now—," I started to say. "Look, you——, smart, huh? Simple question, and last time. You nigger or white?" By this time, my driver was showing every sign of unease. "Well, now," I said, there's been some question about that. On my mother's side—." At this point, I was pulled through the door and stood up. "So, still a smart un, huh? Wanta get pasted, huh? You nigger or white," shaking me by the coat collar. "Well, my dear sir, I will have to tell you that I am colored." Staring at my face, as if to detect my lie, the white cabbie relaxed, then pushed me back into the cab. Feeling that he would bang the door, I hastily drew in my feet. Just before he slammed the door, he looked down at me, spit on me, muttering "damned white nigger preacher!"

The fourth incident, the one that got me fired, involved my teaching. It was some time after Hiroshima and, in class, we were discussing the color line-up in the war. I said that the atomic bomb might possibly have been dropped on the Nazis but that it had not been and asked why. Some student said the Germans were white, and the Japanese were not. I made no comment one way or the other, but asked why the bomb had been dropped on a great industrial center, killing thousands of people, rather than on a barren area as a demonstration. And so the discussion went, with all of us trying to think through a problem that has bothered a good many thoughtful people.

Nothing came of the incident at the time. A week later, I found that I had been quoted in the college paper as saying "whites dared use the atom bomb only against nonwhite people," and that for all time to come "the moral conscience of the world would condemn our use of this most frightful killer." Well, you can just about tell the story for yourself from there on. The alleged quote was picked up by our local (white) newspaper, then by the City press, and then released over the South by wire service. The college board asked for my discharge, without even the courtesy of a hearing, and the president, while sorry, said that I would have to go.

A careful study of life-history material leaves no doubt as to its values in any serious program of intergroup education. While one must bring to it an analytical scheme, content analysis shows clearly the deep-going nature of intergroup experiences, the tremendous impact on the personality of minority- and majority-group members. A simple statistical count of prejudiced and nonprejudiced phrasings can be patterned on a scheme developed for use on another kind of case data,[5] with more complex value analysis requiring time in its understanding and use.[6] While we cannot support the point by evidence, we are convinced by work with life-history data that there are patterns of prejudice with which school and college people cannot hope to deal. Some of the persons who exhibit these patterns are sick persons, in dire need of psychiatric help. Other individuals, by far the greater number, are like the white taxi drivers in the case. They are the product of a normal life experience, an experience typical of their time and place. What can be done to re-educate them is, indeed, a fine problem; yet if it

[5] John Dollard and O. Hobart Mowrer, "A Method of Measuring Tension in Written Documents," *Journal of Abnormal and Social Psychology*, XLII (1947), 3–32.

[6] For example, Ralph K. White, "Black Boy: A Value Analysis," *Journal of Abnormal and Social Psychology*, XLII (1947), 440–60.

is abandoned as unsolvable, educators will have only people of good will, or else the immature, unstructured personality, with whom to work.

SOME FINDINGS FROM FORMAL TESTS

In spite of the known efficacy of formal testing, many college committees gave few or no tests. Other groups, while test-minded, so changed tests about, a phrasing here, a new item there, as to make results invalid for comparative use. Still other testers devised their own study instruments, a practice the College Study staff did not discourage. During the lifetime of the Study (1945–49), good tests—or any tests—in intergroup relations were hard to come by, and if they were available, their use took time. Always too, there was the problem of working with persons who knew no statistics, and staff resources proved at times quite inadequate to this task.

We shall report, first, some of the attitude testing done by college committees, that part which made use of College Study forms, hence gave findings which are roughly comparable college to college. Table 5 gives scores on AS- attitude study tests, all constructed by Dr. Paul K. Hatt in his one year on the College Study staff. Tests were made in the manner suggested by Likert,[7] and had split-half reliabilities of .76 to .89 and standard errors of .011 to .033.[8] Validities were determined by the "known group" technique, with differences in pairs of means in desired directions in all cases and of a magnitude $P < .01$. The principal test, and the one that was generally recommended for college use, is the AS-20 Opinionaire. This is a 40-item check-type attitude test, taking perhaps 30 minutes, and composed of four subscales measuring antagonism toward Jews, Negroes, the foreign-born, and lower-class people. In all College Study AS-type tests *the lower the score, the greater is the degree of positive, liberal, or friendly feeling.*

Table 5 shows scores on a number of College Study tests, with the higher scores indicative of greater prejudice. Lynchburg students, for instance, averaged 45.1 points on an anti-Semitic scale,

[7] Gardner Murphy and Rensis Likert, *Public Opinion and the Individual* (New York: Harper & Bros., 1938).

[8] For detailed discussion, see Paul K. Hatt, "Class and Ethnic Attitudes," *American Sociological Review*, XXIII (1948), 36–43.

TABLE 5

Mean Scores on College Study Attitude Tests, 1946–49
(Possible ranges: AS-10 = 17–85; AS-11 = 10–50; AS-15 = 17–85;
AS-16 = 10–50; Composite = 40–200)

COLLEGES	MEAN SCORE				
	TOWARD JEWS		TOWARD NEGROES		COMPOSITE*
	AS-10	AS-11	AS-15	AS-16	AS-20
Atlanta University					
51 Graduate students					92.0
Central Mich. Coll. of Educ., Mt. Pleasant					
215 juniors-seniors					96.6
102 faculty					86.8
Lynchburg College, Lynchburg, Va.					
228 students, all classes	45.1	19.0	45.0	21.2	
70 B-college students†	44.3	22.4	39.4	19.4	
72 C-college students†	51.3	26.0	48.0	30.1	
152 D-college students†	47.2	25.1	47.0	26.0	
Marshall College, Huntington, W.Va.					
60 freshmen, experimental			45.5		
86 freshmen, controls			51.2		
Moorhead State Teachers College, Minn.					
266 freshmen	50.0	21.4	44.0	22.2	
67 freshmen, experimental group					104.9
124 freshmen, Bemidji, control group					109.0
119 sophomores	48.7	20.1	40.6	21.0	
54 juniors-seniors	43.8	19.0	37.0	20.1	
67 juniors					90.1
146 veterans with overseas service	51.3	22.8	47.0	22.7	
51 veterans, U. S. experience only	47.2	21.4	44.6	22.9	
42 faculty	41.0	19.7	36.7	17.4	
Roosevelt College, Chicago					
120 students, all classes	38.5		33.4		
Springfield College, Mass.					
200 freshmen					95.3
State Teachers College, Eau Claire, Wis.					
97 students, all classes	44.1	17.5	37.0	18.1	
44 graduates		17.0		17.2	
University of Florida, Gainesville					
129 juniors-seniors					115.9
Wayne University, Detroit					
100 freshmen	48.0	20.0	39.5	19.4	
120 sophomores	38.7	19.0	36.9	18.2	
195 juniors	43.4	18.8	37.3	18.1	
210 seniors	43.8	19.1	36.5	18.6	
86 graduates, no teaching experience	39.6		34.3		87.4
412 graduates, in-service teachers	41.6		35.0		89.9

* Attitudes toward Jews, Negroes, foreign-born, and lower class.
† Southern colleges cooperating with Lynchburg College.

in comparison with a low prejudice score of 38.5 for Roosevelt students and high prejudice scores of 51.3 for two other student samples.

Of most interest in the table are the results on the AS-20 Opinionaire, but even here only ten student samples are represented so that findings are inadequate for much generalization.

On inspection of AS-20 test scores it will be seen that student means ranged from a low of 87.4 to a high of 115.9, showing differences significant at the most discriminating level of confidence. The Mt. Pleasant faculty score is notable, not only because it is almost 10 points lower than that of the juniors-seniors but also because of the fact that it was next to impossible in the College Study to induce faculty members to take tests. The Moorhead State Teachers College is an obvious exception, as are members of the Roosevelt College faculty in a vote meter test not shown, of course, in the table. Two years after taking its homemade test, this teaching staff still jests about its request to the writer to carry the test and vote meter to other colleges for a comparable inquiry. Wherever this invitation was presented to a college faculty, it was invariably tabled and nothing came of it.

TABLE 6

MEAN SUBSCALE SCORES ON THE AS-20 TEST

(Possible ranges: 10–50 for each scale; 40–200 for whole test)

COLLEGE	MEAN SCORE				
	Toward Jew	Toward Negro	Toward Foreign-born	Toward Lower Class	Total*
Atlanta University					
51 graduate students....................	23.4	15.7	27.3	25.6	92.0
Central Michigan College of Education					
221 juniors-seniors......................	23.3	22.4	25.2	26.0	96.9
102 faculty............................	22.6	20.0	22.3	23.4	88.3
Moorhead State Teachers College					
67 freshmen, experimental..............	28.3	24.0	27.0	24.8	104.9
124 freshmen, control..................	28.6	25.4	28.0	26.1	108.1
67 juniors.............................	20.9	20.3	23.3	23.4	87.9
Springfield College					
200 freshmen.........................	24.9	20.3	24.6	25.4	94.2
University of Florida					
129 juniors-seniors.....................	27.6	31.7	28.7	27.9	115.9
Wayne University					
412 graduates, teachers.................	21.6	20.2	22.9	25.3	89.0

* Part means may not sum to total means as given in Table 5 because of rounding of figures.

When the AS-20 test is broken down by subscale scores, as in Table 6, there appears to be less antagonism toward the Negro than toward any other group, Florida students excepted. Negative attitudes seem strongest toward lower-class people and the foreign-born, a conclusion that needs wider verification. Differences between college subscale scores, as in other AS-type attitude studies, are usually not large, often not statistically significant, a fact which suggests the presence of basic component factors which underlie and explain the interrelation of specific attitudinal patterns.

To study the interrelations of class and ethnic attitudes, Hatt[9] made a factorial analysis of three selected groups of Detroit re-

[9] Hatt, *op. cit.*, pp. 36–43.

spondents: Wayne University undergraduates, suburban middle-class high school students, and adults in a highly restricted upper-class residential district. He used three class scales (upper, middle, lower) and three ethnic scales (Jewish, Negro, and foreign-born), all Likert-type tests as previously defined and having reliabilities of .76 to .93. What he found, in substance, was five syndromes of attitudes, or, more simply, five types of attitudinal relationships. For example, the major pattern (accounting for 53 percent of the variance to be explained) comprised a favorable attitude toward the upper class, together with antagonism toward the lower class and toward members of all ethnic groups, a relationship exactly reversed at the other end of this same scale. Hatt felt that his findings in full detail provided a basis for reorienting much of current intergroup education, an implication which can be better studied by reading his published article.

Another type of College Study test, but with less appeal to colleges, is the IT-1 Knowledge of Intergroup Relations. While we worked from the first to develop this test for college students, it was not until the third year of the Study that it could be recommended for general use. The IT-1 test is a 100-item, four-part, multiple-choice test, requiring fully 50 minutes to give and about two minutes to score. Items cover five major areas of College Study interest: race, creed, immigrant peoples, rural-urban and class-level differences. If answers are tallied by rows, scores relate to the groups just listed; if tallied by columns, scores fall into the categories of concepts, present status, history, current problems, and proposed solutions. Items are factual, that is, require right answers, and the test pattern is designed to make a systematic coverage of teaching emphases in the college classrooms we have sampled.

Split-half reliability for the IT-1 test is high (.91), as is to be expected in an information test, and validity was checked by experts in constructing items and in coding answers. A "known group" of twenty-eight Detroit social agency heads, with professional training in intergroup work, made a significantly higher mean score (G, in Table 7) than did groups of college students. Standard item analysis shows that about 60 percent of the statements are highly discriminating, and the test is now under revision to improve further its discriminating value.

TABLE 7

MEAN SCORES ON COLLEGE STUDY IT-1 TEST

(Possible ranges: part=0–20; whole test=0–100)

KNOWLEDGE FIELD	MEAN SCORES						
	Atlanta	Mich. Central		Wayne University			Detroit
	A*	B*	C*	D*	E*	F*	G*
Areas of knowledge							
Race..................	7.4	8.1	10.0	7.2	7.0	8.4	14.5
Creed..................	8.5	8.4	8.7	12.0	11.5	10.8	11.8
Immigrants..............	6.1	8.2	9.8	11.1	8.9	9.5	13.9
Rural-urban.............	5.9	7.4	9.0	8.4	8.3	9.2	9.7
Social class.............	5.3	7.1	7.7	6.4	6.6	7.7	10.2
Total†.................	33.2	39.5	45.3	45.1	42.3	45.4	60.1
Kinds of knowledge							
Concepts................	6.7	7.0	7.6	10.0	8.2	8.4	8.5
Present status...........	7.5	10.8	11.8	10.1	10.4	10.8	15.4
History, trends..........	6.3	8.4	9.0	9.2	8.2	9.8	10.2
Current problems.........	6.3	8.1	9.0	8.4	8.5	8.7	12.4
Proposed solutions.......	6.5	6.0	7.8	7.5	7.0	7.7	13.2
Total†.................	33.4	39.5	45.3	45.1	42.3	45.4	60.1

* Following is the key to the letters: Atlanta University, A =51 graduates; Michigan Central College of Education, B =215 juniors-seniors, C =97 faculty; Wayne University (mostly graduates), D =63 elementary education majors, E =77 health and physical education majors, F =343 from all curriculums; G =28 Detroit intergroup agency heads.
† Part means may not sum to total means because of rounding of figures.

Table 7 is read as follows. At Atlanta University (*A*), for example, the 51 graduate students taking the test averaged 7.4 correct answers on the 20 items dealing with race, 8.5 on the same number of items on creed, and so on, making an average correct score of 33.2 on the 100 items when the test is scored by *areas* of knowledge. Scoring the test by *kinds* of knowledge, students averaged 33.4 correct answers, in comparison for instance with the average of 60.1 for Detroit intergroup agency heads.

While the test itself is difficult, the amount of knowledge evidenced by education students does not strike us as reassuring. To date, we are unable to report part scores for any comparable number of noneducation students. In two small samples of Wayne University undergraduates, equated for grade, sex, age, and father's occupation, liberal arts sociology majors made a mean score of 44.8, an average that was significantly higher than the mean of 40.2 for the education majors. In respect to kind of knowledge, lowest scores in the table are rather uniformly in the social class and proposed solutions areas. Highest scores are more varied, yet show some concentration in the present status area. Agency heads are strongest in their areas of daily concern, and weakest on academic classroom materials, facts which if once known have dropped out of use.

In preparation for the last year of College Study work, the staff selected from its fifty-odd study instruments what was judged to be a minimum number of forms for a rounded picture of college student mental content. This assortment of tests, designated as College Study Battery A, comprised the AS-20 attitude inquiry, the IT-1 knowledge test, two EI-4-5 scaled experience inventories, an AS-38 test of stereotyping tendencies, and a PT-10 picture projective test (a series of ten cards each depicting a social situation believed to be familiar to college and high school students). Within the limits of free choice accorded all colleges, every effort was made to secure administration of this battery to a selected sample of juniors and seniors. Our office was to provide all tests, all answer forms, a summary face-sheet, and score and return student papers to each participating institution. First responses from eastern and midwestern schools were favorable, and it looked as if the College Study would be able to supply the education profession with data which it has always lacked—a comprehensive picture of preservice teacher attitudes, information, experiences, stereotyping, and projections. As western and southwestern responses came in, they were uniformly unfavorable. Colorado State College of Education at Greeley, for example, was deep in a community coordination movement and felt that it could not find the four and one-half hours of student time which the battery required.

In consequence of unfavorable reactions, plus the great difficulty of securing rigorously representative samples of students even within the institutions offering to participate, the collective project was abandoned. Only two colleges carried it out, each college on its own initiative, and their major findings are reported in Table 8.

Up to the EI-4–5 tests in Table 8, study forms have been described previously, and no particular comment is needed on test scores. The EI- experience inventories[10] are Likert-type scales meas-

[10] Developed by Robert N. Ford, now in Personnel Division, American Telephone and Telegraph Co., New York, and used by permission.

uring attitudes toward Negroes in terms of community and personal contacts. Weights are assigned so that the larger the score, the more friendly the experiences of white persons with Negroes have been. Mean scores in the table gain in significance when compared with means obtained in other colleges, for instance on the EI-4 test 23.5 and 45.0 at the University of Mississippi and the University of Pittsburgh. EI-5 mean scores at these institutions were 37.8 and 48.0.

TABLE 8

MEAN SCORES ON COLLEGE STUDY BATTERY A TESTS*

COLLEGES	MEAN SCORES							
	AS-20	IT-1	EI-4	EI-5	AS-38			
					P†	C†	J†	N†
Possible range:	*40–200*	*1–100*	*12–60*	*14–70*	*10–90*	*10–90*	*10–90*	*10–90*
Central Michigan College of Education								
221 juniors-seniors........	96.6	39.5	55.0	46.1	43.3	43.6	50.8	51.6
102 faculty (approximate)..	86.8	45.3	....	54.4	....	....	....	....
Wayne University								
343 graduates, teachers....	91.5	45.4	47.1	52.0	43.7	43.1	47.6	48.5

* With the exception of PT-10, a projective test used in individual diagnosis in connection with other test scores and case study data.
† Protestants, Catholics, Jews, Negroes, respectively.

The AS-38 test asks respondents to rate nine groups on a 9-point scale as to average intelligence, emotional stability, general popularity, honesty, cooperation, and the like. Lower ratings indicate favorable attitudes, higher ratings the reverse. Table 8 shows mean scores toward four of the rated groups. Negative feelings toward Negroes and Jews are somewhat stronger than toward Protestants and Catholics. Of more significance is the fact that these predominantly white Protestant students accord Catholics as favorable a rank order position as they give to the Protestant group. Catholics, on the contrary (about a fifth of both student samples) rate Catholics much more favorably than they do Protestants.

In order to check further on self-ratings, or own-group ratings, in comparison with ratings given other groups, an exploratory analysis of variance was run on a random selection of cases from the Wayne sample, all of whom were graduate students and teachers in Detroit metropolitan schools. Procedure was to have each group rate all groups, including itself. The next step was to find the means of all these ratings, after which scores were calculated for each group by finding the deviations of that group's mean

TABLE 9

OWN-GROUP AND OTHER-GROUP RATINGS, AS-38 TEST

RATING GROUPS	CATH-OLICS	PROTES-TANTS	JEWS	NEGROES	LOWER CLASS	RURAL PEOPLE	POLES	MEXI-CANS
49 Catholics.......	4.9	4.3	−1.5	−3.2	− 1.8	2.7	−.1	− 5.6
149 Protestants.....	3.7	3.3	− .9	−1.1	− 3.9	2.4	.3	− 3.7
24 Jews...........	4.1	3.7	2.8	−2.6	− 3.4	1.3	−.1	− 5.9
39 Negroes........	5.6	2.8	.5	.5	− 5.3	−.8	.0	− 3.6

scores from the mean scores of the total sample. Results are seen in a summary table, Table 9.

If read across, Table 9 shows the rating each group gives to all groups; read down, the rating each group receives from rating groups. Of note is the high rating given to Catholics on social-moral behaviors, an index of their *self-feeling,* and of the high position accorded them by other rating groups, an index of their *reputation.* By contrast, Protestants rate Protestants lower than they rate Catholics but higher than they rate any other group. Negro teachers do not appear to think highly of Negroes (.5) if one could judge by this small sample, a finding that obviously needs much confirmation. Mexicans are the least-favored group in the table, with lower-class people next, Negroes third, then Poles, Jews, rural people, Protestants, and Catholics. An F-test difference of 20.4 leaves no doubt as to the statistical significance of this ascending order of prestige; in fact the probability is very great that the ranking will hold for any general college student sample.

PROJECTIVE DATA AND OTHER TEST SCORES

We turn now to the final test in the battery, the PT-10 Human Relations Test, a series of ten line drawings printed on 7″ × 5″ cards and patterned on the Murray Thematic Apperception Test. Each picture presents an intergroup situation, for instance a basketball game, restaurant scene, streetcar incident, a restricted clientele hotel. Four cards have Negro-white content, four Jewish-Gentile, and two are unclued. In group use each subject is given a set of the cards and asked to write a story of a hundred or more words about each scene, telling what is happening, how it got started, what the people are feeling, and how the action finally turns out. At least fifty minutes is allowed for the test, although time can be reduced by omitting the two unclued cards. In individual use each card is presented in turn and the subject is encouraged to talk about it, with the researcher or a stenographer taking notes.

To illustrate use of the test in guidance work, a partial analysis will be made of two graduate students, each an M.A. candidate and with years of public school teaching experience. Student A is male, white, thirty-nine years old, married, a music major, a Lutheran. His father was born in Germany, went to about the eighth grade in school, came to this country in 1908, and worked for years as a farmer. The student was born in Minnesota and has lived most of his life in the capital of that state. Student B is female,

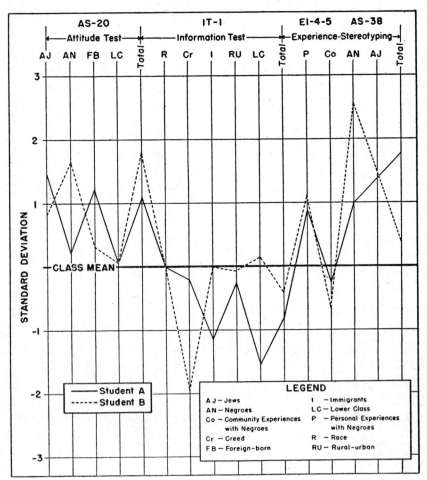

Fig. 2.—Scores of two students on College Study tests, in terms of standard deviations from the class mean.

white, twenty-eight years old, unmarried, a home economics major, an active worker in the First Christian Church. Her father was born in Indiana, finished high school, and is a fairly well-off farmer. The student was born in the same state and has lived for most of her life in one small rural community.

Figure 2 shows the scores of these two students on College Study Battery A tests as charted in units of standard deviation above and below the mean scores of their college class. Student A's outstanding prejudice is toward Jews as seen in both his AS-20 and AS-38 test, although his knowledge score on creed, which contains several items about Jews, is fairly close to the class mean. His views on Negroes, while anything but liberal, are not as intense, and his personal experiences with them have been pleasant. Student B, by contrast, heartily dislikes Negroes, has average knowledge about them, and believes much more strongly than does her class group in keeping Negroes in a subordinate place in community life. Both students, therefore, are well above their group mean in ethnic prejudice and somewhat below it in knowledge.

In the PT-10 test data, Student A identifies Jewish content on all four of the Jewish clued cards, impressing one with his extreme sensitivity to Jewish people. His stories about these cards, in contrast somewhat to those about the Negro cards, are full of clichés, giving every evidence of stereotyped thinking. In all Jewish-Gentile situations blame is attached to the minority group as a troublemaker, but no resolution of any problem is made. This suggests intense personal frustration, unrelieved by any outlet in purposive, planful action. At no time does the student admit that the majority group may be in the wrong or that, as a teacher, he should feel responsible for the reduction of prejudice. His reactions to the pawnshop scene show fairly well his general mode of projection.

Here the man is trying to pawn a vase or a pitcher or something. An antique of great value, I think, and it is valuable to anyone, because he has lost his job and must have a lot of money. So, he takes it in to a Jew *as usual* [underscored in answer] and so here we go again with these miserly people. . . .
The Jew declares it is worthless but offers a little money. This and the stingy, cheap methods Jews employ in business is typical of Jews and it is their own fault that they have the reputation of Shylocks. The Jews like to cry prejudice, prejudice, and get a more favorable

opinion of them. But from experience, I know that Jews are liars and cheats, and this is not my opinion of them. It is shared by all white men, and I have told Jews so, and they don't care if it is. . . .

This pawnshop scene makes me boil, the dirty, lying cheats, and it strikes me as very funny that they [Jews] should be so unlike in character the greatest Jew that ever lived, Jesus. I say that if the Jews would become a little like Jesus, all their unfavorable character would change. Maybe Jesus was not a Jew or even if he was, he whipped the money-changers out of the temple.

Student B shows a very different reaction pattern. She identifies no Jewish-Gentile content in any card and Negro-white content in only one card. Her own repressions, disguised as "fair play," do not permit her to refer to characters in ethnic terms. On the contrary, she uses any number of circumlocutions to avoid ethnic naming. For example, in the basketball court scene, a white player has been tripped or fallen and a Negro player is standing over him in what might appear to be a hostile posture. The student speaks of "a boy on the floor and a boy standing up," or "the boy in dark trunks and the one in white." After the test had been given, the subject claimed it was "most unfair." Her reason was that "teachers should never talk about race, or anything like that." Some people, it seemed, were good, some were bad, and it did not help "to call them horrible names."

While this student avoided the appearance of prejudice, at least in her own self-thinking, her answers showed a great deal of anti-Negro feeling. In general, she refused to make outright blame assignments to either the minority or majority group, an attitude she characterized in an interview as "the proper schoolteacher point of view." In every case, conflict could be resolved through cooperation, "a little good will," and in every instance the projected outcome was favorable to *status quo* relations, that is, favorable to the dominant white group. For instance, one card is a restaurant scene where three Negroes are, apparently, asking service of a white waiter.

"But there is no other place open tonight," plead the three men, all in vain. "I am sorry, Sirs," they are told, "but we would lose all our business if we allowed any of you to eat. This is the policy of the whole community, . . . but we can serve you sandwiches to take out." With a smile of gratitude, these men left immediately for the back alley, where food was brought to them and they ate. . . .

Projective tests are used very little in sociological study, yet we are inclined to predict a future for them. The few tests in existence are designed, as in psychological research, to uncover experiences which the subject cannot readily recall or else is apt to censor. Although the PT-10 is still highly experimental, it has proved helpful in understanding high school and college students. Group scoring methods, while not perfected, hold promise of yielding simple statistical counts which will differentiate students on broad bases. By use of a more analytical scheme, it may be possible to discover personality types as defined in reference to social atmospheres. In two colleges, for example, the religious overcast in student answers was very pronounced. On one card depicting a hotel scene, the young man and woman were said frequently to be college students, unmarried, and "on a trip to a big city over the week end." They try to get a room but it is denied them and, in about half these answers, the individuals "regret their action and return home." This projection is made in spite of the fact that the most conspicuous thing in the card is a wall sign reading "restricted clientele."

INTER-TEST CORRELATIONS

On assumption that the worth of any test is in part made known and improved by correlating it with other test scores, we have encouraged this arduous statistical work among colleges. Again, no full report is possible, because of space limitations, but the general run of findings can be gleaned.

At Wayne University, Dr. Elaine Forsyth Cook has done correlations on all Battery A tests. Briefly, four inter-test correlations were found to be of most statistical significance. Those parts of the AS-20 and AS-38 tests which dealt with attitudes toward Negro and Jew had positive relations of .431 and .542, respectively. A correlation of −.244 was obtained between total AS-20 and IT-1 scores, indicating a negative relation between knowledge and prejudice. Put otherwise, the more the information an average student possessed, the less strong his antagonisms were. A similar negative correlation (−.315) existed between the AS-20 test and the EI-5 experience inventory, suggesting that close personal-social contacts with Negroes tend to be associated with low prejudice scores.

Elsewhere, among College Study institutions, inter-test correlations have been obtained. At Atlanta University, about the same significant relation was found between the AS-20 and IT-1 tests, suggesting that knowledge about people is accompanied by positive feelings toward them. At this same college IT-1 scores had a positive relation (.63) with scores on the California Test of Mental Maturity and the California Test of Personality, especially with the self-adjustment scale (.81) of the latter test. At Springfield College a correlation of —.217 and .214, respectively, was found between the AS-20 and two of the Minnesota Personality Scales, namely, morale and economic conservatism. No significant relation was found between the AS-20 and the ACE Psychological Examination (1946).

At the State College for Teachers, Albany, attitudes toward Negroes and Jews (AS-15, AS-10) were correlated at the 5 percent level of confidence with about half of the eight scales in the Rosenzweig Personal-Frustration Test, leading one to think that prejudiced persons tend to exaggerate personal frustration, to avoid or evade such situations, and to direct aggressions toward other aspects of the environment. At Eau Claire, Wisconsin, State Teachers College students who made low adjustment scores on the Bernreuter Personality Inventory, showed somewhat more antagonism toward Jews and Negroes (AS-15, AS-10) than did students with better adjustment scores.

VARIATIONS IN ETHNIC ATTITUDES

So far, we have reported test means, a standard way of describing the behavior of the so-called *average* college student. Beneath this statistical construct are actual persons, and no two of them are presumed to be identical. Between these two extremes, the abstract and the concrete, a large number of mass variations is known to exist, variations by sex, age, grade level, geographic region, ethnic group, religion, socioeconomic status, and other factors. To suggest their importance in planning intergroup programs, some distributions will be given.

Among the college students tested, men show more prejudice than women when other factors were held constant. Younger age levels, say freshmen and sophomores, were more liberal in viewpoints than were older graduate students, especially in-service teachers over forty-five years of age. There was, however, no uniform change in prejudice as grade level or years in college increased. Teaching experience tended to shift attitudes slightly toward more negative reactions to Negroes and Jews, a finding based on small but equated groups of pre- and in-service graduate students. Elementary education teachers, and probably social studies teachers, were less prejudiced than were teachers in certain other fields, notably in health and physical education where urban conduct problems are often severe.

The anti-feelings of both pre- and in-service teachers appeared to decrease as their fathers' education increased, the striking exception being in relation to attitudes toward the lower class where the reverse was true. While geographic area made a profound difference, the smaller the community in which students have spent most of their life, the more inclined they were toward illiberal views. Aside from Jewish students, who showed less ethnic prejudice than either Catholic or Protestant, church membership left no measurable effect on group attitudes, except a tendency to favor one's own religious group. Students whose fathers' occupation most of their life was farming showed greater negative feelings than those from any other occupational level, omitting attitudes toward the Negro. In this latter case students whose fathers were in clerical and small business pursuits averaged higher antagonistic scores. Students whose fathers were teachers at school and college levels were least prejudiced toward all ethnic and class groups, except the lower class.

Were data complete enough, the same type of variables—sex, age, grade, etc.—would be found to operate within minority student groups, an impression based in part on studies conducted by the three Negro colleges in the Study. Atlanta University in particular undertook to clarify the color factor in campus associations, finding that the lighter the complexion, the greater the prestige of the individual. Preferential ratings on this basis were conditioned, however, by other variables, notably family backgrounds, athletic or other talent, and academic ability. No similar data came from far-western colleges on Spanish and Mexican students, but descriptive material showed considerable variations within these ethnic heritage groups.

SOME COMMUNITY STUDY DATA

At San Francisco, college students made a reconnaissance survey of the city, concluding that their campus was "an island" set apart from the color-line distinctions found in many public services and invitational groupings. In Detroit and Chicago, students did testing for discrimination in restaurants, recreational centers, employment services, etc., and resorted at times to court or other direct counteraction. At Greeley, Spanish-Anglo war veterans, speaking the two languages, assisted the community in its own self-survey by interviewing residents of the local Mexican colony. Elsewhere, in at least four small-town college centers, systematic community studies were made. The commonplace yet basic nature of these student-faculty inquiries can be sensed in a list of agencies and occupations in which a search was made for discriminatory practices.

SMALL-TOWN COMMUNITY SERVICE AGENCIES

Banks	Garages, auto sales	Parks, playgrounds
Barber shops	Hardware stores	Police department
Beauty parlors	Home rental agencies	Poolrooms, hangouts
Bowling alleys	Hospitals	Relief agencies
Clothing stores	Hotels, rooms	Repair shops
Courthouse	Laundries, cleaning	Roller skating rinks
Dance halls	Lawyers	Sheriff's office
Dentists	Loan companies	Swimming pools
Doctors, nurses	Lodges, civic clubs	Taverns, night clubs
Drug stores	Movie theaters	Taxi services
Filling stations	Newspapers	

We know no easy way to summarize community survey findings, no totals, ratios or indexes, for practices differed widely in terms of local factors.[11] In small towns discrimination was most evident where whites and nonwhites met at an equality level, for instance eating in restaurants or attending unsegregated meetings. Intergroup contact was most resented by whites under conditions of intimacy—shaking hands, use of a common swimming pool or dance hall. In large cities human relations were more impersonal and pecuniary, with sentiment yielding in part to profits and efficiency, as in most business contacts. Hostility seemed greatest

[11] For a detailed student survey of a small Michigan community, see Arthur Katona, "Community Services and the Negro," *Social Forces*, XXXVI (1948), 443–50.

over employment policies and restrictive housing covenants, an agreement among property owners not to rent or sell to "undesirables." For sake of record, it should be said that, in May 1948, the United States Supreme Court held that such covenants could not be enforced in court, though they can at this writing be maintained as matter of voluntary individual agreement.

GROUP DESCRIPTION AND SOCIOGRAPHIC STUDY

The idea of making whole groups—the natural groupings in and about school and college—the object of study was strong among Study consultants at the beginning of field work. This interest was not so central in local college committees, oriented as most of them were in moral and psychological frames of reference. Their gradual shift, where change did occur, is in itself an exciting story, but here concern is only with the types of findings derived from group inquiry.

During the initial year of field work, it was not unusual to come upon situations where the individual approach, whether by case study or mass testing, proved inadequate in disclosing the facts needed for corrective action. In a far-western college, for example, a central problem was how to teach a strongly organized minority group that prejudice is a two-way road, that traffic runs in both directions. In ways of which it was not fully conscious, this Spanish-Mexican club was penalizing its members for too close association with Anglo students as in steady dating. It was also matching foul play with foul play, turning back majority-group tricks, and thus endangering its own high campus standing. The need in such cases was for whole-group study, the kind of inquiry that would show social perceptions, norms of conduct and salient motivations.

At several colleges the favored form of group study was either a guided group observation (GS-2 form) or group life history (GS-4), both requiring some understanding of concepts. More popular because it was more easily taught was sociographic study, a series of procedures for discovering the patterns of "attraction and repulsion" inherent in every group. Over time, the College Study staff evolved a seven-page manual on sociometric study procedures, a guide to study-making that was circulated more widely than any other single piece of College Study material.

In group descriptions, some committees focused on "all children," others on racial, creedal, or other deviants within mixed groups. In these latter cases especially, much work was done on leader roles, social isolates, linking individuals, cliques, intra- and intergroup relations, group ratings, conduct codes, and group effects on personality. In group life histories, the range of inquiry was much wider, sending actual and prospective teachers into a group's community backgrounds, as well as into time-trend changes in its life. In urban slum areas the fascist type of child group struc-

TABLE 10

PERCENT OF ACCEPTANCE AND REJECTION BY 96 JUNIORS
AND SENIORS OF THEIR CLASSMATES*

ACCEPTED OR REJECTED AS	PERCENT OF ALL CHOICES	
	Range	Average
1. Best friend	1.8–17.0	6.6
2. Good friend	14.4–44.0	24.9
3. An "O.K." person	20.7–49.0	32.4
4. Unknown to me	3.4–53.8	29.3
5. I don't care for	1.5–30.0	5.2
6. I really dislike	0.3– 2.9	1.1
Total		99.5

* From *College Programs in Intergroup Relations*, p. 252.

ture was more common than any other, and led a committee to conclude that "Here is the clear and present danger, at least in this school district, to our democratic way of life." No differences in group structure were found to run along ethnic or social lines, suggesting that "tough little gangsters on their way to hoodlum status were products of an areal culture, heirs to a tradition which has about it a general antisocial tinge."

Sociographic inquiry, as suggested earlier, made these impressions clearer, adding some findings that were new. Almost every college made some of these "friendship" studies, with half the general committee chairmen affirming that, all things considered, "No other study method was better liked by students or helped them to learn more about groups." At Lynchburg College, to give a concrete example, the sociographic approach was used to explore cleavages on the campus, preparatory to starting integration programs in both curricular and extracurricular fields.

Although we know of no tabular data with which to compare the average percent friendship choices seen in Table 10, there is reason to believe that Lynchburg is "a friendly, fairly well integrated campus," a college strongly pervaded with a Christian (Disciples of Christ) point of view. And yet it was startling to the Study committee to find that about a third of the juniors and seniors were rated by classmates as "unknown to me" or else "I don't care for." Every college campus, even a small college, is a complex universe from a human relations standpoint, a great question mark about which a lot should be known in order to do effective guidance and instructional work.

THE NEED TO KNOW

College Study findings have been hastily canvassed in this chapter, a task made difficult by the diversity of college interests and the unreportability of subjective data. Comparable scores, chiefly test data, have been stressed, thus omitting individual studies well worth detailed presentation. Excluded, too, are pre- and end-test efforts to measure experimental change, a topic discussed in the next chapter.

From a critical standpoint, the studies cited show many of the strengths and weaknesses characterizing present intergroup re search.[12] In general, the major focus has been on verbal responses as indicative of attitudes, and findings have been suggestive rather than conclusive. Study problems have been defined, no doubt, too simply, and working conditions have been far from ideal. Lack of test forms of known worth has been a serious handicap, notably tests that measure salience, the strength of motivations in determining conduct. Inability to secure general college assent in giving Battery A tests suggests the outer limit of voluntary intercollege cooperation, a regrettable limitation so far as presenting a useful picture of teacher attitudes, etc., is concerned.

To say that we have not found all the answers is not to discredit the work that was done. To our certain knowledge, all but a few of the two hundred and seventy-two fact-finding inquiries made by College Study institutions have proved of value to study makers,

---

[12] Best critiques are Arnold M. Rose, *Studies in the Reduction of Prejudice* (Chicago: American Council on Race Relations, 1947); and Robin Williams, *The Reduction of Intergroup Tensions* (New York: Social Science Research Council, 1947).

many being used directly in curricular and other changes. And yet one cannot reflect on our present ignorance without strongly underscoring the great need to know. Research, fortunately, is cumulative, bit adding to bit to extend foundations on which change programs can be built. We are hopeful, not only that our findings may prove of interest to educators, but also that such studies as reported will be repeated and improved.

4. Changing Learners by Means of Academic Instruction

The idea of changing human behaviors is, we believe, the heart of intergroup education, as it is of all social education. To assume that professional educators know how to do this with maximum effects goes beyond the facts as we understand them. Nor does it seem safe to hold that social scientists, psychologists or others, have final answers, for theories handed down by them often prove inadequate in concrete situations. Even to put the educational problem in words acceptable to any number of persons would be an achievement, one on which College Study experience does not warrant any easy optimism.

From a practical standpoint, the problem might take the form of a question. *How can we, in teacher-leader roles, influence people to behave in desirable ways toward one another?* The query seems simple until it is pulled apart. Who are these "we's," the varied teacher personalities? What methods of "influencing" learners are possible, and what skills does each require? What persons are to be changed, and how much is known about them? What new kinds of behaviors are considered "desirable" and by whom? How can the worth of teaching—that is, degrees of change, time-costs, etc.—be assessed? Other questions come to mind but these will show the complexity of the task confronting the intergroup educator.

College Study work has been an attempt to throw some light on the nature of democratic re-education, a term used on assumption that all persons have already done a great deal of social learning. Six approaches to this problem have been made in colleges and schools: (1) academic classroom instruction, (2) group-process education, (3) community participation, (4) use of audio-visual aids and materials, (5) vicarious experience by means of short dramatic plays, sociodrama, fiction reading, etc., and (6) on-the-job teacher education, particularly in student teaching and in the first year of full-time professional service. After looking briefly at the results of all formal College Study change efforts, we shall discuss the first three of these methods, omitting others or relating them to the discussion.

RANGE OF STUDY-ACTION PROJECTS

College Study files contain data on 379 concrete college and school efforts to teach better human relations, the sum of change-induction projects so far reported in the four years and more of work. From the viewpoint of *target,* more of these activities have dealt with prospective teachers than with any other population, including school children. Least work has been done on adult noncollege citizens, a group which has always been hard to reach. While all projects have had the aim of changing people, most of

TABLE 11

AREAS OF DESIRABLE EDUCATIONAL CHANGE

INTENDED CHANGES	IN COMMON SCHOOLS*	IN COLLEGE PROGRAMS	IN THE COMMUNITY
1. In course content, new courses, materials.......	24	59	....
2. In teaching methods, learning experiences.......	22	46	....
3. In extracurricular clubs and activities..........	25	39	....
4. In student guidance and personnel practice......	8	12	....
5. In practice teaching, in-service education.......	11	23	....
6. In school-community relations, area services.....	8	17	12
7. In workshops for teachers, civic leaders.........	12	28	4
8. In official school policy, records, forms..........	3	9	....
9. Miscellaneous undertakings...................	2	12	3
Total....................................	115	245	19

* Nursery, grade, and high schools, public and private.

them have centered on attitudes, next on understandings, and last on motoric action. More than a third have taken the traditional *form* of fact-finding, followed by recommendations. Another third have been "action research" projects where the process itself was regarded as change inducing. Other projects have been marginal to these two types, so that classification is difficult.

A more definitive idea of the 379 activities can be had by tabulating the broad areas in which their directors believed that changes were needed and should be made.

Table 11 should be read with caution. It does not include a large number of activities of a short-run nature, such as one- and two-day workshops, of which there were more than a hundred. It does not take account of the incidental effects of a campus program, for instance, changes in courses made by faculty members who were not affiliated with any working committee. The table is a listing of *official, counted change-induction projects* as reported to us and on which we have descriptive data. While titles are as clear as possible, each heading includes quite different things. For example, changes in educational policy range from correction of small biases in college records or student placement to active efforts to increase the enrollment of minority-group members.

The number of projects in common schools may strike one as strange in a program designed to improve teacher education. Mostly, these were college-led activities, made possible by the active cooperation of affiliated schools. Much of the training needed at both pre- and in-service teaching levels can be done only in direct contact with children, on-the-job experiences where demonstrations are possible. Moreover, as time went on, it seemed that school structure offered less resistance to change efforts than did college structure, for instance in newer course emphases and teaching methods.

Intended changes and actual changes are, of course, different concepts, and in theory the spread can be very great. This sets a complex problem in intergroup education, the task of evaluating success or failure. In 26 of the 379 change efforts, experimenters had pre- and end-test data, evidence to be discussed presently under another heading. In at least 92 cases, assessment could be made from objective facts, for instance, course units, college records, admissions to clubs, and similar evidence. In the remainder of the projects, we have had to depend upon personal observations, observations of experimenters, plus descriptive data in College Committee reports.

What is intended in Table 12 is an over-all estimate, critical yet subjective, of success or failure in College Study work. Biases are in the direction of too much caution, rather than too little, as tested by having college committee members rate those activities in which they had participated. In over half the rated cases, appraisals were a full step higher than those given in the table, that is, from "no change" to "some change," "some change" to "basic change."

In making table ratings, each evaluative category was defined as clearly as possible in terms of the evidence to be gathered. For example, "some change" in course content was judged in part by regular class use of intergroup readings (pamphlets, books), films, or the like in the semester following their initial adoption in a course. In some cases, substitute material (one pamphlet in place of another, etc.) was judged to fulfill the specification set up. "Basic change" in course content was taken to mean a substantial

TABLE 12

IMPRESSIONS OF SUCCESS OR FAILURE IN CHANGE PROJECTS

PROJECT AREAS	ALL PROJECTS	NO CHANGE EVIDENT	SOME CHANGE	BASIC CHANGE
1. In course content, etc..............	83	22	37	24
2. In teaching methods...............	68	9	43	16
3. In extracurricular activities........	64	5	23	36
4. In guidance, personnel.............	20	2	6	12
5. In practice teaching...............	34	6	10	18
6. In school-community relations.......	37	16	12	9
7. In workshops, teachers, others.......	44	30	....	14
8. In college policy, records...........	12	....	4	8
9. In miscellaneous areas.............	17	4	7	6
Total........................	379	94	142	143

innovation, for instance, the repeat offering of a new course, introduction of new work units consuming a third or more of course time, or a new course-related program of community study, field trips, or audio-visual aids. In school and community workshops— to select another example—"some change" could not be objectified well enough for use and was abandoned as a category. "Basic change" was interpreted as a workshop model centering around group-process teaching, with student participation in major decision making and with an effort to evaluate both subjective and objective learning effects.

Simplest explanation of the no-change and some-change columns in Table 12 is the tendency of things to fall back into place, old habits to assert themselves, once a planning group's initial interest has died down. Basic changes, with some exceptions, seemed more likely to be permanent, or rather to carry within themselves the dynamics of further change, since any kind of final program would be unusual and undesirable. Some-change and basic-change totals show that *college efforts at better teaching do pay off*, a finding supported by pre- and end-test data of which a special study was made.

CHANGE EXPERIMENTS

Of the twenty-six pre- and end-test studies of learning outcomes in experimental college and school classes, twenty-four have been selected as fully adequate in design and detail for comparative analysis. Of these twenty-four best studies, ten showed mean changes in either (or both) attitudes or information in desired directions at the 3 percent level of confidence, four at the 5 percent level, but in only a few of the studies was the increase in liberalism or in knowledge very great as judged by test potentials. Seven studies gave no reliable changes in class averages, and two of these showed significant part-test losses in liberal viewpoints. Three studies yielded definite losses for average class members in either attitudes or information as indicated by the College Study A3-attitude scales and the IT-1 knowledge test. In these same classes, of course, some students made positive gains.

Of the ten statistically most significant studies mentioned above, seven were concerned with attitudes only. In five of these, informal teaching methods were used, namely, class planning, project groups, field trips, films, radio, and fiction, and in the other two use was made of factual, academic material, usually textbooks and pamphlets. Three of the above five "group process" experiments did not focus directly on student attitudes—that is, attention was centered on some general topic such as "child growth"—whereas the other two made a direct approach in the sense of discussing attitudes, their nature, bases, changes, etc. End-test results distinctly favored the indirect approach, yielding part-test mean scores in favorable directions significantly greater than in the direct classroom academic work.

Of the three remaining successful studies, all aimed at changes in both attitudes and information. One used the informal method, guiding students, after they had taken the tests, in making a study of the community by giving these tests to a sampling of adults as part of an interview. By contrast, the other two studies were formal and academic, with lectures, readings, and the like. Again, the informal method brought greater attitudinal changes, but it showed much smaller increases in knowledge. Gains in information were, on the average, about ten points less in the informal approach than in formal lectures and book readings.

To make the above comparisons, it was necessary to type the various teaching methods into informal (direct, indirect) and formal or academic; however, this categorization covered up many unique elements in each concrete change project. Reviewers of literature on intergroup experimental teaching have had to do much the same; thus, their over-all conclusions on success or failure leave a great deal to be desired. While Rose's categories differ from ours, his analysis of sixty-six studies shows the uncertainty attending efforts to make attitudinal change.

The main point in Table 13 is that more than half the studies resulted in, or were connected with, favorable attitude change. It cannot be said that one influence was more or less effective than another because of differences in definitions and

TABLE 13
EXPERIMENTAL EFFORTS TO REDUCE PREJUDICE*

INFLUENCE	CHANGE	NO CHANGE	INDEFINITE
A school or college course...................	8	4	1
Specific influence such as films, radio...........	9	4	1
Personalized contacts, trips, visits.............	3	3	3
Correlation of knowledge or acquaintance with attitudes................................	9	2	1
Years spent in school or college..............	8	6	4

* Adapted from Arnold M. Rose, *Studies in the Reduction of Prejudice* (Chicago: American Council on Race Relations, 1948), p. 18.

conditions. Even a concept like "personalized contacts" varied, no doubt, from experiment to experiment. While this by no means invalidates the table, it does leave a reader with no clear picture of means-to-ends relations.

CONCLUSIONS FROM CHANGE PROJECTS

In the above analysis we have used the terms "formal" and "informal," "direct" and "indirect," as words most likely to carry undisputed meaning. While no easy equating is possible, formal is much the same as *academic,* and most academic instruction is direct in that its aims are known to students. Informal education includes both *group work* and *community participation,* and real purposes (changes in students) may be concealed under some guise such as "child study." With this explanation, conclusions can be made to apply to the kinds of education we have italicized.[1]

(1) Under exact conditions, *changes in students in a desired direction are seldom very great in terms of test potentials,* a conclusion subject to the limitations known to exist in standard measurement instruments. As a corollary, it seems clear that (2) *little can be learned about change induction unless testing is followed by case studies.* Who are the changers, the nonchangers, the "average" student? Why do some learners move in one direction, others in another? Why is speed or rate of learning so variable? What kinds of stimuli are most effective for which type of person? Answers to such questions would seem to depend upon systematic interviewing and on the collection of collateral nontest data.

(3) Under pre- and end-testing, it is probable that *group-process education and community participation produce greater increases in liberal views than do academic methods, whereas the latter appear to bring greater gains in factual and theoretical knowledge.* This statement calls attention to a debate of long standing in teacher education, the relative worth of academic and nonacademic types of instruction. Each kind of teaching would seem to rest on its own major assumptions as to the nature of learning, a point to which we shall return from time to time.

(4) Among education majors, *creedal attitudes and social class values have seemed somewhat more resistant to change,* a tentative finding that may be due to circumstantial factors rather than to inherent elements in these two areas of intergroup relations. This problem needs further experimental study for, in theory, a reliable answer would do much toward suggesting prime foci for intergroup educational efforts.

(5) Every experimental change project is a composite of many interrelated elements, few of which are ever analyzed out in detail, so that *over-all means-to-ends relations remain more or less*

---

[1] Like most sharp distinctions in real-life data, this three-way division is set up for study purposes only. Inspection of a detailed report on a college course, for example, the work by W. W. D. Sones at the University of Pittsburgh (*College Study Programs in Intergroup Relations,* p. 111) will show that all three kinds of education may be found in a single course pattern.

obscure. While experimenters deplore this state of affairs, it is improbable that much can be done about it under conditions of field experimentation.

(6) No conclusion in this section should be read to mean that *school teachers en masse are necessarily discriminating against minority-group pupils in their everyday school and life behaviors*. Academic testing does not permit one to make such specific applications of test findings, that is, to predict overt run-of-life actions and reactions. At best a presumption (probability) can be postulated, but even this should be studied in light of criticisms of the usual college classroom testing as discussed later in the chapter.

Nature of Academic Education

In turning now to academic education, the first problem is that of definition. "Academic," in the dictionary sense, has various meanings, but none of these centers thought fully on the content we have in mind. The kind of education under discussion cannot be limited to institutions of higher learning for it is found from the kindergarten through grade and high schools to the university. It is not classical education in contrast to vocational, or theoretical in opposition to practical, or conventional as opposed to experimental. One way to define it is by concrete examples.

Consider, first, two classroom situations in the same large urban university. We quote below the remarks made by one of these instructors to his class at its initial session. The class is a group of last-term seniors and graduate students, many of whom are teachers in city schools, and meetings are held twice a week in the evenings.

ORIENTING A COLLEGE COURSE

This course is foundational to your work in this department. . . . It is essential that you get course content from the start, for otherwise you cannot keep up. You are at a big disadvantage if you work for pay, for your time ought to be spent in study. . . . Drop-outs are very high in this class, students who are unfitted for specialized training by ability and interest. They do not belong here but in some other field. . . . I shall start the first lecture now, and you should take notes with care. Save your questions until the end of the hour, for I want you to see first of all how ideas fit together, how they all get woven into a single big pattern.

This instructor was young, well trained, and confident. From contacts with him, we would say that he knew his business. He knew how to think, to put thoughts into logical patterns, to lecture on these learnings. His classroom role, apparently, was that of a scholar and disciplinarian, a man who worked hard and expected hard work from others. He did not take his teaching lightly, going out of his way after class to help students. His only impatience seemed to be with slow learners, especially with indifferent ones. The help he asked from the College Study was in deepening course content, in providing better readings. All things considered, any other request might have been illogical, for this case gives a glimpse of *academic education.*

Across the hall from this man was another teacher, an instructor in the same social science field. At our request he thumbed through a set of student papers, selecting with care the one he judged most typical of student reactions to the course. These papers were written out of class, unsigned, hence not handed in for grading.

WHAT THIS COURSE HAS MEANT TO ME

Really, I can't say. . . . I've liked the course ever so much. Think at times I'll change my major, but then, again, I don't know. . . . Anyhow, this course has been different. . . . I like best the committee work, the idea of small groups in which students plan how to do a job and then report it to class. . . . All of us have gotten acquainted in this class, and many now meet at the Greek's [restaurant] to talk things over after each evening session. We think you have given an old idea a new twist, the idea of learning by doing. We have learned more about ourselves than any other subject, what we really believe and value in people. We have learned what a group is, or rather can become, and I would say that this can be carried right over into school work.

From reading these papers, one got a distinct feeling about this class. Some accounts glowed too much, some were confused, yet everybody seemed to be having a grand experience in human relations. At times the whole class met, but mostly students worked in small groups on projects. They made trips to interview agency officials and they conducted panels and sociodramas in class. They did a stint of textbook reading, but less perhaps than the reading of newspapers, opinion journals, and current fiction. Whatever this course sought to do, procedures differed from academic instruction. We cite it as an example of *group-process education.*

Academic education is a certain kind of learning. Learning is a change in people, but not all changes can be called learning, for example, those due to maturation and organic malfunctioning. Learning is a *planful shaping of personality,* an interaction between organism and environment which leads to behavioral modification. Of all the kinds of behaviors valued in academic education, the most prized are the closer alignment of perceptions with realities, the use of abstract symbols in problem solving, and the patterning of symbols into systems which give meaning to the flow of concrete events.

Since academic education, like all planful teaching is a situational product, one must generalize details. A visitor to an academic classroom may be impressed with the teacher's command position, his reliance on authority, the compulsion he feels to advance knowledge. He may note, conversely, the "wall" of learner silence, the great dependence on reading, the individual competitive struggle for advancement. The class is more like a human aggregate than a sociological group; thus, it has no goal that is common, being dependent on the teacher to motivate its actions. Symbol mastery is of prime importance, reflective thought the *modus operandi,* with paper-and-pencil tests to indicate success and failure. The teacher is the final judge of progress, awarding grades as a part of his general responsibility.

COURSE WORK IN INTERGROUP RELATIONS

Curriculum revision is widely favored as a way of working on intergroup problems. In College Study experience it was most popular with academic teachers at school and college levels. It consisted almost wholly of course changes, new courses, and better evaluation methods. It would not be far wrong to state that courses were of all kinds, "lab" science and mathematics being notable exceptions. In colleges, changes in social science courses were most numerous, followed in order by those in educational philosophy, curriculum making, fine arts, languages, health and physical education, directed teaching, guidance courses, evaluation, and off-campus courses for in-service teachers. In grade and high school, consultant aid might be requested by teachers in any course area, for all courses were felt to involve human relations.

Over four years one accumulates many examples of academic course changes, so that selection of a few illustrations is a problem. To avoid bias as much as possible, we have opened cumulative files and pulled cases at random, discarding any that were clear repetitions. Cases have been arrayed from low to high educational levels and each one is condensed.

MAKING MAY BASKETS

Some kindergarten children were making May baskets. Terry pasted on a diamond decoration. "Oh, no, Terry, not that way," the teacher said. "Like this," showing him, "because they hold better." Unimpressed, the boy continued in his own way. "No, that won't do," said the teacher on her next inspection, and she pasted all the diamonds on the basket. Turning to Mary Lou, she complimented her. To another boy, Jimmy, she said matter-of-factly, "Now, you've spoiled your basket. See, it doesn't have a handle." The boy replied that he did not want a handle and the teacher told him that he must make one, that "all baskets have handles."

Such an incident would have no place in this volume were it not for two unrelated facts. For one thing, the case suggests how a good many teachers try to shape child personality by direct, authoritarian, compulsive methods. Secondly, a question was asked Terry after class, in fact several questions were asked. It appeared that Mary Lou made good baskets and she was Polish. Terry was "American" and he did not like "Polish baskets." His mother said the teacher was Polish also, which further complicated matters. The impasse in learning seemed to be a matter of social perception, that is, not liking anything "Polish."

EXPLAINING MINORITY CUSTOMS

In a discussion of superstitions, the number 13 came up. A Jewish boy said it was good luck for Jewish boys, and some Jewish girls began to titter. When a Gentile girl asked the boy why 13 was good luck, I explained that, at this age, Jewish boys receive their Bar Mitzvah, or confirmation, signifying their passing into manhood.

In the above 6B class in a heterogeneous urban area, the homeroom teacher was extremely sensitive to cultural differences. While she made no formal study of them, in fact argued against such study, she always dealt with children's ideas as they appeared in classroom behaviors. Her method was that of simple explanation, of treating each incident as a normal and natural problem, and seeking always to widen areas of tolerance and understanding. "When some child said that Catholics do not celebrate Easter, or Christmas, or anything but Mass, I told the children the truth about the matter."

The next case, in truth, the next three cases are lengthy records of high school and college course changes. To describe any one in detail would run to several pages, so that accounts are suggestive only. Emphasis is on procedures, data from which other aspects of a course can be inferred. Again, the classroom teacher is speaking.

HIGH SCHOOL SENIORS STUDY HUMAN RIGHTS

On the first day of class, I held up a booklet, *To Secure These Rights,* a report of the President's Committee on Civil Rights, 1947. Only two students had ever heard about it. I asked the class to name some rights which they enjoyed, and then whether all the people they knew had these same rights. Differences of opinion were numerous, leading to our first assignment. I distributed copies of the booklet, suggesting that each student make a list of "basic human rights."

At the next class meeting, these rights were discussed. . . . I then told the class as much as I could about the history of human rights in this country, their connection with human rights all over the world, reading from a UNESCO report. For the next several meetings, we worked on the problem of why some Americans had these rights and others did not, that is, majority and minority group relations.

With this background, we began a study of six basic rights, for example the right to safety and security, to citizenship and its privileges, to freedom of conscience and expression. The idea was to identify these rights in terms of everyday community behaviors, the things that people did and said and felt. City newspapers were brought to class and analyzed. Trips were made to a number of city offices and agencies, and two speakers were invited in and questioned. To bring things together, we began to build a master list of all denials of fair and equal opportunities to people—in jobs, in schooling, in housing, in social relations, so on.

The last part of the course, perhaps a fourth of the total time, was spent on ways and means of equalizing opportunities. Study was centered on three topics: what should be done, who could undertake to do it, and how might action be started. We began here with things that had been done in the school by different groups of students and analyzed these cases. Next, we had a panel discussion by three community leaders, and finally we turned to the problem of where high school students could do useful kinds of community services, such as settlement-house work and church youth groups. I was able to cite to students various opportunities.

What the course has tried to teach these Seniors is a concern for people, a sense of the common good, plus the duty on their part of understanding the dependence of the community and the nation on good citizenship.

Course changes of this type have long been common in academic education and very numerous in College Study experience. Major emphasis, namely, *to understand* some phase of our collective life, remains the same, but course content is revised to permit teaching in reference to current problems. This is, we believe, the essential viewpoint advocated by most professional educational associations,[2] and the trend is toward a strong intergroup orientation.

The problem of teaching social problems has interested a score or more of individual professors and committees in the twenty-four colleges under survey. Most of these persons profess dissatisfaction with the old-type social problems textbook, a hit-or-miss selection of breakdowns in social order without a theory framework. Many are inclined toward a value-conflict viewpoint, a conception of problems as a clash in group interests and power uses.[3] A detailed outline of one unit in a four- to five-unit course taught on occasion by the writer will show this general viewpoint.

STUDYING ECONOMIC ADJUSTMENTS

I. *The Frame of Common Beliefs*

What do majority-group members believe about minority-group members and vice versa? Students search their personal experiences, interview friends, and comb the literature (including fiction), assembling double columns of popular beliefs. These are then made into a check list, with *A D U* answers, on which students indicate their own present beliefs.

II. *Minority Workers: Economic Status and Trends*

What do facts show? For example, is the Negro "lazy," the "foreigner" replacing Americans in certain industries, the Jews

[2] For example, R. W. Crary and J. T. Robinson, *America's Stake in Human Rights*, National Council for the Social Studies, Bull. 24, 1949 (Washington: National Education Association, 1949).

[3] For viewpoint and bibliography, R. C. Fuller and R. R. Myers, "The Natural History of a Social Problem," *American Sociological Review*, VI (1941), 320–39.

"dominant" in the nation's business? Do minority-group members work for less, do poorer work, refuse to join labor unions? From U.S. Census figures on occupations and incomes, the search ranges over a bibliography of 200 or more titles.

III. *General Work Conditions and Problems*

On close inspection, what are the demands made upon people by various kinds of jobs? The physical, technological, and social conditions of work? The rate of pay, security, advancement, welfare services? Students organize by groups to study areas of interest, for example, agriculture, factory labor, domestic service, skilled trades, small or large business enterprises, and the professions. Schoolteaching is always a popular area with pre- and in-service teachers.

IV. *Economic Progress: Handicaps and Consequences*

What are the universal human handicaps to economic well being, for example, differences in individual skill, talent, and ambitions? What handicaps do specific minorities experience—ethnic, creedal, cultural? How can these two types of factors be separated and tested as to nature and strength? In studying their effects, how can one distinguish between consequence and coincidence? What is meant by saying that the economic side of life conditions all its other aspects?

V. *Furthering Economic Insights and Adjustments*

What are the immediate adjustment needs of specific minority groups? What are their long-range needs? What agencies are concerned with one or both, and what services do they offer? What, for example, does unionization promise? Cooperatives? Where does public education fit into this picture? Why should minority-group members seek a university education? What about quota regulations, jobs after college, relations of the professional person to the minority community?

In College Study colleges such courses have often seemed as good underneath as they look on the surface, depending on teacher scholarship and class industry. They are always analytical in nature, seeking to advance social understanding by contact with factual data and development of study skills. Some work of this kind has been done in every college in the Study, including studies of prejudice, discrimination, group conflict, community institutions, social class structure, the teaching of controversial issues, social action groups, and area-wide community coordination. At no time, to repeat a point, have these units, projects, and studies been limited to social science areas; on the contrary, they have been spread widely through the teacher-training curriculum.

ENGLISH CLASSES STUDY MODERN DRAMA

I. *The Drama as Communication*

How does art differ from other forms of communication? Compare a novel with a scientific treatise, a movie with a stage play. In what ways is society dependent upon communication, or, better, does it exist in communication? What is the public interest in plays dealing with majority-minority relations?

II. *General Plan of Content-Effect Analysis*

Have you seen a Broadway hit play dealing with intergroup relations? How were specific scenes handled? What general plan of study will we use in analyzing current dramas? Is casting important? Major characters? Minor characters? Over-all theme? Can one judge audience reactions and effects on attitudes? In short, by what standards—artistic and social—can a play be judged as to its nature and worth?

III. *A Survey of Leading Broadway Plays*

Does *Abie's Irish Rose* stereotype minorities? Did *Porgy and Bess* point up white virtues by contrasting them with disreputable Negro traits? Do you think *In Abraham's Bosom*, the Negro's struggle for freedom is well characterized? Is *Emperor Jones* a good example of fair dealing with the race problem? What do you think of *Anna Lucasta, Native Son,* and *Rain from Heaven?* Does *Flight from the West* show the spread of nazism in this country? Does *Tomorrow the World* make realistic to you the conditioning of a German boy to democracy in this country? If you were rewriting *I Remember Mama, A Bell for Adano,* or *State of the Union,* what changes, if any, would you try to make?

IV. *The Problem of Artistic and Social Standards*

From an art standpoint, what makes a good play? Must it have a universal theme, a structural unity and coherence? From a social viewpoint, how far can it depart from the biases of its potential public? Can you devise a list of specific fair-play standards? Would these standards diminish a drama's public appeal? Do people really want intelligent, realistic drama?

V. *Need for Nonprofessional, Noncommercial Theaters*

Times Square, New York, has about 40 theaters, and there are about 100 more in the nation. In 1941 there were 25,000 high school drama departments, 700 college theaters, 1,000 community playhouses, and an unknown number of "dramatic workshops." What functions do these institutions perform? What now limits their effectiveness? How much of a force for good will can they ever hope to become?

The above outline suggests the kind of course change made in several types of English or communications courses. At Talladega College, for example, interest goes beyond study into action. Students produce original one-act plays on interracial themes and present them to sizable audiences. The chief limitation has been the lack of good dramatic plays,[4] or rather the creative talent required to write them.

CHANGES WANTED IN LEARNERS

Wherever academic education is found, its stated purpose is to effect changes in learners. Its more specific aims are expressed in terms of knowledge mastery, skill improvement, and attitudinal modification, the latter being defined in nonmoral, nonethical ways. Our impression is that any kind of education in human relations will tend to claim these same objectives so that differences in educational pattern will consist mostly in the classroom methods followed, the emphases made, the evidence sought as to effects. Some of these variations between academic and nonacademic faculty orientations can be seen in the following case.

A PROBLEM IN FACULTY COORDINATION

In this college the faculty faced a problem. Students doing directed teaching were supervised by three persons: a critic teacher who was often the regular classroom teacher, a supervisor of directed teaching from the education department, and a subject-matter specialist in the field of the student's major. Student ratings were frequently far apart, and resulted in confusion to the student and the college. While the problem was not new, it had been sharpened by a general swing in the education department to an intergroup emphasis.

At a meeting on the problem, discussion was started by a math professor who said that "math was math," and to be taught for its own sake, that a student should be passed or failed in terms of subject competency. Other science areas took a similar stand, accusing educators of an "anti-intellectual bias," a sentimental "be good, do good" point of view. Educators replied in kind, so to speak, stressing heavily that children, not subject matter, were to be taught, that teaching should make a difference in everyday life.

In an effort to arrive at some common ground, each side agreed to

[4] See John Gassner, *Human Relations in the Theater* (New York: Anti-Defamation League of B'nai B'rith, 1949), 51 pp.

draw up a list of objectives, points on which to rate student teachers, and to ask critic teachers to do the same. This work took some time for, as it turned out, none of the groups had thought through the complex issue. When reports were made, it was a surprise to find that all lists named all major types of objectives, differing chiefly in wording, in strength of emphasis, and in the kinds of evidence judged to show teacher competencies. Lists included student motivation, social understanding, self-insight, teaching skills, study skills, truth and moral (professional) values.

With the problem now clearer, a joint committee was set up to canvass areas of difference. While its report is too long for summary, its tone of freedom-within-unity can be seen in regard to human relations. Students were to teach, and be graded, in any one of three patterns. One pattern was to suggest the bearings of a subject, for instance general biology, on intergroup problems. Another was to use intergroup materials so far as possible in teaching the subject. The third, the way favored by most educators, was to take the real-life problems of pupils and show the uses of a subject in their solution.

When an intergroup emphasis is based on science, the tendency of scientists is to assume out of existence a vexing problem. This is the question of moral values, the kinds and degrees of human relations desired in society at large. The scientist's concern with value-judgments, as he so often asserts,[5] is either to study them as data or else to guard his studies against their influence, that is, be "objective." In reflecting on this stand, practical workers in the intergroup field feel that social science helps them very little on what is, for them, a major problem—the goals that should be sought in education, the changes most needed in people in order to better their common mode of life.

In discussions of this problem in College Study institutions, social scientists have defended their hard-won, deeply prized objectivity, holding that without this detachment science itself would be impossible. Their only loyalty, it has been said, was to truth; their only interest in cause-effect-cause relations, what things are and how they work. Science has no more affinity with a democracy than with an autocracy; in either case, it must be "free" to follow its own rituals in seeking a coherent view of the universe.

From the counterviewpoint, it is admitted forthwith that science is a positive value, that it is our best long-run guarantee of na-

[5] For instance, Talcott Parsons, "The Prospect of Sociological Theory," *American Sociological Review,* XV (1950), 3–16.

tional security and a peaceful world order. Moreover, for anyone to think, he must have free and full access to data, freedom to make studies and publicize findings. Yet—and this is the issue— such freedom is not absolute for it could destroy the society that nurtures it.

SOCIAL ROLE OF SCIENTISTS

It has long been a matter of some surprise to me to realize that, while social scientists freely use the concepts of "culture" and the "unconscious" in their research, they do not *always* apply these concepts in an analysis of their own relationship to the larger American society of which they are a part. In their sometimes ruthless and cynical criticism of other elements in our culture, social scientists have often failed to reflect the anthropologist's discovery that a society, like a shirt, can split at the seams if it is handled too roughly.[6]

Charles Dollard, from whom the quotation is taken, is a respected social scientist in his own right and president of a large foundation that makes grants for scientific work. He goes on to speak of the aggressions some scientists have built up against a society which believes that "the scholar, like the greyhound, runs fastest on lean rations." To one who has served time in the academic poorhouse, this statement will probably make a lot of sense. "If," the writer concludes, "social scientists work off their aggressions by using the increasingly sharp tools of science to divide American society into armed camps, they will indeed have made a sorry use of their freedom."

Aside from moral values, the practical worker has another reason to question the general academic point of view. This is the assumption that mental processes control behavior, that for average persons they motivate action, even bring the varied elements of personality into an integrated, functional whole. Of course, this may indeed be true, a proposition on which neither side in the issue can produce clear and indisputable proof.

A CRITIQUE OF TEST KNOWLEDGE

Much that is known about intergroup relations, in truth an appreciable part of the psychosocial foundations of education, comes from paper-and-pencil tests. Academic teaching, in particu-

---

[6] Charles Dollard, "A Middleman Looks at Social Science," *American Sociological Review*, XV (1950), 16–20. Used by permission.

lar, depends upon these cumulative evidences of mental content
and change. While tests make valuable contributions to knowledge,
they are not above criticism. At times, to be sure, practical workers
at school and college levels ask more from formal tests than these
instruments can contribute. At other times, there is reason to
believe that testers themselves hold assumptions and/or draw inferences which are invalid. While this problem is too complex for
brief comment, enough can be said to suggest the need for caution
in testing and in using test data.

As long, no doubt, as we have had *intelligence tests,* the tests
have had critics. While no sweeping statement is in order, it does
seem probable that standard IQ tests are heavily loaded with
middle-class biases.[7] If this is the case, universal use of these tests to
forecast pupil school success or failure does a considerable damage
to lower-class children,[8] to large numbers of bilinguals, in sum to
all learners who are not proficient through life experience in certain kinds of word uses and meanings.[9] Nonverbal tests are only
partial exceptions. They stress a time factor deeply ingrained in
urban middle-class life, the hurry-hurry so conspicuously absent
from other parts of our society. Like verbal tests, they reward the
ability to do manipulative tasks quickly and at a superficial level.
If this kind of mental act is to be called thinking, some other term
such as reasoning should be used for the sort of decision making
that rests upon emotional concern and social perspective.

Personality tests, for example the Bernreuter Neurotic Inventory, are equally disturbing to the group-oriented educator. While
all such tests cannot be judged by any one, consider some Bernreuter items.

---

[7] For example, two University of Chicago doctoral dissertations: K. W. Eells,
Social Status Factors in Intelligence Test Items (1948), and W. I. Murray, *Intelligence Test Performance of Negro Children of Different Social Classes* (1947).
Eells shows, for example, that over three-fourths of the items in the most widely
used IQ tests differentiate low-class children from middle-class children, with the
latter making almost consistently higher marks. The question is whether the naming of a "wombat" as an animal is a more complex mental feat, i.e., shows more
intelligence, than, say, the identification of a dog, or whether in both cases test
items simply measure the run of childhood experiences, the culture in which respondents have lived.

[8] For example, Allison Davis, *Social Class Influence upon Learning* (Cambridge,
Mass.: Harvard University Press, 1948).

[9] See Ralph W. Tyler, "Educability and the Schools," *Elementary School Journal,*
XLIX (1948), 200–212. For a study of class bias as it pervades a small high school,
see A. B. Hollingshead, *Elmtown's Youth* (New York: Wiley & Sons, 1949).

TEST ITEMS AND ANSWERS

1. Do you see more fun or humor in things when you are in a group than when you are alone? [Required answer, i.e., a sign of normalcy, is "no."]
2. Can you usually understand a problem better by studying it alone than by discussing it with others? [Required answer is "yes."]
3. Do you usually face your troubles alone without seeking help? [Required answer is "yes."]
4. Do you like to bear responsibilities alone? [Required answer is "yes."]

Here, one might say, is a tester with a firm faith in individualism—in man alone, free, strong, non-grouped. On this test, subjects who preferred to work with others, who found satisfactions in team effort, are judged abnormal, that is, weak, dependent, or maladjusted. They seek group help, engage in group activity, because they feel inadequate, unable to cope with life by themselves. We doubt if any greater distortion of human nature can be found than this extreme personalistic emphasis, for man in all his time has been a group man, a pack member. Whether this has been a source of strength or weakness, it has been the human way of survival, diminished more in present mass living than at any other period of history. To use such personality tests to rate learners, to interpret learner responses from a socially atomistic viewpoint, can be debated as a dubious educational venture.

Of no less concern to educators is the general question of *attitude testing*. One might think, in view of a tremendous literature, that social psychology *is* attitude testing, though this would be in error. If attitudes are defined as what present attitude tests measure, namely, degree of mass acceptance-rejection of a list of items, then our comments will not be relevant. However, if one wants to know about people, what they are inclined to do in life situations, then current attitude tests leave much to be desired by workers in intergroup projects.

A small but classic study will point directly to one central issue. On a trip across the nation, LaPiere[10] and two Chinese friends stopped at one hundred and eighty-four restaurants and sixty-six hotels and cabins for overnight accommodations. A little later

[10] Richard LaPiere, "Attitudes Versus Actions," *Social Forces*, XIII (1934), 230–37.

proprietors of these places were mailed questionnaires asking whether they would serve Chinese or accept them as guests. Well over 90 percent of the replies were negative; and a control group of places, which had not been visited, sent in almost the same percentage of "no" answers. This suggests, of course, the great difference between attitude (test response) and action (life behavior).

Unless one thinks a moment, he may not realize how common such inconsistencies are in intergroup relations.[11] A teacher gets all the "right" answers from pupils in a discussion of Brotherhood Week, but notes that, outside of school, the "wrong" behaviors continue. Youth workers at interracial camps find that children draw close together in their activities; yet on returning home, they resume the usual patterns of a segregated life. Delegates to intergroup conferences may say goodbye before boarding trains to take them home, thus avoiding "embarrassing" situations. A school superintendent adopts an "intercultural policy" for the city schools; yet he assigns Negro teachers only to Negro areas. A college professor lectures his classes on democratic values but is a member of a property owners association excluding "undesirables" from his residential area.

Inconsistency in life is a commonplace, a reflection, no doubt, of our schizoid culture. Everyone is caught in conflicting pulls and counterpulls, pressures and counterpressures. To expect complete consistency is unreasonable; yet this admission should not obscure the point of present interest. If people are not minded to do in life what they say on tests, if their life behaviors are really unpredictable, of what value are the tests? To state forthwith that test data do have uses, that one can, through teaching, try to change student test scores, is again to dodge the major problem, *the task of educating for better human relations in actual life situations.* From this standpoint, academic teaching—so far as it depends upon classroom test data—can readily overrate its understanding of people-in-living, the general carry-over of its findings and inferences to the run of everyday events and affairs.

To document the point just made, consider some contrasts be-

[11] See "Consistency and Inconsistency in Intergroup Relations," *Journal of Social Issues,* V (1949), 1–63. In addition to this whole issue, much relevant discussion is found in almost any recent book on testing, for example, Lee J. Cronbach, *Essentials of Psychological Testing* (New York: Harper & Bros., 1949).

tween the classroom testing situation and real life, the push and haul of human relations on the campus and outside.[12]

The basic aim of classroom testing has been to create a response situation where the subject's "true" attitudes can come out. What this means is that "real life" is greatly distorted. For instance, social issues are clarified on a test, ambiguities and the like ironed out. In life, issues come buried in other issues, and their unscrambling is a problem. In life, phrases are loaded with many potential meanings, but in a good test words mean what they look to mean within the limits of common usage. In life, whatever has happened, or is happening at the moment, sets in part the context for decision, whereas on a test every effort is made to control carry-over effects from item to item. In life, the subject is held accountable for what he says, but on a test the respondents are anonymous. In a classroom, the atmosphere is conducive to calm thinking, in contrast to the heated arguments found outside.

Other contrasts between life and formal testing situations derive from the statistical procedures used in testing. For example, the reliability of attitude scales and opinion polls is usually based on the fact that, for a large number of subjects, the findings will be stable. However, this does not mean that the attitudes of any particular person are measured reliably. Moreover, the usual practice is to "sample" a population segment, for instance college freshmen or labor union members. They are treated as an aggregate in the sense that each person's reaction is assigned the same weight as that of any other person in the sample. While conclusions can be drawn for the total sample, findings say nothing about the psychological weight of any individual, the effectiveness of this person in influencing a groupwise point of view.

One could pursue this analysis further, but the important thing is to remember its bearing on the educator's job. The point is not that present testing practices are inadequate, or that attitude testing should be scrapped, or that testing in general has been oversold. On the contrary, our first concern is with the nature of science, the use and misuse of its findings in practical affairs. Secondly, we hope that scientists can be interested in designing classroom tests which, so far as possible, will incorporate the life

[12] Based in part on Herbert Hyman, *Journal of Social Issues,* V (1949), 38–42.

situations where predictability of attitudes and overt behaviors are desired. Experiments of this sort would have both practical and theoretical values, making formal test data much more useful in educational programs than they now are.

SCIENCE, CONSISTENCY, AND REALITY

In the discussion of tests and their uses, the matter of consistency and inconsistency in human behavior was passed over. Our language shows many words for people who say one thing and do another, for example "two-faced," "undependable," "hypocritical." Such actions are excused by calling them "expedient," which means more or less "inevitable" when all the facts are known. To approve such behaviors, we label them "flexible," "progressive," even "diplomatic." What, after all, is consistency? Can anyone be consistent in human relations, and where do the social sciences fit in?

As we understand the issue, consistency-inconsistency must refer to the direction of movement, that is, toward or away from some inclusive goal. It cannot be defined, therefore, in terms of form or content, but rather in reference to purpose or intent. In intergroup education immediate and remote goals are assumed to be democratic human relations as discussed in past chapters. Inconsistency would be any action in conflict with these goals or even tangential to them.

If facts are known in any concrete case, most human inconsistencies are understandable. They derive from the situational pressures facing an individual, or from the uncoordinated levels of his thought, or from a subconscious desire to live in confusion as an escape from such freedom as the personality could command.[13] Thus, a person may be unable or unwilling to weigh and balance pros and cons, to extend the applications of a principle, in sum to rationalize a clean-cut course of action. It is here that science enters in, first, by clarifying the conditions of action, and, second, by predicting probable effects of alternative response patterns.

Scientists argue this issue often in terms of their own experiences, what happened to them as they absorbed scientific teaching. From their say-so, it is possible to develop a great faith in the

[13] The classic study is Erich Fromm, *Escape from Freedom* (New York: Rinehart & Co., 1941).

precise truth of science, the critical self-insight which it brings. They have been forced, they aver, to take themselves in hand, to discipline their thought, to take charge of their own mental-growth processes. Thus, science appears to function in personality, hence in society at large, as a kind of *reality principle,* conceived as "the best adjustment of the organism as a whole."[14]

For some learners, notably the talented few, we are inclined to assume that this reasoning holds true. But it does not seem valid for present heterogeneous school and college populations, with their many and varied backgrounds, intellectual abilities, and social orientations. Most of these persons do not seem interested in erudite matters, in the cold take-it-or-leave-it mood of the scientist. While every teacher has ways of compelling learner attention, those relying primarily on group process and community participation may have stronger motivational forces than does the scientist as a scientist, a speculation which if true would hold only for the masses of students.

In conclusion, academic education is our oldest and most respected way of transmitting knowledge. It functions best, we believe, in uncovering causal relations and in organizing them into theoretical systems. To be educated in any science is to be disciplined in logical thinking, to stand aloof from the problems of men and bring intelligence to bear upon them. In academic classrooms, moral values are presumed to be excluded from study-making and instruction, a point debated pro and con by both academic and nonacademic teachers. To the intergroup educator, values are central in the learning process, the pivotal points about which initial decisions need to be explicitly made. They function, too, in the use of study findings, the applications of science to practical affairs.

[14] James W. Woodard, "Some Implications from Our Present Knowledge Concerning Prejudice," *American Sociological Review* (1946), 345.

5. Group-Process Teaching: Cases and Theory

It is told that the Wind and the Sun had a contest of strength. To demonstrate his prowess, the Wind undertook to strip the coat from the back of a man who was walking across a field. As this story is recited to children, the Wind blew and blew and blew, but the man only pulled his coat more tightly about him. When the Wind shrieked and howled, the man buttoned up the garment to his chin. And then the Sun took his turn. He beamed benignantly on the man, wrapping him in warmth. The walker unbuttoned his coat, spread it open, and finally took it off.

In a chapter on group process teaching, one may begin with a parable, taking the Sun as his hero, but it proves nothing about any way of influencing people. In fact, the story rather supports the charges made against group-work educators, teachers who "speak in tongues" (confusion) or make claims for which data are lacking. It is not our aim to write the present smallness of group-centered learning into something large, though its growing popularity seems evident. Our purpose is to examine this newer teaching method in human relations, to illustrate it by College Study cases, analyze and appraise its worth.

GRADE AND HIGH SCHOOL CASES

When one first starts teaching, it may seem that fact is fact, that right is right, and that affirming such simple truths should be enough. Chances are that a teacher will grow exasperated when, having had his say, people persist in the ancient error of their ways. And then may come an insight on teaching, mostly that truth and right have no one meaning, that clamor about them causes any voice to be discounted, that some people do not seek these goals at all in their daily living. It is then that one sees the difference between announcing facts, as in an academic classroom, and teaching them, as when learners are guided in making their own discoveries.

OUR CLOTHES AND WHERE THEY COME FROM

Mary Efstratis, aged seven, entered the home room late and just as the teacher got a note to come to the office for a moment. When the instructor returned, Mary was in tears. The teacher asked for no explanation, nor did she scold the class, knowing simply that the child had been teased about her Old World attire, that a chronic situation had built up to a serious problem.

In a day or two, when it was time to take up a new unit of study, the teacher directed attention to the clothes that pupils wore, so many different colors, different styles, and the like. Where did all these pretty things come from? Was it nice for people to wear garments that were different, things that had real meaning to them? What would our nation be like if everybody dressed alike, and spoke alike, and wanted only the same clothing?

In this fashion, a unit was opened on "Our Clothes and Where They Come From." Mary, though quite timid, took a fairly active part. Clothes she had worn every day (for, like several of these children, she had little choice) became objects of favorable attention—her shawl, dress, beads, and so on. So with youngsters of other nationalities, and of native rural backgrounds, and the class was given a situation in which to plan a number of projects. Hearing of school interest in clothing, some parents sent garments for display, and two mothers gave talks to the class.

The teacher was wise, we believe, in not making an issue of the group's treatment of Mary, but rather taking up the problem as soon as possible as a normal part of schoolwork. Here we assume a difference between *policing* and *education,* with the first resorted to only as an emergency measure. Educators are not policemen, though at times they are forced to be, for otherwise education may have no chance to get started. To the extent that policing carries a hostile attitude, a threat of punishment, it makes self-learning difficult or impossible, a caution against its use in group-process work.

To continue with cases, a more complex individual-to-group situation can be seen in an educational film which is well worth study and analysis. The problem is much the same as in Mary's case, the integration of an isolate into a classroom group.

THE SOCIALIZATION OF ADA ADAMS[1]

In this film, Ada, a high school freshman, enters English-I late on

[1] McGraw-Hill film, *Learning to Understand Children;* also *Broader Concept of Teaching Method.*

the first day, drops her books, fumbles about, obviously ill at ease. She looks funny in her sacky clothes, straight hair, and with an awkward walk, drawing laughter from the class, a group of well-off boys and girls. To get acquainted, the teacher asks students to tell about their hobbies, which they do in great style. Ada has no hobby, nothing she says that she likes to do, and she is so shy that her answers are hardly audible. After class two girls approach her but she turns away from them.

The film continues in true-to-life detail as the teacher assembles school data on Ada. The girl's IQ is normal, her reading rate bad, her health poor, her home a prime problem. In her classes she is failing in every subject, with the math teacher the most explicit. Ada "just hasn't the brains for math" and the man can see no hope for her to pass the course. Her art work is good but "the child is so queer," so much an isolate in her peer group.

Meantime, in the English class, students are making reports on some book of their choice. When Ada's turn comes, she walks slowly to the front and, with eyes downcast, begins to speak. She talks in a very strained voice, then chokes up and, in panic, tells the teacher that she cannot go ahead. Instead of covering for her by drawing the attention of the class, the teacher tells Ada to take her seat. While this is a kindly act, it accentuates the girl's separation from the group. The teacher could have taken over the narrative, or told a related story of her own, asking her now and then for brief comment. If Ada had recovered poise, she could have gone on with the report. Otherwise, an excuse could have been granted in a face-saving way.

Though very guarded in her brief talk with the teacher after class, Ada is heartbroken over her failure. On assumption that she needs self-confidence, that a word might help, the instructor tells her that she is "as good as anyone in class," an exaggeration which Ada sees through. When the teacher asks about visiting her home, the girl is again near panic. Since she cannot prevent the visit, she agrees and the conference ends.

The home visit is the big turning point in the story. Mrs. Adams, the girl's mother, is hard-working, long-suffering, impoverished, and full of self-pity. She is suspicious of the teacher, greeting her with: "Well, what has Ada done now?" Her husband, she says, is a worthless scamp, and times are hard. Ada is of no particular help, "moonin' about," and "wastin' time on them pictures." As the girl starts to take her baby half-brother upstairs, she stumbles about, knocking over a portfolio of sketches. In retrieving them, the teacher looks them over. One after another, they are marvelous, much better we suspect than average. The instructor now has a key to unlock Ada's isolation. The thing to do is to use the girl's art talent as a way of changing her group role and status.

The first step in the program is to show these drawings to the English class. The teacher starts this but, as surprise and wonder deepen, Ada takes over. One can feel the great lift she experiences as she looks into this new group mirror, sees herself as classmates now see her. Her self-feelings might have ended there had it not been for a run of circumstances, a series of developments not wholly of the teacher's own contriving.

Students are reading Shakespeare and decide to give a play. Their choice is *Twelfth Night* and they organize in a businesslike manner. Ada accepts membership on the costumes committee, where her ideas and designs meet with acclaim. Everything runs smoothly, maybe too smoothly for reality, until the committee meets at one of the homes. Ada is astonished at what she sees. Her classmate has so much, maybe all the girls have pretty rooms, pretty clothes, maybe . . . maybe. . . . The task at hand is to fit costumes, and Ada is persuaded, much against her will, to try one on. To do the job right, a friend unpins the girl's long black hair, letting it fall over her shoulders, and everyone exclaims over its beauty.

Ada is impressed with her change in appearance, so much so that she decides to risk her mother's scolding. While she is sneaking in the door at home, her mother sees her. "Now look at you! What ever will you kids be doin' next?" Ada pleads for her new hair-do and Mrs. Adams, taciturn but not indifferent, relents. Encouraged, Ada asks if there is any way she can get a change of school clothes. Her mother agrees to make over one of her old skirts, but cautions the girl against wanting anything else.

At school, things are beginning to happen to Ada. Her classwork is better, so much so that even the math teacher believes she has a chance to pass the course. Her speed of reading improves, and she is much freer, more spontaneous, in recitations. One judges that she has several close friends, that she is coming to be regarded as a nice person.

The play goes on before an audience of school children and parents, with actors missing cues and muffing lines as usual. Ada had counted so much on her mother's attendance and keeps watching the door for her appearance. While Mrs. Adams does not come, Ada smiles when her committee is praised for its work on the costumes.

This is, in substance, the story of Ada Adams, a film that has been used in almost all the colleges in the College Study. While it has nothing to do with race, creed, or the like, it has a lot to say about people, many specific answers to questions on how group work is done. Though it has some bits of unreality, for instance, its focus on a talented child, its over-all effects are quite convincing. Students speak of seeing it as "an experience," an indication of their own emotional involvement.

If teaching is defined as what academic teachers do, the Ada Adams case can be ruled out of order. However, it would be hard to rule out the standing challenge of the *social isolate,* the marginal child always on the fringe of things. This person is an unhappy person and, like Ada, a poor learner, a prime problem in many classrooms.[2] A full third of a thousand teacher papers collected by College Study consultants in every part of the nation dealt with these withdrawing, misbehaving young people. In them, "mind" is no free floating entity, nothing to turn on, turn off, at a teacher's say-so. It is an aspect of personality, varying markedly with its possessor's social adjustments, the job satisfactions he finds in going to school, the situational pressures of daily living.

All teachers use what can be called their personality in teaching, the sum of their life experiences, their aspirations and frustrations. All employ too their scholarship and professional training. Group-process teachers have still another teaching instrument, the learning group. This is to them much of what a textbook is to an academic educator, though all kinds of learning are highly dependent upon systematic reading. To sharpen this point, *the planful use of the group to influence behavioral change,* we want to draw upon a type of case that is admittedly debatable from a teacher standpoint.[3]

THE SPINACH EATER

The time is noon, the place Corpus Christi. Among the Spanish and Anglo first-graders eating lunch, one little rebel will not touch his spinach. He looks down at his plate, looks around at peer mates, then up at the teacher. The impasse, apparently, is an old one, and the boy is not moved by routine admonitions. A visitor, who has been observing this situation, asks the teacher's permission to talk with the children.

Yes, the visitor has come from far away and he would like to tell about Detroit, a big auto-making city. But he has just heard a new song, fun to sing it, too. It is all about "Popeye, the Sailor Man," how strong he is, how good, and how he eats his spinach. It goes like this. . . .

As each verse was sung by the children, the visitor moved up the table toward Angelo. At the end of each stanza, each ending with some

[2] See Lawrence K. Frank, *Mental Health and Ethical Conduct* (New York: New York Society for Ethical Culture, 2 W. 64th St., 1950).

[3] For various short cases, Lloyd Allen Cook, "The College Study in Intergroup Relations," *Journal of Negro Education,* XVII (1948), 27–41; also "Group Guidance Techniques in the College Study," *Social Education,* XII (1948), 209–12.

reference to spinach, the leader would make a great to-do—look at someone's plate, exclaim that the food was all gone, feel the child's arm muscles, etc. This caused increasing excitement, with children never tiring of the silly doings. They twisted and squirmed to see, asking the visitor repeatedly to come and look at their plates.

As the leader drew near the boy, the latter began to stare at his plate, head down, not singing. A companion whispered to him, but he did not reply. A few seats away, the child looked up and caught the adult's eye. He began to toy with his plate, to grip it, then let go. One child distant, with his turn next, Angelo took the plate in both hands and bolted down the spinach.

The song over this hero was a rather special matter. Why, one could almost feel his muscles bulge! The child's scowl disappeared; he looked around the room and grinned. Everybody grinned back at him, and he joined slyly in the last and most noisy verse.

Debate in this case can become sharp and informative. It may turn on educational *ends* as well as means. Maybe the boy did not like spinach, maybe spinach made him sick, maybe he had learned that one can live without eating it. As to *means,* who effected the changes in Angelo's behavior—the teacher or the group? Or was it the teacher working through the group, using the force of group pressure? Is this a bad thing to do? If so, how can one account for the boy's habitual rebel role at the table and otherwise? Did the consultant help him do what he was, in reality, trying to do for himself, namely, to win a higher status rating within his school group?

Every case is but a moment of time in the complex life of people, a pinching-together of people-in-process. In view of the little that is known about democratic behavioral controls, the follow-up on results would seem to be an inescapable imperative in group-process work. While we shall not always do this because of space limitation, the teacher's comments in respect to Angelo were altogether favorable. A week after the incident, she wrote that Angelo "had stopped finding foods that he did not like." A month later, she said that "his general behavior is greatly improved."

A CLASSROOM DISCIPLINE PROBLEM

Invited to help solve some "discipline problems," the visitor asked the teacher to be specific. She named a run of things, mostly behaviors that violated classroom order. One little boy (third grade) was pointed out as "the ringleader," kicking children as they passed his seat, tripping them, and the like.

On being presented to the class, the visitor said he was, indeed, interested in young people, that he had just come from a meeting where a first-grader had told a student council the big gripe of all first-graders in the school. It was that other children called them "babies" and they wanted, please, to have this stopped!

As the class laughed, the consultant went on talking, explaining his interest in how people treated people. Sometimes this was good, but sometimes it was bad. Did they know any bad ways that some of their classmates treated one another? Several points were made, until someone mentioned "kicking." Here the speaker seemed puzzled, saying that he did not know what this meant. Instead of asking for an answer, he pulled two chairs together in front of the class.

"Now," he continued, "I would like to see this kicking. I wonder who will show me how it goes?" Several pupils spoke in chorus, urging that Blackie (the ringleader) undertake this task. At the speaker's urging, Blackie slouched up and was seated in one of the chairs. "But we need another pupil, don't we," and the class shrieked "yes!" When no one volunteered, the visitor selected a second pupil, a hardy type, and walked with her to the second chair.

By this time, the class was in a hubbub of excitement, so much so that the speaker, grinning all the while, spread his hands out for quiet and then began to view the chairs from various angles, to fix attention of the group. When the moment was right, he turned suddenly to the little girl. "Now kick him, go on, kick!" Impelled by the suggestion, she let go a little tap, and the boy, surprised because he had expected to do the kicking, cried "Ouch!" Neither child made any move after the kick, except to eye the visitor who had, apparently, lost all interest in the matter.

Now the visitor gave every evidence of disappointment, asking if the children had been fooling him all along. He saw nothing about kicking that should worry any one. When assured vehemently that he was wrong, he approached the girl and, suddenly, asked her again to show how kicking went. This time she registered a real kick and the boy let out a yell. Even the class quieted down, and the visitor, apparently, was surprised and disturbed.

This was the teachable moment, the experiential basis of learning. The visitor, very solemn, said he saw why kicking was bad. "It hurts, doesn't it?" turning to the kickee, who replied with a strong "Yes." Kicking hurt and it was bad, and did he think that it should be stopped? Standing now with the visitor's arm about him, taking pride in his martyr role, Blackie was sure that kicking must be stopped, a view in which the whole class instantly concurred.

It was no trouble to work out with these children an antikicking plan.

Basic aims were to get the kickers committed to non-kicking, non-tripping, etc., in front of their peers, to make Blackie in particular the leader of group action, thus to shift as much responsibility as possible from the teacher to the class.

We could not maintain contact with this teacher so that we have no knowledge as to how the situation turned out. While "kicking" cannot be recommended as a classroom procedure, the general theory underlying this type of group-process work is worth comment.

In an effort to persuade housewives to buy cheap but little-used meats during World War II, chiefly glandular meats such as liver, an experimental test was conducted. Three groups of women were given attractive and authoritative lectures, and another three groups were led in group discussion, followed by group decision. In the check-up later, about 3 percent of the women who had heard the lectures were serving one or more meats they had not used before, whereas 32 percent of the other women were trying one or more new meats.[4] The point to stress is *group decision,* the affirmation of a plan by a group's own leaders, as was attempted in the Blackie case. While public commitment can be used with any age group, we have found it most effective in large meetings, for example, the community audits and self-surveys reported in the next chapter.

A SCHOOL CAFETERIA CAMPAIGN

The scene was a school cafeteria at noontime, pack-jammed with high school students grabbing a bite to eat; close, smelly, and noisy. One boy, an undersize Negro youth, lingered from table to table on his way to a seat. A Negro teacher, supervising the lunch period, took him by the shoulders, hurrying him along, then pushed him into a vacant place at a table.

As the instructor turned to go, the boy stood up, threw his tray of food into the air, and jumped on the teacher's back. The latter shook him off, fell on him, and a crowd gathered. The principal was called, ordered students to their tables, and took the boy to the office. Here the latter was first reprimanded and then questioned, repeatedly questioned, on the cause of the disturbance. All that he would say was that "ol' X" called him "a little white monkey," and that he "will not take that from nobody."

[4] Cited by Kurt Lewin in T. M. Newcomb and E. L. Hartley (eds.), *Readings in Social Psychology* (New York: Henry Holt & Co., 1947), pp. 330–44.

When the teacher came in, he confirmed all the boy had said, adding details. Again an effort was made to find out why the phrase, "a little white monkey," was so insulting, and again no reason could be uncovered. At this point, a social studies teacher entered the office and, seeing the boy, spoke to him. Sensing that this was a serious matter, this teacher went on about his business. By this time, word was passing through the school, and the social studies teacher heard several versions of the cafeteria incident.

After stating these facts to a college friend, the social studies teacher asked what could be done. He was advised, first, to forget about the "little white monkey" phrasing. It could have been red monkey, or green or blue, or anything, for this was most likely a symptom, not a cause, of disorder. Next, he was asked about his own twelfth-grade Problems of Democracy course in which the Negro boy chanced to be enrolled.

To shorten the case, the development of the next unit of study in the social studies course can be condensed. The project centered on the cafeteria. What was wrong with it? What could good school citizens do about it? Ideas came from the class, for the place was a kind of bed lam, not created by anyone, disliked by everyone. First, the class set out to see, to look it over, and then began to make a plan. As this work ate up more and more class time, committees began to hold meetings after school, and then, later, to meet at noon in the cafeteria to observe the effects of their efforts to make changes.

What the class did, first off, was to elect a chairman. Thinking in team language, he was called the captain. One committee on food values was set up, another on rowdyism, a third on posters, and a fourth on entertainment. Later on, when the campaign met its toughest going, when gains were not an easy matter, two other committees were created. One was on publicity, the other on leadership, and both were school-wide groups. All committees sought and found administrative and faculty suggestions and support.

Any reader can supply details as to committee work. The food committee, for example, checked samples of trays as they passed the cashier's desk. Students got figures on the dominance of hot dogs, cokes, desserts, etc., also on the dearth of solid foods and the relative absence of fruits and salads. These data were turned over to the posters committee which, in cooperation with the art department, got out slogans, signs, and cartoons of comic characters, each playing on some health, prestige, or other theme.

The school leader committee came late in the project, devised as much as a morale builder as anything else. After initial enthusiasm had died down, after daily gains grew small or turned toward losses, the whole project was restudied. What had been done, and why, and what good bets were being missed? It was here that a conception of the school was outlined for the class, *an idea of school as a system of inter-locking groups.* Since every group has leaders, how about assembling these leaders and trying to lead through them?

This put the campaign on an all-school basis and there it was carried on until the semester (and school year) ended. While statistics are not lacking, they tell very little of what happened to these citizen-workers, what they learned about real citizenship. In all of this, the Negro youth first mentioned gave some evidence of change. For just cause possibly, since he had a severe personality problem, he had not been liked by his classmates, in fact had been the victim of a good many heartless pranks. Having no talent which could be discovered, he worked along with two groups. He made some friends, lost some of his hypersensitivity, and seemed a little more secure in his group role.

One point of emphasis in this case is the tendency of school people to overrate the worth of words, to treat them as basic when they are only symptomatic. Many case materials show the extreme lengths to which a principal or a teacher will go to find out which child told a "lie," or used profanity, or peddled school gossip. While such pupil conduct cannot be condoned, the significant question is not who but why—*why was this done?* What made the act proper, perhaps necessary, from the actor's point of view? In short, what is the logic of group relations underlying such surface manifestations?

The school cafeteria case may justify another comment. Even the best movies, like the McGraw-Hill films, tend to oversimplify the mechanics of group-process teaching. One may get the impression that, once group action gets started, about all an instructor has to do is to walk about, look in a moment on this group or that, speak an encouraging word. At times, indeed, this is true, but such times are as rare as when, in an academic classroom, a pupil on his own initiative reads through a whole library of material. *Group-process teaching is teaching,* involving an array of professional skills. It is not well done as a rule when a teacher believes that these abilities can be picked up casually on the run. It is leadership, a leadership of emotional concern, intellectual insight, group work techniques, and good judgment in risk calculations.

Finally, while no case, or series of cases, can be taken as defining what we have called the "group process," such examples do suggest what this kind of teaching is not. It is not the study of parliamentary law, or the organizing of school patrols, useful as both can be. It is not a matter of breaking a big group into little groups, each with its own problem, although this may be done. It is not the manipulation of learners, or their indoctrination in civic virtues, yet we have seen both things happen. Group management, like any teaching method, is pretty much what a teacher can make it, the degree of insight and skill one is able to put forth. At its best, it is a learning-by-doing, a group-motivated effort to accomplish a socially meaningful task.

COLLEGE GROUP-PROCESS CASES

College cases are as variable as those found at grade and high school levels and, again, selection is random. From many incidents in the field of extracurricular activities, two will give an idea of group-guidance problems and procedures. The first occurred in a state teachers college in a metropolitan city, a group-making proj ect that is still progressing.

TOWARD INTERCREEDAL UNDERSTANDINGS

It was registration day at college. A double line of students was passing an outer desk where each was handed a card. Curious about this card, a professor assisting with registration found that it contained a jagged, bloody picture of the head of Christ, plus an invitation to attend a student meeting of "Fundamentalists."

At this meeting the professor was impressed with the group's faith in their fundamentalist creed, in their attack on Catholics and Jews, in their announced aim "to clean up the campus and the town," and in their urgent bid for student converts. The group had no affiliation with any outside organization and existed under the rule of complete freedom as granted to all campus associations.

Presently, the professor had an invitation to address these students. Instead of a speech, he proposed a talk session. What were some of their beliefs? Did they believe in one God? Did they believe in life after death? Did they believe in the Ten Commandments? Were good thoughts best expressed in good deeds? Had they ever visited a Jewish synagogue or a Catholic church? Were any of their close friends Jews or Catholics? Disturbed by what he found out, he decided to talk to the College Committee on Intergroup Relations.

Within a short time, a call was issued by the dean to all student religious leaders to meet in his office. Students were not invited to represent their organizations, nor was anything said about religion. The college, it seemed, was interested in student services to the community.

Since there was no student service organization, could such a club or council, with a speakers bureau, be set up by the students and run by them?

The idea took hold at once and, for the first time, campus religious leaders were united in a common cause. As personal contacts increased, student friendships developed, and presently, individual students began to swap creedal points of view and talk over organizational problems. Meantime, needing a sponsor, they invited the professor who, unknown to them, had started this integrative action, to fill that office. By the end of the year, they had greatly extended their community services. More to the point, they were discussing in their meetings the common problems and closer unity of all religious faiths on the campus.[5]

This is as near perfect an example of indirect approach to intergroup problems, as defined in the past chapter, as our files show. Academic education is obliged by its very nature to raise issues, to think critically about them, to formalize the learning situation. Group-process teachers are inclined toward somewhat different assumptions. For one thing, they rely more upon big muscle action, *the integrative effects of a common cause.* Of course, they want changes in student perceptions, the restructuring of a field of vision, but they put main emphasis, not on logic, a cold war of mind on mind, but on feeling, the motivational power of a combined team effort. To hold that intellect is not operative in such teaching is to show several misunderstandings. There is the matter of collective vision, for example, a dream of how some situation could be made better. Next comes group planning, the fusion of pieces (people) into a new whole (the group) that differs from any of its elements. And finally, in firstrate teaching, the entire process will be intellectualized at its conclusion. Learners will be asked to retrace the road they have traveled, for otherwise their perspectives will be blurred, their carry-over from one experience to another considerably lessened.

Any kind of teaching involves hazards, for there is a point at which learners must be left pretty much on their own. They can either swim or not swim, or swim under certain conditions, and in spite of all the evidence one may gather, he cannot know this point surely except by test. We shall condense a great deal a case from

[5] From *College Programs in Intergroup Relations,* p. 359.

a committee report, our worst case of failure, if it was a failure, in the years of College Study work. The college is small, white, and Southern, an institution devoted to Christian ideals. The experiences given occurred within a three-year program where many good things happened. The focus now is not on these hard-earned rewards of group effort but on a serious slip-up, a misstep which a little more planning on our part could have prevented The writer is a senior at this college.

INTERRACIAL STORM AND AFTERMATH

At its first meeting of the year, the all-campus student-faculty committee reviewed the past year's work. It was decided that face-to-face contacts between white and Negro students had had the greatest pay-off values and should be stressed during the new year. This meant a continuation of past practices, for example, inviting Negro speakers to the campus, and a much greater stress on intercollege visits. . . .

On the first occasion of this latter kind, Negro students from a nearby state college came to the campus. They were housed in local dorms, ate in the dining hall without segregation, took part in social activities, visited classes—in short, moved about as any students would. All of this was very novel for our college, but the subcommittee studying campus reactions assured us that the visit was a marked success.

It took a full two weeks to show us that this judgment was in error. . . . As things turned out, we were in for a lot of trouble, and all because of one very unfortunate and unscheduled event. I shall tell this in some detail because, for some of us, it proved to be the most educative experience in our four years at college.

All resident students eat at a college dining hall which is also a student center. Before and after meals, especially dinner in the evening, we have an informal social hour. We read, visit, play records, lounge about, talk, and dance. As told by a principal participant in the affair, a close girl friend of mine, here is exactly what happened.

"The next I saw of our Negro guests was at lunch. Two ate at our table and everyone seemed to have fun. The same two boys ate dinner with us that evening, after which we all went into the hall and stood around, talking. We walked out to the porch and then returned to watch some students jitterbug. We stood around some more and then a white girl asked one of the Negro students to dance. The other colored visitor asked me if I cared to dance and I accepted. It was a fast number which I cannot do very well but I was afraid that, if I declined, the boy might be offended."

This, then, was the incident, and trouble was to follow. But at the time, and for several days, nothing much was thought about it. Our subcommittee made its usual campus check-up, and reactions were very favorable to the Negro guests, so that we planned our next event, a trip by our students to Talladega College. It was at about this point that the storm broke, and it broke very fast.

What had happened was that news of the dancing had trickled out into the community and, no doubt, been garbled in the telling. Some one, possibly a parent, had told a city paper which proceeded to write up a rather lurid story. This article, and others, appeared on the front page, often under boldface headings. They spoke about "inter-racial dancing" at the college as if it were a commonplace. They urged that a meeting of the college board be called to inquire into "the state of affairs" and to take "immediate action," steps which were taken after a fashion. . . .

In his statement to the press, our president reviewed the whole experience and connected it with the general program of intergroup work here and in other colleges across the nation. He explained that no social event had been planned for the Negro student visitors but that, during a brief period of recreation, five of our students had "offered injudiciously" to dance with the colored students. He added that the incident was "exceedingly regretted by the college," but went on to assert that the college, a church-related school, was devoted to the Christian ideals of a democratic life. He stated frankly that the college mission was to further brotherhood among men.

Of course, no further intercollege visits were made. The committee felt that the incident was most unfortunate, that it really never should have happened. The campus itself was fully as pro as it was con in its reactions, more so if our studies can be trusted. Typical of favorable interview data is the comment of a girl who was not a member of our interracial committee.

"Now that it is over, I am glad it happened. I have learned more about race relations, about the mores, than I have learned in years of classroom study. I want now, more than ever, to go into the work of furthering good will and brotherhood, of which race relations are a definite part. Come what may, this college must still lead. It is a Christian college, not a godless school. If we are sincere and have faith, we can march on."

These were Southern young people, liberal in the true sense, yet they misjudged their South. Their mistake, perhaps, was in taking too lightly some clear cautions against mixed dancing. The South is changing, no matter how anyone may feel about it, and the direction of change is not a prime issue in most college circles. Change is toward democratic human relations, and faster now with federal pressure on states and localities than ever before in recent

years. From an educator's viewpoint, the issues are speed of movement, circumstances, leadership, and strategies. What an outsider
can do in any local situation is not much unless he is accepted by
all parties in a dispute. A case from another Southern college will
center this value-judgment for discussion.

SUCCESS OR FAILURE: A TEST CASE

In a white Southern university a group of school heads and in-service
teachers asked for a demonstration of the sociodrama. With time short,
several persons offered to sit as a panel, and a search was made for a
problem to discuss. Since no one came up with anything, the consultant
suggested that "We talk about race relations." While no person openly
disapproved, still no discussable issue shaped up; in fact, no panel
member seemed inclined to talk. Again, in violation of good sociodrama, the leader proposed that thought be centered on the then
pending bill for federal aid to education, a topic of great interest in
all Southern states.

"Well," said a school principal, "I am opposed to any federal aid to
education if it is to be equalized between white and colored schools."
This view met ready acceptance up and down the panel, with talk
consisting of reasons for its support. One could not, it appeared, trust
Negroes to handle public funds. Negro schools were not too bad, better
in fact than colored people had ever had before. Whites were ready
to help Negroes on their health and job problems, "without the
interference of the North."

Whatever these views added up to, they did not involve a debatable
issue in the minds of these school people, so that the consultant took
another tack. What about the coming election (county option) to vote
on whether or not farmers, who grazed stock, should be required to
fence their lands? "Now," said the principal, "you do have something.
In my community, that is a real battle. . ." From this point the discussion moved off into a swift exchange of opinions, depending on
whether a speaker took the rural or the urban point of view.

While the fencing problem was very real, a great deal of time had
been spent in finding it. Little time remained for demonstration work,
so that the leader tended to lecture on different ways of handling dis-
cussant roles in the sociodrama. All the while, he had a distinct sense of
failure, of failing to make good use of time in discharging the assignment he had been given.

On the way home after class, the professor in charge of the class
chided the consultant with failure to do anything about race relations,
an experience that he had also had. The visitor replied that it did, indeed, look like a clean-cut failure, yet that education was a curious
business, that tomorrow might tell us more about the evening's work.

Next morning, the first person the consultant met on the campus came up and introduced himself. He had been present at the evening session, in fact was a university staff member, but had neglected to introduce himself. During the morning two other persons introduced themselves, both graduate students. Both were extremely friendly, with one wanting to talk over a problem of his own.

At lunch, a participant in the sociodrama came up to the visitor's table. She spoke with some enthusiasm about the evening meeting, adding that the same program should be repeated. When this student was told that, in the consultant's opinion, the demonstration had been a failure, she asserted quite the opposite. When she was asked for evidence, she said that talk was going about the campus. Again, upon being asked to be specific, she hesitated and then decided, apparently, to be frank in her comment. "You may not believe it," she said, "but you are the first Northerner in our experience who has not come here to solve our race problem!"

One may judge this meeting a failure, since the consultant was unable to get a hearing for a liberal interracial mode of thought. Or one may wonder simply what the point is in this rather unclear case. From a group-work standpoint some measure of success can be claimed. It consists in the fact that a relationship of confidence was established with some few persons, an essential foundation for further work. One must, at least as we see it, *win the right to educate people,* to invade their areas of privacy. To do this, he must secure and maintain a degree of group respect and trust.

Of the three college cases cited, only the last one was an in-class affair, a regularly set up instructional program. This might lead to a very false conclusion, namely, that group-process education at the college level goes on chiefly in extracurricular activities. This view would, we believe, be far from the truth. Most consultant time has been spent on course revisions, much as in academic education. It has taken the form often of helping an instructor arrange better group-work experiences for the student, or else of analyzing with him the theory underlying group-process work. An excellent illustration is the project conducted by professors and agency heads at Trenton, New Jersey, reported in the *College Programs* volume, chapter 3.

SOME FOUNDATIONAL ELEMENTS

It may be some years before we have a systematic theory of group-process education, one as complete as that undergirding academic instruction. In this latter system, classroom relations are impersonal, formalistic, and competitive. One goes straight to the top if he is built for climbing; otherwise his station is on the ground. If a learner becomes a good scholar, he will be by the same token a good teacher, or so the theory runs. If, now, he teaches as he has been taught, the circle is closed, the system is self-perpetuating. One beauty of this pattern is its clarity, another its precision, its harmonic part to whole relation. It would take a hardy soul, or an incautious one, to say as much about group-process learning.[6]

Group learning of the kind described in chapter cases is not what some authorities call "freedom for children,"[7] as we understand their thought, nor is it lacking in what average teachers call "classroom discipline." It is not "child-centered" as in extreme progressive education, although it does use interest to motivate effort. It is a long sea mile from traditional textbook-centered teaching; yet it makes much use of reading materials. It is, to repeat a point, *group-oriented and life-related,* the idea being first to teach groupness as, for example, in the intercreedal case, and then, through group process, to teach a good many other things. This kind of learning does not apply, therefore, to all phases of a school program, but rather to those aspects which are social in both content and method. Its central thesis is the idea that an individual, if he would change himself, *must change his groupings.* Put in teaching terms, new groupings must be built, old ones discarded.

What makes any assembly of students a group? Not the presence of learners in a given place, or their similarities, or the teacher's reiteration that now a group exists. Such conditions do not create groupness, as the disorderly, destructive, or inert behaviors about schools and colleges make quite clear. Groupness is a relationship among people, a mental state and feeling tone in which all persons share. While it is many other things, *the sharing of concern* is the

[6] For example, in a current book, Ronald Lippitt, *Training in Community Relations* (New York: Harper & Bros., 1949), it takes 220 pages to analyze a two-week intergroup workshop, a novel experiment, yet one that might have been studied in much less space had theory and concepts been clearer. This is no criticism of the author, who is well known for his group-dynamics work.

[7] See Howard A. Lane, *Shall Children, Too, Be Free?* (New York: Anti-Defamation League of B'nai B'rith, 1949), 33 pp.

foundational base to remember. If there is no sharing, no inner picture of togetherness, there is no sociological group, no unity of interacting persons.

This, then, is the first item in group-work theory, a point that explains much of the shoddy effort, the dreamy play-acting or hustle-bustle which passes often for group-process education. The fault lies in the inability to distinguish between activity and participation. Students can carry a heavy load of action—taking orders, running about, making talk—without feeling any substantial personal involvement in outcomes. Learning is superficial because energy expenditures do not really matter. One can do this, do that or the other, as long as he is in motion. In our language there is no *functional participation,* no sharing in over-all planning.

With this much theory, a college teacher[8] can study the fitness of an aggregate for groupness—its size, physical makeup, social backgrounds, degree of interpersonal acquaintance, and the like. He will know that every individual studied is a member of various functional groupings, for example, a family, church, political party, clubs, union, and so forth. He will know also that the learner has other dynamic belongings, such as race, nationality, social class, and age-sex identifications. Armed with such data, a teacher can formulate two more items in group-work theory, each of practical use.

One principle is that *social meanings come from groups,* the meanings on which students tend to act.[9] One will never grasp this point well until he begins to study classroom behaviors in terms of student backgrounds, to figure out why this was said or that was done, that is, on what past experience student perceptions, attitudes, and the like are based. One can, if he listens closely, hear a wide range of invisible characters speaking, the models on which learners have patterned, the frustrations they have suffered, the phases of culture they have managed to acquire. The "little white

[8] Much that is said applies to teachers at any grade level. Since some situational frame is needed, comments are directed primarily to college teaching.

[9] For example, Walter Coutu, *Emergent Human Nature* (New York: Knopf, 1949), chap. 10, "Meanings Come from Groups." The classic work is M. Sherif, *The Psychology of Social Norms* (New York: Harper & Bros., 1936).

monkey" case illustrates the point, the phrase—while used by the teacher—irritating the boy because of its past use by the group as an expression of derision and hostility.

The second idea is not easy to state in a sentence. It involves the organized character of modern living, the *interconnectedness of all a society's parts and pieces*. Touch this student, regardless of his age and a teacher touches the National Association for the Advancement of Colored People, or the Anti-Defamation League, or the Civil Liberties Union, or the NAM or CIO, or some church body, or other social action organization. Interpersonalism, an exclusive teacher-to-pupil relation, is yielding fast in mass society to intra- and intergroup relations, a situation where people are organized and stand guard to protect and advance their conception of group rights and interests.

Functions of Groups in Life

To dig still deeper into foundations, a group-work teacher needs to reflect many times on the functions of groups in social life. Group pride, group process, group loyalty, group integrity! What do they mean? It is a curious fact that one can be in groups, *in, for,* and *of* them, all of his life and never learn much about them that is significant He can move in and out of groupness without giving it an analytical thought—pulling it apart, inspecting its pieces, putting them together in ways that will produce more satisfactions for more people.

From experience, one knows that groups are effective in controlling the behaviors of their members.[10] Why is this? A simple answer is that *people, who would be liked by people, must be like people.* What one will do in order to be liked, respected, loved, and so on, is a rough measure of group control over his attitudes and conduct, though this principle has obvious limitations. Unliked persons also exercise a measure of control, for instance the most disinterested members of a class. No one knows the energy expenditure, the concessions, and strategies made by teachers and others just to keep such malcontents within the group.

---

[10] Much can be learned by reversing this proposition, i.e., through studies of deviant and non-responsive group members. For a study of an adamant little clique leader, see the writer's "An Experimental Sociographic Study of a Stratified 10th Grade Class," *American Sociological Review*, X (1945), 250–61.

One's groups are, as Lewin points out, "the grounds on which he stands,"[11] the foundations from which he views the world. They give him perspective and security, a cushion against shock. They are the matrix of social personality, the molds in which human potentials are cast. If these molds become too narrow, if one feels squeezed in, he may break out, headed for other groupings or else toward a kind of psychotic aloneness called "anomie," a rootless kind of life. Groups form, therefore, the greater part of one's *Lebensraum,* the "life space" in which he moves. Groups are means to ends, as well as ends, the only way to achieve a number of common social wants. And finally, the fact of group membership often means some degree of clash between personal and social goals; hence groups give imperative training in arts of leadership and adjustment. Every case in the chapter illustrates these several points.

It is these functions of groups in everyday life that underly group-process education, that make possible the teacher's use of the group to motivate behavior, to re-educate people in human relations. They correspond after a fashion to the mental processes and authoritarian controls undergirding academic learning, provided allowance is made for a considerable overlapping between the two educational systems.

THE PROBLEM OF GROUP BUILDING

One may agree fully with the points made and still fail as a group builder. In psychological terms, the problem is *to create in individuals the role of the generalized other,*[12] a phrase meaning in teacher education an inclusive concern for the common good. Early in life, children begin to imitate things, animals, and persons, to play their parts in imaginative ways. Presently, in their team games they face a harder learning task. To play any part well, a player must coordinate with his teammates, imagine how they will act, take their respective roles as need arises. Thus, the concept of team (group) takes on content, becomes an entity in thought

[11] Kurt Lewin, *Resolving Social Conflicts* (New York: Harper & Bros., 1948), pp. 85–86.
[12] G. H. Mead, *Mind, Self and Society* (Chicago: University of Chicago Press, 1939), pp. 178 ff.

and feeling. Ability to take the role of the total group, that is, "the generalized other," is of course the basis of all altruistic citizenship. It is, obviously, the prime motivation in the inter-creedal and school cafeteria cases.

From a sociological viewpoint, group building is *planful action designed to increase group-worker output*. Output may be material things, such as shopwork articles, or intangible products, the creation of an atmosphere conducive to learning, the development of fair-play standards. Whatever form it takes, it is a function of communication, the interchange of meanings without distortion or defense. It is, secondly, a result of efficiency, the most logical means-to-ends relations that can be devised. In any complex undertaking, for example, a community action movement, high group output will depend upon a division of labor and the continuous coordination of unlike work tasks.

That group-process educators know these things, though vaguely one might guess, is seen in several ways. For instance, by language usage. In "How does the group feel about this," or "What do you [collective] think about that," teachers tend to bring group consciousness into being by assuming its existence. Even more convincing are the informal behaviors about a classroom, the sense of camaraderie and shared concern. "We always felt," said a student about a certain professor, "that something was doing in his classroom, that we were going somewhere though just where we might not know."

One can, to be sure, overdo informality in group work. One may see in mixed groups minority representatives who are, apparently, quite overwhelmed by their reception, the back-slapping good will or obsequious hospitality accorded them. Good manners call forth good manners, until real people and real issues are buried under an avalanche of formalism. The payoff comes later at some moment of frank talk. How can persons, who know so little about one, like him so much on sight? The truth is, of course, that they cannot. Their behaviors are ritualistic, limited in meaning so far as group process goes.

What has just been said applies almost wholly to adults. Children are notably frank in their interpersonal relations, honest to the point of unconcern and cruelty. From parents, as someone has said, they learn "the morality of constraint," the good manners, right conduct, imposed by authority. From their peers, the push and pull of street-corner life, they learn the morality of cooperation, whether it be of the jungle type or "civilized." From the school, they learn—what do they learn? This will depend, we suspect, on the kind of educational system in which they happen to be caught.

Group Structure and Processes

In the growing literature on group teaching, two concepts are usually made central—structure and process. While structure is the product of action, it tends to shape further action, much as banks channel a river's flow. It is structure that makes for order in a group, for predictability of member interaction, even as it does in society as a whole. To begin then with structure seems logical, although in group-life history, the action process comes first.

Teachers do not think much, or think well, about *group structure*. One reason is the tendency to confuse it with "red tape," another to view it as the loss of "freedom," and a third to push it aside as an academic matter, hence of no practical use in teaching. The essence of structure can be glimpsed by drawing dots on a bit of paper. If these marks symbolize people, they can be connected by lines which will show how persons relate themselves to one another. Structure is the framework binding people together, the pathways their actions have left over a period of time, the offices in which authority and responsibility have been lodged. In a college class, where there is no past history of collective action, structure would comprise the sum of group agreements, the complex patterning of member roles and statuses.

A student of any particular grouping would be interested in a detailed analysis of these group-member roles, the functions persons perform, the efficiency of their actions, role conflicts and coordinations. He would be concerned with status ratings, the relation of prestige to power, and of power to over-all group leadership. Some group structures, so analyzed, would be found to rest upon a primary (intimate) face-to-face basis, a kind of relationship between people where each person is emotionally irreplaceable, where no substitution is possible. Other groupings, per contra, would be of a secondary nature, an impersonal, efficient social system.

Within every group, various *social processes* go on. Every member is obliged to position himself in relation to other persons. Whether his behavior is action or inaction, efficient or inefficient in terms of group goals, integrative or divisive, positioning takes place. This is a continuous sifting and sorting, an unending shakedown of interests and talents, concerns and abilities, into patterns of leadership and followership. Positioning is, in substance, a competitive process; yet it occurs under rules which are, in themselves, evidence of a vast amount of cooperation. To ask which is "natural" to man—competition or cooperation—would appear to be either an unwise question or an unsolvable one, for both work together to produce an end effect.

Inspection of group struggle at close range, for example, the ongoing changes in a college class, will show a great deal about human nature. Persons are nowise alike and equal, and time increases their inequalities. Some excel in rational thought, others in emotional concern; some in practical judgment, others in organizational skill. Some rate high in several things, others seem to live on low, even levels. Some move ahead if given opportunity, others drop out or get lost in the shuffle. In all of this there is much headache and heartbreak, and no teacher can change it as he might like. He can try to see that chances are even, that tests of worth are fair, that rewards are based on merit.

It is out of this process that group leaders arise. A leaderless group is, we believe, a self-evident contradiction. Grouped, people will be and they must be, and the real issue is the quality of their headmen. Teachers need to know that office-holding is not, necessarily, leadership, that their own leader role in democratic group work is not a gift but an achievement. It is a situational product, rather than an official imposition, an award of honor conferred by the group for services rendered. A democratic leader is a leader, not because of his office or the authority lodged in him, but because he has met the tests a group has set. He can do more to further common goals than any other group member, and he holds this power position just as long as these responsibilities can be met.

A group leader is, first of all, a caretaker of the group, a person concerned with its physical well-being. In classroom teaching situations, this function covers a range of familiar items, mostly external conditions such as seating which make good work possible. The leader is also an initiator of action, a coordinator of ideas, a maintainer of process, an evaluator of product, and a representative of the group to other groups and interests. The quality of leadership, whether democratic or otherwise, will give shape and content to these various functions.

THE TEACHER-LEADER

With this as background, a teacher-leader can anticipate some of the organizational problems every group will meet. For instance, a common goal. We have spoken about group members being different, having many separate aims, purposes, motivations, and the like. Is it likely that they, if let alone, will integrate these differences, organize about agreed-upon goals? Can they lift themselves by their own bootstraps, take full charge of their own reeducation? To read some writings on "group creativity," one might think this is an everyday occurrence. Authorities seem to say, as did a military commander, "There go my men. I must catch them, for I am their leader!"

Here we face a disturbing paradox in group-process teaching. There is about democracy much permissiveness, much spontaneity and freedom; yet we are not inclined to think that letting people alone can effect the kinds of changes needed in them. What *laissez faire* does create under experimental test is extreme frustration, aggression, and anarchy.[13] If this is true, what is a democratic group leader to do? He can manipulate a planning process, giving participants the impression that they are running the show. He can blackmail them into acquiescence, vaguely threatening punishment. He can kill time with petty matters, settling big issues under cover outside. He can engage in endless inanities, all irrelevant, or he can run away from the problem, taking cover in a crisis in the authority vested in him. He has, in fact, many alternatives from which to choose, each making group process a farce, each an

[13] See Kurt Lewin, Ronald Lippitt, and Ralph K. White, "Patterns of Aggressive Behavior in Experimentally Created 'Social Climates,'" *Journal of Social Psychology*, X (1939), 271–99.

insult to anyone who believes in the use of intelligence. For this kind of leader, more honesty would be a healthful thing.

A group leader who wants to be democratic faces the problem of what kind of guidance to attempt. One guide to guiders is *the logic of the situation* in which they are called upon to work. In a factory, for instance, we would assume the moral worth of production, for that is what a factory is set up to do. In a school we would take for granted the focus on learning, the idea being that the more of it, the better pleased everyone should be. We would assume group acceptance of these situational demands, establishing a common ground on which to discuss controverted issues. If our assumptions were questioned, as they might well be, our inclination would be to explain them as in keeping with the reality under which group work could be done. What this means is, of course, that a leader would be well advised to expect failure in social settings where there is no basic common ground (a point of major interest in the chapter on community education).

Second, a teacher-leader can further delimit a field of action by being clear in his mind on the *kinds of learnings* to which he feels committed. For us, in group work, these values would be democratic human relations. While this assumption would indicate the direction of desirable movement, it would leave many issues to be settled—the nature of democracy, whether this practice is democratic, how much democracy is wanted, and the like. Points of this sort would be regarded by the teacher as debatable, matters on which study would be needed.

Third, one must keep in mind the learning process, *the way in which the behavioral changes wanted can take place*. This is, of course, a factual problem, and it could in theory be resolved by scientific test. While College Study data are not conclusive, as explained in the past chapter, a number of experimenters have worked on what was felt to be a promising hypothesis. It is, in brief, the idea that the kinds of learnings most needed in intergroup relations must be experienced by the learners as things they elect to do. Where this does not occur, as in academic education, new learnings are unlikely to assume in personality the position of a superego, a moral conscience motivating behavioral change. This is, we believe, the most basic issue in current intergroup education and one that should be subjected to crucial test.

Finally, a leader cannot lead without followers. Here a number of *reality principles* must guide educators as long as they operate as educators, rather than in some other role. A teacher will seek changes in all aspects of personality—mind, emotions, actions, and so on, educating wholesale rather than piecemeal as in the intense cultivation of mental processes. Yet—and this is the point—he will not lose touch with the group, or with any learner in it. Readiness to learn, speed of learning, assessment and reteaching, will all set limits which a teacher will have to take into account. He cannot march ahead, covering ground, and call back for students to follow if they are able.

For learners of low comprehension, whatever the cause, a simple level of group work is called for, simple in content and procedures. Average students need more complex learning experiences; yet they can profit from a learning level that is set too low for them. For the best students in a group, a good teacher must extend himself. Learner capacities are great, very great, a judgment hard to quantify because it depends on experiences. Most group-work teaching we have seen is set much below top talent levels, and this raises a question on which educators are far apart in their values. In view of time-cost factors in schooling, in view also of society's dependence on technical knowledge, where should a teacher set his main sight? On least-able students, on the average, on the talented few, on the most gifted?

From our standpoint, group-process education need make no clean-cut choice. It can work in realistic ways with very heterogeneous groups, assuming that three requirements are met. One is that the objects of group activity, the targets at which to shoot, must be such as to make use of various kinds of interests, skills, and talents; thus a mental picture is created of not one big hill to climb, the intellectual, but several other steep ascents as well. Second, every group member must have some real job to do, some task involvement of his own choice and liking. Third, the group rewarding system must follow these same lines, so that the payoff for effort (praise, grades, self-feelings) is fitted to this over-all pattern, in fact, motivates it. A learner will know then what to do, where to take hold, for he will see that it takes different kinds of abilities to run the world, that his school will reward them all.

In this chapter we have begun the analysis of group-process teaching, a task that will be continued in the next chapter on community education and later in a study of the consultant's role in college change programs. We have spoken as clearly as possible because theory issues are not always easy to grasp. Without theory, however, no group process can make much sense, nor does it contain dynamics which make necessarily for its own improvement. It can run on over a long period of time, low grade, inefficient, a system in which mediocrity or worse perpetuates itself. What we have discussed is, in effect, a way of working with people that is very old in community life and education, the foundation of a democratic social order. What has been sought in the chapter is the improvement of this kind of education so that, in time, it may rank along with academic learning as a respected approach to problems in human relations.

6. Community Education and Coordination

We have discussed two of the principal College Study approaches to learning problems in intergroup relations. One was academic education, the other group-process teaching, and both overlap the third, community education. By this is meant college and school programs which focus on local area life, its nature, changes, problems, and planning. One type of activity is to acquaint learners with this life, another to guide participation in it, and the third to work for its improvement. The latter is in part a matter of coordinating resources, a topic treated in detail in chapter 9. All educational institutions in the Study, in fact such institutions everywhere, are actively interested in life-centered learning. Many take initiative in organizing area services, councils, and campaigns.

The rationale of community work in education would appear to lie in a viewpoint that cannot be explored here in any serious way, namely, that the problems of most concern today are not the narrow, technical problems of education. On the contrary, they are *the problems of our society* as they flow over into the school, the problems of a changing social order as it pulls itself along by its own bootstraps, seeking ever a greater measure of democracy in its common life. We shall begin, as usual, with a spread of concrete cases, taking them much as they come from the files, and then go on to theory. This chapter will be less sharply centered than the past two, both because of the nature of the topic and of placement of material in a later context.

SOME CONCRETE SCHOOL CASES

Schools have never found it easy to make and keep good contacts with foreign-born parents. These parents are often handicapped by language difficulties which make them shy, self-conscious, and confused. Their energies go rather fully into making a living, and they may have had little formal schooling. It is difficult, at times

132

quite impossible, for them to keep abreast of their children, to guide them in acquiring American ways. Various College Study institutions have done good work in adult education, for example, the language classes at San Marcos in Texas, and the home visiting program among the Mexicans conducted by the Central Michigan College of Education at Mt. Pleasant. Rather than review the kinds of adult teachings that have been tried, we shall report two informal ways of bridging the gap between parents and their children.

THEN AND NOW: A SCHOOL GAME

At this lower-grade school in an urban area, parents were invited (personally pledged) to attend a series of school parties. Mostly mothers came, and as each entered, she was asked to sit in an outer circle of chairs, just behind her own child. Children sat in the inner circle, except the one who was "it." He sat in the center on the floor, an arrangement much enjoyed by the children.

For the first meeting or two, the teacher asked the questions. Of the child who was "it," she would ask what he had for breakfast, how he spent his evenings, which games he liked best, what he felt was most exciting about the city—one question of this sort to each child. After the child had spoken, the mother was asked to tell what things were like in her life when she was the age of her child—her breakfast, games, evenings, etc.—so that "now and then" comparisons were possible.

It was the teacher's role to help the children understand and appreciate parental backgrounds, to try to catch some idea of change and its problems. She guided parent-and-child discussions over tensional issues, trying always to widen areas of mutual respect and affection. If an adult started to scold, she was led to talk about some other topic. If a child became smartly critical and disrespectful, the teacher would ask for information on some other phase of his life.

Later on, as children and parents became better able to talk together, the teacher tried to build some norms of conduct through total-group agreement. In most cases, this proved to be difficult, and yet over a semester of work some gains were made.

Judging by attendance records, as well as by participation, these meetings had positive values. They made for as much sharing of ideas as possible among people so far apart in age and culture. Most parents had ambivalent attitudes toward the school, including dislikes which the teacher tried to get expressed in words and to alleviate.

Big-city schools in foreign language areas are criticized, perhaps unjustly, for their use of legal pressures to exact parental cooperation. Some teachers get results by more persuasive methods, for instance a cautious introduction of American customs.

CHANGING DRESS CUSTOMS

Children were eager for school play. We wanted them, of course, to use the playground, but the girls were not dressed to slide down the chutes or climb on jungle gyms. They came in long white dresses and underskirts, no bloomers underneath.

Our first step was to secure some serviceable panties and to make a fuss over them. Children handled them, admiring the lace edgings, and presently some girls wanted to put them on. We explained how much easier it would be to romp about and they liked the idea. We anticipated trouble with their older siblings and their parents.

We called in some of these older boys and girls and showed them how cute the little ones looked, how they could slide, climb, and run. A burst of laughter met us. "Girls wear pants here?" We insisted that the garments were not pants but panties, nice, fine panties, very much in style. "And do teachers wear panties, you wear panties?" If worst came to worst, we were prepared to show them what we wore.

After one more lesson of this kind, the issue seemed pretty well settled. "In America, girls and women wear pants, too." At the children's insistence, we suspect, mothers began to copy the pattern and to turn underskirts into "briefs" for their lively little girls.

In College Study travels we have met a score of teachers like this one, "little mothers" to an area's children. Unless a person has studied such cases, it will come as a surprise to see the affection in which these teachers are held by local residents, children and adults alike. In one rural school district, young men and women in World War II kept up regular correspondence with a teacher who, in turn, communicated with their parents. In a big-city slum area, a very tough district, certain teachers visit homes at will, without fear of being molested. They do not hold with much of the street life which they see and hear; yet they are respected persons. Their relationship to people, like that of rabbi, priest, or pastor, is one of trust and intimacy.

With few exceptions, colleges have encouraged schools to make full use of parents, lay leaders, ministers, social agency heads, civic officials, and so on, in planning school services and programs. This has been notably true on so-called controverted issues, areas of living where custom and/or law decree that schooling shall not enter. The school is called a "residual institution," meaning that its functions are delegated to it, that it tends to do things not well done by home or other agency; yet it is hard to tell exactly when a school should start some new kind of instruction.

A COURSE IN RELIGIOUS EDUCATION

In this far-western community, a high school faculty became concerned with the indifference of young people to religious teachings. They believed that a common core of ideals and basic morals could be worked out which would meet the approval of local churches. They felt that such teaching should decrease the high youth dropout rates at these churches and, at the same time, reduce juvenile perplexities and misconduct.

When the school board was requested to approve an elective course of this kind, it set a date for a public hearing. All local churches but one sent representatives, usually the minister, and other local groups had spokesmen. While most of the speakers favored a trial at religious education, there was a vigorous opposition. At their next meeting, the board approved the course by a narrow margin, chiefly on the strength of its faith in a very popular school principal.

The school staff knew that it would need to proceed with utmost caution. What was done after some further thinking was to call a meeting of parents, young people, and others, to talk over the general problem. At this meeting the instructor named to give the course was asked what she proposed to teach. Her reply, plus her obvious interest in all religions, greatly disarmed the opposition. She said that she did not know what such a course should contain, that its content and conduct should be a matter of school and community agreement.

At this point the principal suggested that a committee be appointed, to consist of two representatives of the school, the ministerial association, the P.T.A., and the high school seniors. This was approved by unanimous vote, and the principal was asked to make the committee appointments. This committee met biweekly throughout the semester, reviewing the literature on religious education in public schools, studying local church doctrines, and sampling adolescent needs and problems.

The end result of committee work was a six-unit course outline, each unit very flexible, with a great deal being left to class interest and teacher judgment. Units dealt with the faith problems of young people, church views of conduct, boy and girl relations, good citizenship, intergroup relations, social change, and religion. Of more concern here was the way this course was conducted. Committee members were expected to attend class as often as possible. This group approved a list of persons (doctors, ministers, young married couples, etc.) to meet with the class from time to time. The teacher spoke to each of the larger sponsoring organizations, summarizing student reactions.

Any kind of public school religious education is a hazardous undertaking. This appears to be due chiefly to the strong secular trend in our culture, the loss of core (unity) values in many communities, and the general view that public schools cannot deal fairly with all creedal points of view. The project described was free from sectarian bias, with no church given a preferential rating. It was opposed on this latter ground by one church and was weakly supported by three others, because of their conviction that such teaching should be the task of the home and the church. Religions were not taught as of equal or unequal worth but rather as different, with each making its own approach to problems of faith and conduct.

Small pilot surveys in College Study centers show that this type of course would be disapproved in many communities; yet it seemed to do well in the situation discussed. One strength of the project was the competence of the instructor, another the cooperative planning, a third the fact that control rested in a representative committee. Other strengths were the use of local resource persons in instruction and a policy of keeping the sponsoring organizations well informed. Any school project of this kind might well be regarded as a compact with a community, hence as subject to regular audits and changes.

Units and courses designed to acquaint young people with their community were common at every school level. They took the forms of area trips, agency visits, fact-finding studies, assembly of artifacts for school exhibits, agency services, and programs given at churches and civic clubs. They took the form also of bringing the community into the school by means of a number of conventional practices. One novelty was the use of sociodramas depicting intergroup relations, parental teachings about these child contacts, and the friendships developed across color, creedal, or other line. The most memorable occasion was, however, a community "audit," a big turnout of people in a small city in the South.

A COMMUNITY AUDIT

At this meeting, grade school children had been seated in one section of the auditorium, high school youth in another, young to middle-age adults in a third, elders in a fourth. It was explained that few communities were perfect, that most places wanted to be better, that an "audit" was one way for the people themselves to assess the area's strengths and weaknesses. On a big blackboard the leader had written:

> What is good about our town?
> Who should get credit for this?
> What still needs to be done?
> Who can undertake to do this?
> When can this work be started?

The idea was to move back and forth across the auditorium, taking in turn one problem from each section. This problem was listed on the board, discussed as to need, what action should be taken, at what cost, and by whom.

Of all the age levels, the grade school group provided the most excitement. They passed their first turn, unable to state a problem but, on second trial, they threw the auditorium into uproarious laughter.

One little girl stood up and said she had a problem. Asked to state it, she said that "the town was corrupt." Not sure he understood, the leader quieted the audience until she could repeat. The town was indeed "corrupt," for her papa had told her so that very evening just before supper!

As the two-hour meeting broke up, down the aisle came a very distraught mother, her small daughter in hand. "Stop the people, tell him Ellen, stop . . . tell. . . ." she kept saying in the same breath. A mistake had been made. In reading a news headline, Ellen had met a word she did not know, and papa, busy with his own reading, had failed to understand. The town was not "corrupt" but "bankrupt," so its trustees said. Once this was cleared up, the only casualty was the little girl, who was crying silently to herself.

Good points were made at this meeting. For example, a high school boy said that he was from the country, that his parents would have come had the roads not been so bad. A county board member spoke on this issue, answering questions. Notes were kept on all such items, and the local paper ran a full account of the evening. People liked this kind of meeting in preference to a speech. "It gives us a chance to know the town," a businessman said, "and to praise some people for the good things they are doing."

From an action standpoint, such meetings need a thorough follow-up; yet they hold potentials for getting projects started. As an educational experience for young people, we can strongly recommend them. They can cut deeply into the civic ignorance of youth, the sense of being shut off from adult concerns, the lack of identification with any community action program that is real. We have found "audits" best in uncovering material lacks and needs, as in the bad roads incident, and least useful in unifying people on human-relations issues.

COLLEGE TEACHER-TRAINING PROJECTS

Most college time in community education has been spent in improving the use of the "area 'round about" as a training laboratory for students. In theory, some learnings in human relations can occur in classrooms, some only in field contacts and experiences, while others take a close linkage of the two.

At the State Teachers College at Trenton, New Jersey, student community experiences start in the freshman year in a club-leader program and continue until the prospective teacher is graduated. The last event is a period of residence in some community of the student's choice, preceded by a semester's work of community study. During the period of his residence the student is guided by regular field visits and campus conferences. While this program and others in Volume I of the College Study report are too involved for summary, they are useful reading in connection with the present chapter.

To meet in groups and work in groups is an old American custom, one that antedates formal schooling in this country. It has been commented upon by foreign observers from de Tocqueville and Dickens on, notably by Bryce. What is fairly new, as suggested in the past chapter, is the idea of using technical skill to improve action processes, a viewpoint College Study workers have carried into many school-community groups. The following comments are by a P.T.A. member, a parent.

IMPROVING PARENT-TEACHER MEETINGS

At our P.T.A. meetings, things have perked up. The reason is, I think, that we have been wasting time. . . . You have to learn how to work in groups, just like you learn other things. . . . The principal started us on a group-improvement program, but we run it now, ourselves, with the help of some students from our local teacher-training college. . . .

We have two kinds of group observers. One is the group-process observer who studies our meetings from the angle of how we treat one another, who takes part in discussion, who gets mad or hurts people, who is liked and why that is. The other observer studies the business side of our meetings, what we set out to do, how well we did it, what the principal called "the product" of our discussion.

While I am positive that we settle down to business faster, and that there is a much better feeling in the group, any kind of group observation and reporting is very hard to do. . . . College students who meet with us are studying these things in class but they are not as good at them as some of the parents. Our principal is the best of all. He sees things we do that nobody else notices, and he can say things in a very nice way.

There are a lot of ways to improve P.T.A. meetings, to get a satisfactory turnout, so that this case should be kept in perspective. Process and product observation can be a bungling job, hurting people a great deal, or it can be a fine art in the exchange of productive ideas. To immerse young people in this flow of adult doings, to open their eyes to the performances that go on, is in itself a liberal education in the dynamics of social change. Any kind of observation and recording has the function of furthering group action, not distorting or impeding it, and the rub comes most often in the "feedback," the observer's report to the group.

A PROBLEM CLINIC, ROLE-PLAYING

In a middle-states small city, a two-day conference was held for all directors of all the voluntary sociocivic, educational, and religious organizations in the community. This "problem clinic" was held under joint college and agency auspices, and as a part of the active public service program of the college. While many paid agency officers were present, they did not conduct the program. This was done largely by a professor, an outside consultant, college students, and a few lay persons.

Since we had no exact count on the number of board members, directors, etc., in the area, it was a surprise to find almost four hundred persons assembled for the initial session. Most of them were representatives of their church, lodge, club, council, or the like, and had been instructed to report back on the meetings.

In a brief address, the role of sociocivic bodies in a democracy was explained, how every community in the nation depends upon them for many essential services. Board members were praised for their willingness to serve their groups, often at real personal costs, but it was added that few directors have had any training for their jobs. Would it be possible for them to do better work if practices could be seen and ideas thought about?

With this, the consultant began work. What, really, was a board member's job? What did all board members have in common? To start at the beginning, how did they come to get their jobs? When a board member started to answer, he was invited to come to the center of the room where, on a low platform, a table had been set up. Three college students, each coached for a particular part, sat at the table with him. He was asked to show, "just as in a real board meeting," how prospective board members were discussed, accepted, or rejected.

These sessions brought, of course, several laughs. Midway in them, a woman spoke from the audience to say that things were not run that way in her church group. She was asked to join us at the table and went on to explain how the choice of board members was made outside of meetings—in homes, at clubs, in stores, etc.—and then announced when the board convened. While it would have been instructive to have found the frequency of this practice, no effort was made to follow up this point.

Well, that was half the story of board member selection, the other half occurring when the selectee received his invitation and made his decision. How did this take place? These sessions brought more laughs than any other ones (a point made here because people at such meetings must have a great deal of unstaged, spontaneous fun).

When the consultant began to feel that roles were coming dangerously close to reality (for example, a union man simulated a phone call to a CIO executive, asking if he should take office), he defined the situation once again as a role-playing job. What we wanted to illustrate were "common practices," simply to set them forth and to let the audience see if they were good or bad.

At successive meetings the functions of board members were explored, ending with a memorable sociodrama on a board member trying to sum up the values he had found in a lifetime of board work. In all, five sessions were held, morning, afternoon, and evening, and attendance increased steadily. After the second session it was evident that the meetings could be counted a success. The consultant had messages and phone calls from persons who wanted to tell him of some scandal in board operations, some wrong that should be straightened out—one sign that our work was sinking in.

This was a new venture for the writer, a use of sociodrama that has been improved since that time. The sociodrama can be adapted to a great variety of intergroup situations, wherever role play can be used to explore issues and give practice in better techniques. The example was selected to suggest to educators a much neglected area of community service. The country over, there are thousands of board members who have had no special preparation for the posts they fill, public servants whose training needs are very real. Second, we want to pin another comment on this case, a point to be read into a great many concrete examples. We did not parcel out colors, creeds, and so forth, in this problem clinic, because they were not highly relevant to the work undertaken. While all such facts are useful, people should be treated like people wherever that is possible, with no labeling at all unless the context makes it relevant.

Various colleges have been interested in community coordination, some on a long-term basis, as at Greeley, Colorado. Here the principal intergroup problem involved Anglo-Mexican relations, with the so-called "colony" an object of concern.

COORDINATING AN AREA'S GOOD-WILL FORCES

At Greeley, in 1947, a meeting of over four hundred persons was held on the college campus. It was sponsored by the college, city and county school systems, community agencies, and government offices. Participants included college students, faculty members, schoolteachers, the mayor, a newspaper editor, agency heads, and other prominent persons. Directors of intercultural programs came from as far away as California and Texas, for Spanish-Anglo problems blanket the whole Southwest.

The meeting culminated a year of arduous fact-finding, detailed studies of Mexican life, living conditions, Anglo attitudes, and discriminating practices. These studies were made by college, school, and agency committees, and have been summarized in a 240-page mimeographed report by Dr. Earle U. Rugg, chairman of the project. They are mostly simple and factual in nature, showing the kinds of evidence (health statistics, crime rates, school progress, etc.) practical persons regarded as important and were able to obtain.

At the meeting, reports were made by each committee chairman, brief highlights on salient findings. What further could be done? Answers pointed in three directions. One thing to do, a central value in the year's work, was to see that these facts got into the teacher-educating program, for the college sends teachers over the entire southwest region. Point two was to publicize findings, with the *Greeley Tribune* undertaking the local job. Point three was to do something about local conditions, and to date a number of specific changes have been made.

What may prove to be of great importance has been the effort to get the Anglo-Mexican problem made central in the work of a local unity council, or community coordinating body. While progress is being made, outcomes are still unclear, and it would be unwise to venture guesses as to the future. Many persons, including the project chairman, have worked hard on community coordination, feeling that intergroup relations will require a long-range point of view. Opposition has developed, some initial zeal has been lost, all of which are commonplace occurrences in community work.

That the Greeley studies have had no dramatic finale, that action is still in process, make the project more typical than would a smashing success, for realistic community coordination is hard to achieve. Facts have a way of calling for more facts, so that new studies are under way; yet good works are also present. These include better roads to the colony, improved civic conditions, and bus transportation for Mexican children to Greeley schools. The case in full detail is a good example of "action research," in contrast to traditional fact-finding (a distinction to be discussed later).

Colleges have been described as a way of keeping young men and women immature and dependent, of fending off the strains of fully adult living. Whatever the merit of this view, it applies with least force to community education, especially in its social action phase. Under this title we want to call attention to the student movements reported in the *College Programs* volume, activities illustrated by a very brief case. The reporter is a graduate student and a part-time schoolteacher.

STUDENT INTERGROUP ACTIVITIES

I feel that students are well organized at our college to work on intergroup problems . . . provided they can keep out of trouble with the college administration. The city is full of problems, mostly interracial, that need correction. I wouldn't say the faculty is much interested, only a few of them are, as we are finding out now in planning our biggest campaign up to this time. . . .

Back in 1944, when the Student Intercultural Council was started, we began to work on restaurants, movies, bars, and the like. The idea was to end Jim Crow, to get fair and decent treatment for all patrons, regardless of race. . . . And then, presently, we had a speaker at the Council who talked on housing, then another speaker on jobs, and we switched over in our work to these areas. . . .

Last year in particular, we tried to rethink our program, what we should be trying to do in race relations and how we can get some changes made. About half the group has been gathering facts for Council use, often as term papers in some college course. We have tried to find out what it costs this big city to "keep the Negro in his place," just the facts about housing, welfare, medical care, leisure pursuits, jobs, and education

Take education, for example, or rather one issue in education. Our schools have a swell intercultural policy, one with a lot of say-so but little do-so, as we have found. What burns us mostly is the fact that Negro teachers are not assigned to any schools except those in Negro districts. In a big public meeting in which our Intergroup Council took part, this policy was admitted and defended by the superintendent of schools.

The superintendent took the stand that "race, creed, or national origins are not to be considered in the hiring or promotion of teachers," as the Schools' Intercultural Policy states. He said that no part of this statement, nothing in the policy, applies to the assignment of teachers to jobs, that this placement is guided by racial considerations. "The school board," he said, "has never indicated that it wanted us to pioneer or crusade in breaking down neighborhood racial patterns." He added that, "This does not mean that we are to stand pat, to do nothing about the matter." When the superintendent was asked to explain, he called attention to the "intercultural program" in the city schools.

We think "the intercultural program" is pretty much the bunk. Many of us are teachers, or we know teachers to whom to talk, and what we can find out does not add up to much, except fine talk. Show us a school, in a cosmopolitan city like this, that does not have a Negro teacher on the staff and we will show you a school that needs one, the same school. To learn about people, you can't simply read books. You have got to have contact with them, see them at work, interact with them.

Well, the campaign to break this assignment business is swinging into high gear, with a lot of city organizations behind it. Just now, we are circulating petitions, getting all the signatures we can, and these will be presented to the school board. We are also encouraging school districts to ask for at least one Negro teacher, some carefully selected person who can pioneer for good will and understanding. It is likely that some kind of court action will be needed, but that is out of our hands. We hope the thing can be worked out but, win or lose, we feel that the fight itself is important.

In some College Study centers, student activities operate through an intergroup council, with a detailed program of campus and community services. Elsewhere, students have adopted aggressive tactics in their fight on discrimination. They may picket business places, report color bars to law enforcement officers, work with civil liberty and pressure groups, stage hearings with public officials, bring their own part-time employment problems before an FEPC commission, fight openly against any semblance of a college quota system, go on strike to end classroom and/or campus segregation, agitate to remove anti-somebody clauses from fraternity or other charters, and force declarations of official college policy in such areas as athletics, social clubs, and honorary elections.

All things considered, our impressions are that such efforts to secure equal rights and equal justice are growing rapidly. They appear to indicate an increasing impatience with routine official moves against prejudice and discrimination, to suggest an ever-mounting pressure on college administration. As we write, a news item shows a situation that is not confined to any section of the nation. At the University of Texas,[1] the ban on Negro students was to have been put to student vote. Two days before the poll, the test was called off. Antireferendum forces had argued (1) a vote to keep the ban would give Russia another chance to publicize our prejudices, and (2) a vote to lift the ban would bring enraged Texans down upon the university. While student tactics in general are as yet not much to speak of, neither pro nor anti sides in campus controversies are unmindful of the national spotlight they can focus on any educational institution.

NATURE OF LIFE-CENTERED LEARNING

An adequate theory of community education would take account of at least three philosophical dicta. One is Dewey's oft-quoted half-truth that "education is life," another is Hart's neglected addendum. "The problem of democratic education," wrote Hart,[2] "is not that of training children" in any narrow, academic sense. It is that of "making a community in which children cannot help growing up to be democratic, intelligent, and disciplined to freedom." After this, he expressed a disturbing thought, "a school cannot do this; only a community can do it," a view we take to mean *a vital school-community unity in the educational task.* And finally, there is Darwin's functionalism, the foundation of modern stress on "functions of living," "felt needs," "life situations,' and the like, in school curriculums.

[1] In *Time*, March 27, 1950, p. 85.
[2] Joseph K. Hart, *Democracy in Education* (New York: Croft-Appleton-Century, 1918), pp. 370-71.

To follow these three leads and combine them into an organic whole would be an involved process.[3] Suffice it to say that the community point of view in education is like group-process teaching in certain basic particulars. Both testify to a loss of faith in the academic method as a way of democratizing emotionalized attitudes and behaviors. Neither viewpoint believes that such changes in

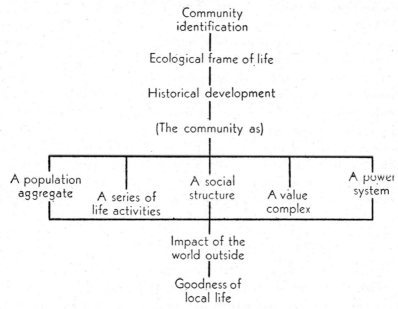

Community
identification
|
Ecological frame of life
|
Historical development
|
(The community as)
|

A population aggregate | A series of life activities | A social structure | A value complex | A power system

|
Impact of the world outside
|
Goodness of local life

Fig. 3.—A general plan of community study (From Cook and Cook, *A Sociological Approach to Education*, p. 64. Used by permission of the McGraw-Hill Book Co.)

people can be made by preaching eighteenth-century moral ideals, or by teaching parliamentary law, or by detached inspection of human struggle patterns. And yet both community and group-process education want social science in the picture—a science, however, related to practical experience and to the tested values of democratic cooperation.

Textbooks list various kinds of community experiences which can, in theory, be provided pre- and in-service teachers. They cite directly, or hint vaguely, at several kinds of learnings, although not

[3] Lloyd and Elaine Cook, *A Sociological Approach to Education* (New York: McGraw-Hill Book Co., 1950), chap. 16, "Using Community Resources."

under pre- and end-test controls. Worse still, they do not attempt to define conditions under which "life" appears to educate, or to discuss the types of students who seem to profit most by direct, perceptual experience. Finally, no educational institution with which we are acquainted has any systematic plan of community study, any comprehensive view of what a community is and how it functions in orienting intergroup relations.

While each community study in the College Study experiment was a discrete project, all these undertakings fell within a broad conception of community as outlined in Figure 3.

Concepts in Figure 3 are, to a degree, self-explanatory. Of special interest are the views of community as a value complex and a social power system, ideas which if related would force basic changes in the study of values as that study now goes on in average education classes. No explanation is needed for concluding the outline with "the goodness of life," for this is the educator's prime interest in community study. He studies community for the purpose of assessing its effects on people, for replanning with them the conditions of a better way of life.

STATUS RESEARCH AND ACTION RESEARCH

If College Study educators have made any worth-while contribution to community education, it may lie in a way of thinking about organized group action. We would not give the impression that college staffs have been united on this point. On the contrary, some professors have argued that the school should confine its activities to the school, that it should not meddle in community affairs. Others have taken an opposite stand, pointing out what they called the unreality of "the hilltop view." Whether one's interest is that of an analyst of social action, or an adviser to study groups, youth councils, adult activities, and the like, the issue just raised merits serious thought.

A start can be made by contrasting status research with action research. Status research is traditional study-making, the finding of facts, their interpretation and communication as a contribution to knowledge. It purports to be, as stated earlier, "valueless" research, the student's only loyalty being to truth within the rituals of his science. On "practical problems," a researcher may break over these limits to the extent of popularizing findings, speaking at mass meetings, and otherwise trying to motivate corrective action.[4] Here the effectiveness of effort, one's total *modus operandi,* comes into question, plus the assumption that he can slip in and out of conflicting roles (traditional scientist, skilled actionist) without one role doing damage to the other.

In action research, the people making the study are the ones who have considerable power to effect a change in conditions, for example, a whole town seeking to control prejudice,[5] housing project dwellers trying to stop the spread of rumor,[6] an industrial shop force wanting changes in their work situation,[7] a youth group engaged on some community service project. These people are not experts, as status researchers often are. They must be able to revise plans in process and to learn from a never-ending wake of mistakes. They have, as a rule, a professional consultant, but the project is not his, nor will he be led to assume responsibility for it. His major function is advisory, so much so that, in years of school-community work, we recall no more than a score of cases where basic ends seemed to us a serious impasse. In these instances we have tried to cause people to face up to issues, to meet reality demands in light of likely consequences. Failing in this, we either went along with group decision, whatever it was, or else withdrew from the project with a sense of personal failure. A consultant is, day in and out, a technique man, a helper in devising plans and evaluating progress, all within the frame of democratic values which he assumes that participants accept.

It seems plain that status research is based on the academic assumption discussed earlier, namely, that organized knowledge will affect attitudes, that study findings will result in civic changes. In action research, stress is put on participation—active, varied,

---

[4] An excellent example is the 91-page booklet *Segregation in Washington,* by Joseph Lohman and committee (Chicago: National Committee on Segregation in the Nation's Capital, 4901 Ellis Ave., 1948.

[5] "Prejudice in Seaside," *Human Relations,* I (1947), 2–24, a summary account by the staff of the Commission on Community Interrelations of the American Jewish Congress.

[6] Leon Festinger, *et al.,* "A Study of a Rumor: Its Origin and Spread," *Human Relations,* I (1948), 464–86.

[7] Everett C. Hughes, "The Knitting of Racial Groups in Industry," *American Sociological Review,* XI (1946), 512–19.

and inclusive participation—so that, in theory, everyone is "task-involved." The study-change process is kept flexible, adjustive to continuous "feedbacks" of data as things happen. Aside from technical details, this is the way that pioneers in intercultural education have tried for many years to solve intergroup problems.[8] Atlanta University's "get out the vote" campaign (*College Programs,* Volume I, chapter 13) shows that this technique need not be limited, as someone has said, "to little groups of little people."

RESOLVING A SOCIAL CONFLICT

To get a fairly complete example of action research, we shall take an incident outside the College Study. The case selected involves an industrial conflict in a small garment factory, a type of *status clash* which we have met time and again in community work. The narrator is Alex Bavelas, an industrial consultant attached at the time to the Lewin Group Dynamics staff. The actual case is greatly abbreviated, and the italics are ours.

SETTLING A STATUS CLASH[9]

As I walked past the boss's office, I saw Paulson (mechanic) and Sulinda (supervisor) standing in front of his desk. All three were ill at ease. . . . "You're just the man we're waiting for," was the boss's greeting. He explained that Paulson and Sulinda were having some trouble because they could not agree on which machines should be repaired first and that an operator was playing them against each other by gossiping about each to the other.

I said that it was not uncommon for operators to gossip, citing an experience in another factory. Since I wanted to get the supervisor and the mechanic back to work, I added that I had to talk to one of the girls about some matter, after which I would like to talk to each of them. Both agreed to see me at any time and I walked upstairs with Sulinda to the shop. She confided that what made her mad was Paulson's telling lies about her and the operator's calling her a liar to her face. Without taking sides, I told of a similar instance and added that the whole thing might have grown out of some simple misunderstanding.

In the next few minutes, I interviewed the boss who said that Sulinda was ready to quit her job when I walked in and that Paulson

---

[8] See Rachael Davis DuBois, *Get Together Americans* (New York: Harper & Bros., 1943).

[9] Based on Kurt Lewin, *Resolving Social Conflicts* (New York: Harper & Bros., 1948). Used by permission.

also said he was quitting. The boss hoped I could smooth things over, saying that this kind of thing had been happening right along but that now it was worse. Both workers were very independent, lost their tempers, and shared a mutual dislike.

In the interview with Sulinda, she said that Paulson was not a good mechanic. Often he didn't know what was wrong with a machine, would tinker around for ages. He would blame the operator, or say the thread was no good, or make other excuses. Just that afternoon, Sulinda said, a girl had come to her and told her that Paulson refused to fix her machine. She had gone to Paulson at once and told him what the girl had said, adding that he had to fix the machine. He got very angry, denying that he had made any such statement. He went to the girl, accused her of lying, which she denied. She said that Sulinda was lying, whereupon Paulson took her to the supervisor. It was here that Sulinda had picked up her coat and went down to tell the boss that she was quitting.

[*Since the machine operators were dependent on both Paulson and Sulinda, it was the unclear line of authority between the two that made the lie such an important issue. If Sulinda had admitted the lie, she would have lost face and weakened her position with the girls. For Paulson, the lie had involved a threat to his honor, and to his authority with the girls.*]

Sensing this dilemma, I said no more about the lie. I asked Sulinda factual questions about the number of machine breakdowns, nature, etc., all of which made it clear that Paulson was kept very busy. Sulinda agreed that, if he had time, he would do better work. I asked her whether she thought it would help if I talked to the girls who were carrying tales, and she agreed. I asked if she would like to know what they said, and she replied yes.

In my interview with Paulson, he started by explaining how hard he had to work, only one pair of hands, etc. After easing the situation with a joke, I found it easy to arrive with him at the point of attributing the trouble to the impatience of the girls and the lack of mechanic time. He, too, thought it would be well to talk with the girls and that it would help to know just what they thought.

[*Paulson, like Sulinda, had defined the situation in terms of right and wrong; he was right, the supervisor wrong. He was led in the interview, as was Sulinda, to perceive the problem in objective terms—the insufficiency of mechanic time, the natural irritation of the girls. While both interviews uncovered facts, their major function was to change perceptions, thus to start the problem-solving process. Neither person was asked to face all the facts, including their individual behaviors, which might have ended their further cooperation with the consultant. Being conscious of status strivings, the consultant secured their consent before he approached the girls.*]

I then called in several girls for a short interview. They all agreed that Paulson was O.K., but that he had too much work to do, hence could not do a proper job. I asked each girl if it would be a good idea to get all the girls together who had made complaints and see if something could be worked out to reduce the time they had to lose in waiting for repairs. They all agreed.

When the complainers (trouble makers) were assembled, I talked about the problem, stressing the lack of mechanic time. Since it was unlikely that another mechanic could be hired, the question was how to use Paulson's time. Through group discussion, we arrived at this plan. When machines had the same importance, that is, other machines not depending on them, the first to break down should be the first repaired; otherwise the most critical machines should be fixed first. It was further agreed that this plan would be presented to Paulson and Sulinda. I was to report what they said.

[*Conflict is viewed by the consultant as a three-way affair, with the girls its most active promoters. It seems to center on unclear lines of authority, on a status clash, due chiefly to a faulty organization of production. Machine operators themselves are made the social action group, not all the girls but only the "trouble makers," those having greatest power to effect a change in the situation. The consultant has created a hope that the problem can be solved.*]

In reporting to Paulson, I assured him that the girls had nothing against him personally, that they felt he had more work than one mechanic could do. Feeling good about this, he looked over the girls' plan, saying that it was exactly what he wanted, if only everybody would stop bossing him around. He was, I said, a skilled mechanic, and he should not be bothered about deciding which machine should be repaired. Sulinda could cope with this, a matter on which he agreed. He doubted, however, if Sulinda had enough brains to do this.

On talking with Sulinda, she thought that the plan was exactly right; in fact it was what she had proposed long ago, but no one could tell Paulson anything. I said that Paulson was ready to accept her decision as to the order of repair and that the girls thought the whole matter was very clear and would cooperate in every way. She agreed to try the plan but was skeptical.

After telling Paulson that Sulinda would go along on the new scheme, I called in the girls for a short meeting where we went over the plan and the procedure involved. I said we would give it a test run, that it could work only if the girls made it work and that all of us would welcome further ideas. . . .

A few weeks later, the boss and I were talking, when he asked me if I had noticed a change in Paulson. He said that Paulson seemed to have much less work to do, that his report showed about a third less repairs. The boss was certain that he got along better with Sulinda, that the girls were less restless than before. On my speaking to Paulson, he felt that work output was higher than it had been. In his opinion, "the music had a lot to do with it," referring to a loud-speaker system he had just installed. As for Sulinda, he felt that the girls had gotten the impression that "we hate each other," when "no enmity had ever existed." Of course, he had "bickered" with her, but the two were really "the best of friends." Feeling secure in his job, he could afford to be charitable toward the supervisor. She could, in turn, laugh and joke with him.

Time has been taken with this case because it shows a good many features of basic action research, wherever it is found. The problem involved human relations, a status situation where authority was unclear. Solution of the issue depended on attitudinal changes, which rested in turn on social perceptions. The dispute was settled in line with reality principles, the demand to keep production up. Planning was initiated with the group lowest down in the status hierarchy, the group with power to make or break any kind of plan. The "lie" was disregarded, as in our "little white monkey" case in a past chapter, and an attempt was made to get beneath symptoms of unrest to its causes.

To be certain, the case raises questions. Is action research *research* in any fundamental sense? If fact-finding is defined as formal study, then this did not occur; yet in an informal way a good many facts were searched out. Did these data have meaning in any systematic, scientific framework? We are inclined to believe so on the grounds that a science of group dynamics is now developing in which all such situational evidence will be meaningful. Was the consultant's work objective, that is, can it be communicated as are other scientific procedures? We can see no reason why management techniques cannot be abstracted and generalized, much as scientists treat other aspects of complex situations.

SOME COMMUNITY STUDY-ACTION METHODS

While any discussion of action research is at present controversial, we would not pass the topic without suggesting that not all group work is, by any means, as informal as the Bavelas example. Informality is the rule, however, and possibly this indicates a need to move in the direction pointed by an ancient couplet.

Those rules of old, discover'd, not devised
Are nature still, but nature methodiz'd.
                                        —POPE

Although thorough discussion of method is beyond the scope of present interest, a listing of the techniques most used in College Study projects should help further to clarify the field of community education.

GROUP STUDY-ACTION METHODS

Study Methods

Action indicators, what-would-you-do types of tests
Anecdotal records, diaries
Area surveys, polling techniques
Attitude tests, scales, etc.
Audience reactions, analyses
Change barometer, trend data
Documentary and primary-source material, print analysis
Community life history, reaction to crises
Group interviews, fact-finding
Group study, case history
Inventories of interests, problems, time uses, wishes
Opinionaires, knowledge tests
Projective tests, situational, photo, and print forms
Sociometric charting, individual and group sociograms

Action Methods

Activity projects, teamwork
Area trips, visits, agency services, apprenticeship
Community audits, clinics
Community coordination, the area council idea
Complacency shock, stress test techniques
Conference procedures, around-the-table-bargaining
Group assessment, process and product observers
Group discussion, decision
Group experimentation, controlled change factors
Pageants, festivals, displays
Panel discussion, round table, symposium, etc.
Workshop techniques, small- and large-group coordination

Study methods are fact-finding techniques and devices, and hence they differ from action methods, the aim of which is to secure behavioral changes. That differences are real is a fact of psychology as well as logic. For example, in study methods much scientific ritual is for the purpose of objectifying operations, whereas in group-process teaching methods of any kind one must maintain close rapport with people. Where an educator must be skilled in both types of methods, the training task becomes complicated by the role conflicts to be discussed later.

Viewpoints toward Community

In concluding, it might be useful to inspect the two main viewpoints from which community educators approach their task. One is sentimental, the other realistic, if such terms will point the way toward an understanding of a much debated issue in community education.[10]

From a sentimental standpoint, community disunity and conflict are regarded much the same as war. War is unmitigated evil, doing untold harm to victor and vanquished alike. It is abnormal, a periodic breakdown in world order. It is a barbaric way of problem solving, where might makes right, no matter what other scales may say. Since no thoughtful person wants war, the thing to do is to outlaw it, even if a war must be made to end all wars. Our concern here is not to debate war, certainly not to defend it. It is to suggest that, when this viewpoint is carried over to community life, it becomes unreal in the sense of misjudging a good many solid facts.

In the now disappearing primary community, the village or town area of horse-and-buggy days, people were few in number. Their mode of life was simple, their human relations intimate, their interests much the same. Neighboring was, in itself, a rather complete code of conduct resting on a consensus of feeling, a commonality of experience. To assert that this social pattern has changed, that the big-city way of life is ever more dominant, is to state a truth the implications of which no community educator dare ignore. The secondary community, the metropolis with its footloose thousands, its heterogeneity and impersonality, its complexities and stratification, is not like the little town. It is not a small place grown big, but a new way of life in man's long history. It is a mass society founded largely on competition, on the clamorous struggle of special interests, the jungle ethics of conflicting power groupings. Such a society is finely poised, dynamic, searching, seeking.

If this viewpoint were accepted, what changes would occur in community education? Speaking broadly, one might anticipate three developments, each related to the other. The first would be

---

[10] A discussion continued in chaps. 9 and 10.

a change in teacher mind-set, the general outlook on social life. If one sees a giraffe once a year, it remains a spectacle; if he sees it daily, it becomes part of the landscape. So with group conflict in community life. It appears inevitable, an incident in the ongoing social process, and it would be helpful if it could be faced as matter-of-factly as any other natural event.

Second, to say that the clash of group with group is normal in our way of life does not mean that efforts to control it should slack off. A society can exist only in unity, in common loyalty to core values, for otherwise cooperative action is impossible. "The danger is," writes Angel,[11] "that in the struggle of opposing groups, the loyalty to common values will be lost." If this happens, as it now is happening, the principles of democracy and common human rights will be denied in the interest of programs aimed to benefit particular groups, the power elements in our society.

Finally, educators would put more stock in Dewey's dictum that "democracy begins at home," home being in one's own groups. We say that "cooperation is beneficial to all concerned," that "minorities are a source of strength," that "people learn through participation." Who has ever tested out such propositions in a conclusive way, proved them in a science sense? If democracy can be made to rest on science rather than on preachment, and we believe it can, the best proving ground will likely be our small and intimate community groups.

[11] Robert C. Angell, *The Integration of American Society* (New York: McGraw-Hill Book Co., 1941).

Part III

IMPROVING TEACHER-LEADER
TRAINING

7. The College Study as In-Service Training

The formal goal of the College Study was to effect changes in the young people who were entering teaching. Past chapters have dealt with matters relating to this theme—the nature of intergroup relations, majority-minority cleavages, theories of prejudice, student attitudes and learnings, academic instruction, group-process teaching, and community participation. While some attention has been paid to the teachers of these prospective teachers, we want now to review the College Study specifically from this angle. Teachers are the people who are in position to make intergroup education permanent, to develop it as a part of all education; hence their continued training on the job and off the job is very important.

Had the College Study had the time and money, it might have made a "job analysis" approach to in-service training problems, a systematic study of human relations in and about schools. Lacking such resources, it was obliged to do much less, chiefly to work in terms of what was known, felt, wanted, feared, and hoped for, much as does every field intergroup program. In this chapter, the aim is to analyze the College Study as a field experiment in the education of college teachers, a complex group process on every campus. In the next chapter, attention turns to so-called "centers of human relations," the assembly of in-service teachers for intensive training. The concluding chapter in this Part is concerned with a most crucial problem, the question of strategies and tactics in community change programs.

THE COLLEGE STUDY WORK PATTERN

In four years time many changes come and go in college intergroup programs, alterations which we cannot hope to detail. While no two campus situations were at any time identical, the general work pattern can be seen in a fairly typical small-college case. This case will show the way one college faculty proceeded in its first

year. The material is abstracted from the report of a college committee chairman, the person in general charge of College Study
work in his institution.

A YEAR OF WORK, V-COLLEGE

This year has been, in some ways, a satisfactory work experience,
but it has not been perfect. . . . It has been hard to keep our committees
on the ball, to keep leaders actively interested, to meet deadlines for
reports, and so on. Half our projects are still in process as this is
written, but they will be completed by the time of our year-end meeting.
The other half, or rather their findings, have been passed on to the
faculty, so that we are now at the stage of determining the projects on
which we want to work next year.

This is, as you know, our first year in the College Study, and I shall
try to tell the story from the beginning. After speaking to you [College
Study director] at the N.E.A. meeting, I began to get busy on the
campus. The president was interested and so were faculty members, so
that I wrote you for further instructions. I passed out the bulletins you
sent and then we held a meeting. It was agreed that we should explain
the project to the total faculty and make a motion that this college
draw up a formal application.

The visit of your associate director to our campus was a most stimulating experience. . . . His talk to the faculty was well received, making
us think more than ever that we wanted to participate in the project.
On that day and the next, he met with us individually or in small
groups, asking about our interests, what studies could be undertaken,
who would lead study groups, and the like. That last evening, we had
a general meeting at which I was elected faculty chairman, and an
intergroup committee was appointed.

I think the organization of all committees here was pretty routine
so that little need be said about it in my report. What we did first was
to appoint a college planning committee. It was the job of this committee, as per advice in your letter, to canvass the faculty for ideas,
suggestions, and needs. After these were tabulated, we had to decide
on a priority rating, for it was impossible to work on all these ideas at
the same time. Incidentally, that has been our greatest handicap, the
fact that everybody is so busy, so caught up in other things that any
new work is just an extra burden.

After agreement was reached as to project areas, we asked that every
faculty member who was interested accept membership on some one of
the eight committees. Students were brought into several of these
groups, and in some cases school heads and social agency representatives. Groups ranged from about six to twenty persons, and each had
a regular schedule of meetings. This was the point we had reached at
the time of your first visit to the campus. . . .

I think your talk at the student assembly, and the discussion that evening at the faculty meeting did a lot to clear up our confusions. Your four points were well chosen—what is intergroup education, how do we develop teamwork, making use of consultant services, and the company (other colleges) we are keeping. The bull session following the faculty meeting was the real clincher for us . . . the interest-getter of your trip.

After this period of stimulation, my problem was largely that of assisting the project groups in their work. You may recall that four of these groups were making studies, three were engaged in action programs (learning human relations skills), and one was concerned with checking up on our college policy in respect to minorities. Groups met once a week during the month after your visit, and then changed to a two-week meeting schedule. We had a general meeting of committee chairmen every two weeks and then, later on, every month. . . .

I was able to help, or to find help, on study techniques, especially on attitude testing and sociographic charting. . . . Where we needed consultant help, as I told you in my letters, was on the actual demonstration of human relations skill. Your next visit to the campus was devoted almost entirely to this problem, as you may recall. The movie was good and well received, but the role practice sessions found more favor among students than among faculty. We still need some good literature on this, for the faculty is not at all sold on the idea of group process teaching. . . .

The best thing that happened in this phase of the program was the workshop held here last May. In addition to Dr. Hatt [associate director of the Study], we had Professor Raths from Ohio State. We had Dr. Edgar Dale earlier in the year, and both men were exceptionally good. . . . I think the idea of skill training is catching on, in fact I know it is with some professors, but it should be stressed heavily next year.

Your Bulletin No. 26 called our attention again to the need to work on the problem of involving other people in this project. The workshop for college committee chairmen and others at Wayne University in February helped me on this problem, mostly by showing us what other colleges were doing or had done. You will remember that community meetings were discussed, along with newspaper publicity, campus groupings, services to schools in our teacher-placement area, and minority groups on the campus.

On your visit in March, time was about equally divided between work with our project groups and planning with the general committee for its appraisal of the year's activities. The idea of the "feedback" (making use of findings and experiences in the general education program) caught the interest of all our teams, leading to recommendations which we presented to the faculty and the student council. There were twelve of these recommendations, which I shall now discuss. . . .

I want to tell you how we are thinking about the coming year. By unanimous vote, the faculty wants to continue with the work, so that the president will send you a reapplication. We believe that the general chairmanship should be rotated each year, both because it is a lot of work and to get new ideas. . . . Five of the committees should go on with their studies, and they wish to do so, but the other groups should be disbanded. . . . Three new groups should be started, as follows. . . . I would add that we are just beginning to get the swing of this thing and that next year will be a big year.

We have deleted specific content, for example, the areas of committee interest and committee findings, because our concern at this time is with the ways and means by which college faculties did intergroup work.[1] In a very abstract form, the picture for an average college would be about as shown in Fig. 4.

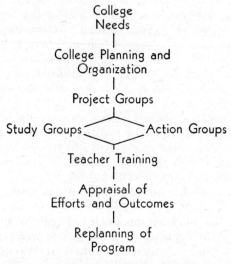

FIG. 4.—General plan of college study work

In Fig. 4 the beginning of faculty thought is with college needs in intergroup relations. What should this college do; where could staff work be most productive? Usually this led to a quick, informal survey, the effects of which were four. One effect was to start talk about majority-minority issues, to focus attention on

[1] With space at a premium, college committee chairmen stressed content and findings in their chapters in the *College Programs* volume, with an understanding that a chapter on "work process" would appear in this report.

them. Next came a diagnostic study of problems and a selection of those to be worked on. These two activities imply a third, that of involving as many persons as possible in the initial planning of the project. Finally, such actions showed better than words the localistic nature of each college program, including the kinds of "needs" to be worked on for some time to come.

Once problems were selected, college organization took the form of a general coordinating committee and small teams or project groups. These groups varied from four or five per college to perhaps twelve. Some were study groups, some action groups, some training groups concerned only with providing students experience in the practice of human relations skills. It is the work of these various groups that fills the pages of the *College Programs* volume, statistical and other findings which need not be reviewed here. On occasion, each college conducted special activities, for instance, workshops and conferences, but the small team groups were the real backbone of the national College Study effort.

Preplanning in the College Study

To understand the work pattern described, as well as the problems that arose, one needs some perspective on preplanning activities in the College Study staff. The healthy birth of a field program and its growth into a mature work effort is a complicated matter. It is, first of all, a function of planning, or so the College Study staff and sponsors assumed. In theory, either under- or over-planning could be disastrous, yet no field-work staff can know or find out ahead of a test the exact amount of planning needed. One must work by guess as to a faculty's action potential, his guess and those of other persons, as checked against two kinds of criteria—the staff's past experience (standards), and the emergence in process of group morale signs. In many cases, too little planning is done ahead of field work, because of the excessive haste shown in most large projects to get started, to set all the wheels in motion.

The central function of preplanning is to set the stage for effective field participation, to create a basic framework in which further local planning is imperative. In theory, two planning levels can be distinguished, the formal and informal. Since formal planning—budget, staff, selection of colleges, general procedure, etc.—

has been discussed in the earlier volume, we shall not detail it here. Informal planning is an attempt to anticipate concrete field difficulties, to prevent their rise or to devise and teach ways of working on them.

In the College Study, staff shortage alone would have made a good preplanning job impossible.[2] We make the point, not to expand upon it, but to indicate its obvious effects, thus to argue for a larger staff in any undertaking similar in scope to the one under review.

Staff shortage endangers a field program at crucial moments, times that seem bound to come. At these instances, it has seemed imperative to the College Study staff to break schedules and get to danger points. Crises are not always to be deplored, as one might think, for they can be great landmarks in a growth process, times of stress in which people learn more than in long periods of routine effort. Even under normal conditions staff inadequacy reduces college work output, with the result that average groups function below their potentials. Finally, research is pushed so far aside that even simple participational statistics are not kept, due dates on reports cannot be met—in short, college programs close without leaving data that are adequate for their analysis.

Haste in getting field work started is not the real reason for indifference to research considerations. In various field "experiments" that could be named, there has been little interest in research or else a superficial conception of it. For example, here is a large-scale citizenship education study, running five years and costing half a million dollars. Evidence would suggest that its history is a general negation of social science knowledge in social education. It has been disdainful of theory, ignorant of group-study methods, taking pride in its naïve "fact-finding" and "calls to action." Its reports are propaganda documents, mixtures of good intentions, showy head-count data, simple recipes, and clichés. If professional education is to continue to have the respect of science-minded people, it must, we suspect, conceptualize its field-work problems a little better. It must budget research as a basic function,

---

[2] Staff consisted of the writer, on half time for the four academic years with one minor exception, and full time for summers; an associate director, an unpaid advisory committee, and such consultants on a per diem basis as could be afforded. Planning had to be done pretty much in process, a situation not to be recommended.

coordinated at every step with change activities, and pay the costs that this implies.[3]

To return to the College Study, every effort was made within time limitations to get the project before selected advisers. Long before college visits were begun, the staff had sensed a number of alternative roads and emphases. Three of these possible lines of development are illustrative.

1. To the staff it seemed that action projects should be given high priority, that the great need in intergroup education was to test out ways of effecting changes in people, of making ideals work. At times, this view met ready faculty reception, orienting most of a college's projects, but in many cases it came off a poor second best to academic studies. When, on repeated trials, this preference for academic studies proved real, the staff adjusted to it.

2. We had been told by various leaders of educational thought, persons highly respected in the profession, that intercreedal differences were important, that cleavages here were growing, and that they were a genuine threat to national unity on moral matters. We had also been told that college groups would not care to work in this particular field of human relations, that risks were too great. With one exception, a college at which basic work was begun, this latter prediction was very true, all of which was contrary to staff efforts and expectations.

3. We have spoken of action potentials. Under favorable circumstances, it was expected that work efforts would be considerable, for the intergroup field is very much alive, much in the forefront of national thought. But what surprised us was the performance of several colleges under most adverse conditions, the work output of greatly overworked faculty members. There is no easy way to objectify this finding, except to say that our sponsoring bodies, after examining data, agreed that it was true. We are uncertain, in spite of study, as to why some whole colleges caught fire and others merely smoldered, a point to which we shall return.

[3] Costs of experimental research in human relations can be seen by comparing a small workshop project (see next chapter) with the College Study. This project, by Kurt Lewin and others, involved forty-one rather average "trainees" in a two-week session. It cost more than a fourth as much as the College Study over a four-year period, yet its contributions seem substantial. Good research takes money, whether it is long range or short term.

STUDY, ACTION, AND TRAINING

Once it was decided to center College Study activities along study, action, and training lines, we began to work with college teachers on categories of needs. Listings were made under each of these three headings, with each list showing projects, experiences, and so on, which could be used to teach prospective teachers the content and skills of intergroup education in practical school and community situations. At times, categories of needs—for example, fact-finding skills—were worked on separately, each large category an object of committee effort, but mostly needs were blended into organic life projects. Learning became linked with problem-solving, as a concrete case will suggest.

THE CONTROL OF HIGH SCHOOL FRATERNITIES

I want to state first that this problem was not of our making, that it just happened to us. . . . Our committee on Social Activities had met several times and had a full work program with college campus groups when a committee member thought we ought to give some help on the high school "frat" problem. . . .

We invited the high school principal to speak to our committee at a special meeting called that next Saturday morning. "Any port in a storm" he must have thought, because he spoke very frankly of his being on a spot and he earnestly sought our help. In substance, here were the facts in the case.

"The high school fraternity problem is not new in this community. Repressive measures in the past have simply driven it underground and, from time to time, it reappears. The present crisis was brought on by a grade school P.T.A. president who believes that the state law against fraternities should be tested for constitutionality and repealed. She wants her daughter, who will enter high school next year, to pledge to her [the mother's] sorority, and is organizing a movement to change the state law.

"This mother has been opposed by other mothers who want the principal to enforce the law, to abolish frats. . . . The issue has been discussed enough, and publicized enough, so that the whole adult community is taking sides. Several phone calls come each day, asking me what I am doing on the problem, advising me to expel pupils or not expel them. The school itself is excited, with students and teachers talking of little else in their out-of-class contacts. Something must, definitely, be done, and I find it a most awkward situation. . . ."

Once our committee saw that this problem fell within the scope of its activity, that the case demanded immediate action, other business was put aside. We divided first into study groups. One group was to investigate the state law on high school fraternities, another to make a cautious inquiry among the high school students, a third to study adult attitudes, and the fourth was to canvass other schools to see what they had done. Each committee had two or more college teachers on it, from five to ten college students, with some school teachers in three of the committee groups. The principal became a member of our general committee.

We had assumed that these four inquiries would be relevant, an assumption checked against the facts as they came in. The state law, in particular, was hard to understand, leading to two meetings of the total committee. Three sections of the law were at issue, and we sought a good bit of help in their interpretation. . . . The principal himself had made a study of these sections, securing legal opinion, and he placed this study at our use. . . .

One section states that "it shall be unlawful for any grade or high school pupil in any public school . . . to organize, join or belong to any school fraternity, sorority or secret society." Every such fraternity, etc., is declared "an obstruction to education and inimical to the public welfare," but nowhere is fraternity defined, save to assert that it is "a secret society."

The second section specifies that it shall be the duty of each school board "to prohibit the organization or operation of such fraternity," etc. The board is given power to "suspend or expel" students who join, or pledge to join these "secret societies," and it is implied that the school principal, as the board's agent, shall enforce this act. The third section specifies punishment for the school official if he is remiss in his duty, namely, a fine between $25 and $100 and, we might add, the possible loss of his job.

The question we had to decide was what is a high school frat? The more we turned the matter over, comparing these groups with other school groups, the more we came to believe that a fraternity or sorority has four distinguishing characteristics. It is a secret society in that it exists without official school knowledge and approval. It has a Greek letter name. It is an autonomous group, meeting in parent homes and elsewhere but without adult sponsorship. It is exclusive in its selection of members, basing choice largely on status factors.

The committee studying the high school brought in two kinds of evidence which I cannot treat fully here. One type of data came from asking students, presumably both in and outside of fraternities, what the reasons were for and against belonging to a frat, how the pupils themselves saw this matter. The other kind of evidence was descriptive of fraternity activities, the kinds of parties given, the nature of regular meetings, anything else that would throw light on the programs of these groups.

Before summarizing these findings, I might add that no such data could have been collected had the principal not made it clear to pupils that we were no wild-eyed group. All of our interviewers were college students, a hand-picked lot, and most of them were members of college fraternities and sororities. We were a group of scientists trying to help out in solving a difficult problem and we acted exactly in that manner.

Well, what was found out? Frat members, that is, students who so identified themselves, expressed motivations along twelve different lines, their reasons for belonging to these groups. Mostly, they wanted to meet in some peer-level association free from adult control. They wanted to decide policies and make plans by themselves. They felt that they were a highly selected bunch, enjoying the prestige attached to membership in secret societies, each with a pin, grip, and the like. Members used their organizations to run the social life of the school, throwing the biggest parties and dances. They felt that parents took pride in their belonging to exclusive groups, and some students no doubt got fun out of breaking the state law.

Their activities were limited rather strongly to regular business meetings and social events. Their parties were "great fun" and, by their own admissions, "rather wild." A recent party in particular was much discussed, a "brawl" at the home of one of the members, with parents away from the house until after midnight. . . .

After these facts were digested by the total committee, and the interviewers sent back to the school for more, a report was heard on parent attitudes. This subcommittee could find no way to identify the parents who had children in fraternities, but it could ask the question if the adult had ever belonged to such a high school group. Of the parents who answered "no" to this question, two-thirds were opposed to high school frats. Of those who answered "yes," about half were opposed, a fourth were favorable, and the remainder "didn't know," or did not feel able to state a point of view. In terms of numbers, there appeared to be no strong community support for fraternities. Women favored them more than men, but even so the anti vote outweighed the pro.

Committee Four had easier going than the other groups. A member wrote to the director of the College Study, who sent materials and said he hoped to come along in time to help with the plan of action. Grade and high school frats, it seemed, were pretty tough problems, with more failures than successes in their democratic control. . . .

When the director did come along, we had two grand committee meetings. I cannot detail here our lines of reason, only the decisions as to action that were reached. (1) Direct, remedial action would have to be channeled through the high school students. They must see the problem from its human relations angle and want to take steps toward its control. (2) This work should be done with as little publicity as possible, for publicity can only excite community groups. (3) The principal must not be put in the position of knowing about, or condoning, law violation in the school. (4) Parents themselves will have to be reached, preferably through their children.

It was decided to make an action plan along these lines, with provisions that (5) if it did not work after fair test, we would have to check the intake of frat members well upstream, namely, in the upper grades of the public schools. If this failed, (6) all that seemed to be left was to enforce the law with more severity than had heretofore been the case in the high school.

We felt better after these decisions but the real job was still to do. To start with, we had a closed meeting of high school students, asking them [frat members] to consider the facts we had found. This meeting was well attended and there was no question but what the students did not want to continue in violation of the law, yet they did want to preserve the values in their in-groups. This set the problem on which a student committe was invited to work, with our offering any aid we could give. For two meetings, we listened to the report of this committee, with each of its proposals debated by the students. I served as a kind of clarifier of issues, watching out for such consequences as we all could anticipate.

Committee recommendations numbered ten in all. The first one stated simply that students favored intimate, friendship groups (or clubs) in the school. Such groups would accept in principle the ideas of a regular school audit of their finances and adult (one parent, one teacher) sponsorship, provided each student group could select its own sponsors from an approved list. Clubs were to continue to elect their own members but to eliminate the "blackball." Students became eligible for membership in their sophomore year, and freshmen were no longer to be "pledged." Club goals were defined as of three types: to provide social activities, to further scholarship, and to render community services. Greek letter names were to be abolished and other kinds of club names to be devised. An inter-club council for the whole school was to be organized, and all students in the school were to be encouraged to join an existing organization or to start a new one for themselves.

Each statement, as we have said, was roundly debated, until it could be shaped into a form acceptable to the students. Put more clearly, we did not stop work on any item until there were no more objections to its intent and phrasing.

The next problem was to get these recommendations before the student groups themselves for adoption. This was done through a student training program. We did this work through mock sessions in which each student would present an issue to us and we would help him in his presentation. . . . After this, and a little late in the process, we had sessions with students on how to approach their parents. . . . The grand windup was a dinner meeting of the P.T.A.'s of the community, at which the high school students made a presentation and then took questions. While the newspapers have been most cooperative on their publicity, there is still pro-fraternity sentiment in town and we do not know what the future will bring. . . . The school has organized an interclub council for social activities, and the principal is hopeful that the council can help all the clubs in the management of their affairs.

This case is long but nowise as long as it should be in view of the seriousness of the grade and high school fraternity problem, especially in well-off suburban schools. We believe that study-action processes are fairly clear, and we want to raise only one question on the material. Assuming that such work went on in every College Study institution, what would participating faculty members learn? Of what, specifically, would their in-service education consist?

This question is the concern of the chapter and, at the moment, we want to speak of one phase only. Reference is to the training category, to the demonstrations of study-action processes. One type of teacher-training consisted of factual inquiry—the setting-up of a problem for study, the kinds and amounts of data needed, the gathering of facts and their processing, the various ways (tables, charts, diagrams, etc.) of reporting findings.[4] Another kind of training related to group-action skills, the sort of work done in the case just cited and illustrated repeatedly in the two-volume College Study report.

SOME TEACHER GROUP-WORK SKILLS

1. To see one's self as others see him, i.e., to become group-responsive, change perceptions of self-effects and roles in relation to other persons.
2. To work cooperatively with others on intellectual and emotional levels, i.e., to exchange meanings without giving or taking offense or distorting personality.
3. To influence people in their viewpoints, feelings, and actions, i.e., to learn the control of means and their limitations in maximizing group productive effort.
4. To make realistic appraisals of group process, i.e., a group's intake of ideas, degree of sharing, feeling tones, end-products and their worth.

[4] For details, Lloyd Allen Cook, "Methods of Community Study," in W. C. Reavis (ed.), *The School and the Urban Community* (Chicago: University of Chicago Press, 1942), pp. 201–14.

5. To use consultants in the learning process, i.e., the ability to ask for and receive the kind of help needed, to assimilate technical knowledge.

Our idea was not to impose this type of theory on college teachers, but rather, as occasion arose, direct attention to these training needs. If talk started, if someone felt concerned, then two things might happen. We could use normal work tasks, routine activities, and meetings to teach group-work competencies, and we could devise special situations as they were necessary. Devised situations might take any form, but our hunch was that they would tend toward role-practice sessions.

SAMPLE ROLE-PRACTICE SESSIONS

1. A meeting within a meeting, to show how meetings, good and bad, are organized and conducted.
2. Patterns of nonparticipation in meetings, assessment and discussion of nonparticipant roles.
3. Problem-solving sessions, to show the parts that people play (agreer, disagreer, initiator, etc.).
4. Exploration of gripes and tensions, assignment of roles so that release and analysis is possible.
5. Survey of community knowledge, i.e., how would a union leader behave, a minister, housewife, etc.
6. Bell-ringing interview, how to approach people in any kind of field study or project.
7. Resolving social conflict, re-enactment of conflict, role reversals, soliloquies.
8. Rewriting of movie plots, fiction, plays, etc., by showing how the story "should have turned out."

We cannot pass this point without stressing again the contributions that can come from sociodrama.[5] Consider, for example, a situation we recall at Atlanta University. At one stage in their big "get out the vote" campaign, the problem was to teach block workers (students, teachers, etc.) how to make an interview contact. The typical instructional scheme is to assemble workers, in this case several hundred, and to brief them on their job. Some high prestige person makes a speech, mostly an appeal to "go out there and fight." By actual test, role-practice training stands to double

---

[5] For example, Ronald Lippitt, *Training in Community Relations* (New York: Harper & Bros., 1949).

worker success. What kinds of persons will one meet in door-knocking and bell-ringing? To what motivations will they respond? How, *in word-for-word ways*, should they be interviewed? What does one do, if . . . if . . . if? In years of field work, we have found no substitute for situational tests (including sociodrama) where skill learnings and improvisations are at issue.

REALITY LEVEL OF COLLEGE WORK

College people are people, meaning that they are variable. In respect to their readiness for serious work effort, we had thought of having to get along with a range of individual and group differences. We believed that most faculty members would be like those in the V-College case with which the chapter started. They would be extremely busy people, diverse in viewpoints, alert to the times, unclear as to the intergroup field, interested in cooperative action, willing to team up and see what could be done. In all but a few instances, this was the situation on campus after campus, a fact that might encourage the organization of new and larger projects in college intergroup work.

Thinking further about backgrounds, we had anticipated finding all the "P-D" (prejudice-discrimination) combinations discussed in chapter 1, with many faculty members in middle categories, the "gentle people of prejudice," the expedient adjusters to the turn of events. Beyond this basic division, we had imagined various types—the starry-eyed idealist, the work dodger, the radical, etc. The problem in procedure was to devise study and action projects that would appeal to all these types, for participation was to be as general as possible.

What we wish to do is to analyze at some length the *reality level* at which the College Study tried to function, an important dimension of any undertaking in a field so full of sentimental action as is present-day intergroup education at school and college levels. To do this, we shall cite some rather atypical cases, cases that are extreme in the sense of showing organizational problems not found in average colleges. Average cases are easy cases, suggesting that college people are nice to be with, a fact we strongly affirm. But it is the "un-easy" case, the hard-to-solve case, that gives a better measure of a project's strengths and weaknesses.

We shall quote first from a rather unusual document, a diary kept over one year on X-College happenings. This diary was written by a local faculty member for reasons of his own. Its existence was unknown to us until after the College Study had ended. The college itself is small, southern, and not well financed. Its staff is mixed Negro and white, mostly the former, hard working and intellectual. While the College Study here has had a stormy history, there is no doubt of general good will toward it. Even less doubt exists as to the worth of this college program. Every consultant has showed an eagerness to return to the campus, to participate in its stimulating debates. Dr. C in the case is the author of the present volume, and we are grateful for all that was taught us by this school.

GETTING WORK STARTED, X-COLLEGE

October 6. All hands present this afternoon to hear Dr. C, a representative of the College Study. Said much the same as we had read in some canned stuff that had been passed around. Interested in "democratic human relations," etc. Spoke too much and said too little for many of us, for we know better than he does what the South is like in race relations. . . . But what the heck, we voted to go in. . . . Another Boy Scout good-will tour. . . .

October 7. Meetings scheduled with the CS director. Much talk about what the college should try to do, the general point of the year's work. Three faculty members and two students at the meeting in my office, one quite impossible for anybody to work with. Director listened to ideas, contributing few of his own. Seemed reluctant to evaluate ours, saying he needed to catch the feel of campus thought.

Met that evening in full glory at the J Home [president's home], and I am sure the meeting had been rigged. Not sure that the CS guy had a hand in it, though he ate supper with the J family. The president led off with an old joke, followed by his usual pep talk. After this, our general chairman announced seven projects, asking all of us to identify with some one. He asked also that each group meet during the coming week, make a work plan and submit a budget of expenses.

I must say that Dr. C did not seem overly pleased at all this easy sailing, in fact seemed suspicious of it. He asked several times if the faculty had given enough thought to the year's work, felt certain of its goals. He cited other colleges in the Study where a quick survey of problems, needs, etc., had been made, followed by a discussion of priority demands . . . But no one wanted to open up, to joust against the power alignment in this school, so the meeting closed.

Our perception of events in these two days, as noted in file record, agrees very well with the views expressed above. We knew that men like the diary writer were seasoned veterans in race relations, suspicious of a stranger's motives, not very hopeful for any change in things. We knew that factions existed on the campus, that a power group was backing the president's desire to see the college make good on its application to the College Study. Aside from suggesting a self-survey of college needs, we knew of nothing to do, except to wait. Our guess was that the college had a real action potential but that things would have to get worse before they could get much better.

REJECTION AND REPLANNING

October 16. Well, the fat is in the fire. I have, personally, organized faculty and students in opposition to the "research projects" foisted upon us. They are not in line with our needs and they call for time and skills which we do not have. We upset the applecart this evening, at a general College Study meeting, by voting the projects down. Our side was given, in turn, an assignment from the president through the college committee to propose a new list of projects on which to work. . . .

Being told of these developments by letter, the author asked the college chairman for details but received no reply. On the next trip to the campus, five committees were found at work. The first general chairman had resigned and the diary writer had been elected, a man characterized by the president as "a tremendous worker." All the old projects but one, a "social action" project, had been discarded and new ones started. We shall skip several pages in the diary in order to focus on another crisis.

REALITY THINKING, A STRESS TEST

November 4. Dr. C came in this morning and has been meeting with our project groups. Addressed the chapel, saying some things we don't like. Met with sophomores to demonstrate role playing, the problem being to "keep communication going" across interracial lines (baloney!). He met this afternoon with three project groups, advising with them on their plans. Not much help for he takes a compromising stand, "get what you can, settle for that, then try to get some more." We do not deal with human rights that way. It is equal rights or none, something we shall have to teach our visitor!

Took a walk with Dr. C late this afternoon. He asked how the day's work had gone. "Not good," I said. He asked how he had done and I let him have it, but straight. . . . He replied with equal frankness, saying that he knew he had not been going over, that his views seemed to clash with committee thought. I spoke to him about our own anti-caste viewpoint, saying that we could not go along with any compromise in respect to human rights. We kicked this around a while, then C asked if I knew a good consultant whom we would like to have? Now what can you do with a guy like that! I told him no, we had not given him up, that we would convert him before he knew it! We both laughed at that. . . .

Supper this evening at my home and the usual bull session. Eight faculty members present, along with C. All colored but two. Things dull at first, nothing to talk about. C began to tell of experiences in another Negro college. Nobody much interested. C told then of an argument at a bull session like this. Some prof had said that no white speaker could tell a Negro joke to a Negro audience and not offend Negroes. Somebody disagreed, et cetera, et cetera. Prof. L, our new English man, said "very interesting, *very* interesting," as sarcastic as the devil, and there we let it rest. C got the point all right but didn't take offense.

C kept on talking about so-called interracial "humor," saying how much a study of it was needed. Then he told a joke which he thought was funny yet would give no offense to Negroes. Said he got on a bus in Detroit and took a seat behind two small colored boys. Listening to their gab, he heard one say to the other: "How ol' is you?" "Dunno," said the other. "Dunno how ol' yo' is," said the first. "Well, is yo' fouh or is yo' five?" "Ah dunno," the boy repeated. "Yo dunno is yo' fouh or is yo' five?" "Naw, man, I don't." "Well, is yo' goin' with de gals?" "Naw, I ain't." "Well, den, yo' is fouh!"

With this crazy tale, the whole gang hit the ceiling. "Man," said someone, "you ought to know better than that. You ought to have more sense than to tell that kind of story. It is an insult to every Negro and you know it, damn well."

Dr. C was, obviously, disturbed. He said he didn't see where the joke was so bad. Everyone was hot and we rode him but good. Told him off on the story and then really opened up. Asked him what he thought he was trying to do at X-College, anyway. Did he think we would go for his lily-white compromising stand? I must say that he did not get sore. Simply took it and asked for more, so I guess everybody gave him plenty. . . .

Don't know how it was but we got off on Cox's "Marxian point of view," then into Warner and Myrdal. Argument was even hotter than it had been, for we split right and left. We never agree on anything, except against an outsider, but C came right along, raising this point and that. Well, the meeting got chummy again, breaking up at midnight. We had learned at least one thing, that it takes all kinds of people to make up a world, not excluding the C's.

Here was a difficult situation, a group of intellectuals soliloquizing on what the world should be like, how people should treat people. To preserve their faith in radical action, their "no compromise stand," they had withdrawn from the illogical life about them, escaping its debasing demands on nonwhite people. The college itself was a cultural island, having almost no interactive contact with the locality, wanting none under the terms offered it. While college committee members had accepted College Study goals in spirit, they were now denying them. These goals could, of course, have been quite wrong, for they pointed toward expedient action, a planful risk-taking in improving minority-group conditions. However that may be, we did not feel inclined to walk away from this situation. Walkouts make consultant work a kind of sight-seeing tour, a holiday adventure, dashing here and there, taking credit where no credit is due, riding trends instead of influencing them.

The immediate problem was to get these people to talk, to precipitate tensions, and clear the air for an exchange of thoughts. At times a quick shock will do this, for example, the fictitious bus incident; yet this is always risky business, hence to be used as a last resort, if it should be tried at all.[6] Once group catharsis starts, the group worker must take "insult" without rebuttal; he cannot become ego-involved, status conscious, or the like. He must remember what he is trying to do, what its costs are, how the process goes from stage to stage. The hardest task is to move out of the target spot, to direct attention elsewhere, perhaps to begin reintegrative action about some common goal. If the meeting does not end on a friendly note, one may count that group "lost" so far as its work output is concerned.

The next entry in the diary is particularly interesting, though we shall not quote it in whole. The diarist observes that "the day's work went some better," that "meetings were more worthwhile." At the bull session that evening, "people were in good humor. Prof. L asked C, laughingly, if he knew any more Negro stories, and then told him a rip-snorter." Talk centered on "the liberal in race relations." Why is he? What makes him tick? How did he

[6] See, for example, Leland Bradford and Paul Sheats, "Complacency Shock as a Prerequisite to Training," *Sociatry*, II (1948), 37–46.

get that way? What torments are in him, driving him on? How does he act under fire? Who mourns him when he is gone? What should he do about conservatives? Does society need them? Is there a mid-position, gradualism? How far dare one compromise basic principles and not lose integrity as a person? We did not, to be certain, find answers to these questions. Some are under study with members of this group, two years after the incidents related in this case.

Another "stress test" case comes to mind, one that is looked back upon now by the Y-College group as "a definite contribution to the success of the project on our campus." At the moment, however, things were fairly tense. The following report is based on consultant field records.

COMPLACENCY SHOCK, Y-COLLEGE

By traveling a thousand miles off schedule, the consultant was able to make a planning meeting at the Y-College, to be followed by a full day's work on the morrow with project groups. At three o'clock, meeting time on the first day, three college professors were present. At 3:20 P.M. another one came in. At 4:00 o'clock the consultant prepared to leave. He touched casually on how busy everyone was, on the need to cancel tomorrow's schedule since he felt it best to catch a plane that evening for work long past due at another college.

The committee chairman, who was among the four faculty members present, was surprised and hurt, saying that we should wait, that faculty members would be along, that the schedule on the next day could not be canceled. With sincere regrets, the consultant spoke of the exacting demands made upon his time, the difficulties of continuous and rapid travel, affirming his need to leave town that evening.

At this juncture the committee chairman asked the consultant to stay a minute and he left the room. He stepped across the hall to the president's office, where this officer and the dean were in conference. Presently, both men returned with him, and we could hear a secretary telephoning faculty members. By 4:20 o'clock, all committee members (twenty-four persons) except two were in attendance and the chairman called the meeting to order. He began on some routine matter when the consultant suggested that he wished the group could talk over a problem that had him deeply puzzled.

Asked to explain, the consultant went over some recent history. He stated that little use, and poor use, had been made of his time on the campus, citing several incidents. For example, on his last trip, the schedule made out by the committee chairman called for him to speak at a certain class at a certain time. When he knocked on the door, he did not know the professor nor did the latter know him. When this teacher learned that the visitor had been "assigned" to his class, the consultant was invited in. The professor thought a speech on "groups and things" would be fine, just fine, although he still did not connect it with participation in the College Study. The "speech" was very brief, of course, since it obviously interfered with whatever the class had planned for the period.

The question in the consultant's mind was whether College Study work was worth doing. Were professors too greatly overburdened? Did they simply have to cut somewhere? Had they been pushed into the project against their better judgment? Would it be better, all things considered, to close the books and admit failure?

Placed in such a situation, any man who is a man will talk. He has been charged with failure, been remiss in duties, and his ego is hurt. Chances are that he has been working at what he regards as his level best, that he feels unappreciated and misunderstood. His impulse is to strike out, to tell someone off, to get a load of worry off his chest.

With a few more twigs, the fire did burst into flames. It was to be expected that aggression would come our way, but this was not the case. It turned on the dean, a man who had had to run the college in the president's frequent absences. In faculty opinion, he had been operating in "a high-handed way," a phrase that covered a good many specifics. The president professed ignorance of how things had been going, taking the dean to task. In the scramble, the College Study was lost sight of, until someone brought us back to the beginning of the argument. As human relations began to straighten out, it was not hard to create policy for the Study. No one blamed it for a situation with which, in the dean's words, "we should long ago have come to grips."

It takes very little to get mad, no skill, no training, no intelligence. While it is a very human thing to do, it does not solve problems. Assuming that a *redefinition of a situation* is needed, the thing to do, once grievances are out, is to pick up some positive idea, some item overlooked in the heat of argument. One then restates this view, with group members shaping it to their satisfaction, after which another item is added. Everybody feels some measure of blame, some loss of dignity, some urge to get on with business. Given impulses of this sort, it is no particular problem for a group to realign its actions and energies.

In the next case, the institution is large, heterogeneous, and impersonal. Face-to-faceness has gone out of fashion, with "office memos" taking its place. Leaders of student-action groups print letters to the university president in the student paper before the president sees them, and he prints replies in kind. A teachers union, concerned with its own drive for members, petitions the administration, with many whereas and wherefores, rather than ask for an unpublicized conference. In this frosty atmosphere, one cannot expect the intimacy of relations found in smaller places, nor is it necessary. Yet an intergroup program can disintegrate to the point where it means very little.

As background to the incident told, it should be said that the College Study had acted favorably on the application of this college to go ahead in the Study for another year. At the time of the consultant's visit, the general committee had held two meetings, but no one had, or presumably would, accept the office of general committee chairman.

GROUP FEELINGS AT Z-COLLEGE

At the third meeting of the college committee, with the consultant present, the college dean began to write items on the board even before the meeting was convened. He listed areas where intergroup work should be done, naming project-group chairmen and assigning faculty members to these groupings. The performance was an exact duplicate of the way in which some school heads organize their faculty for curriculum study.

The college dean moved along in dead silence until he wrote down the name of a certain professor. She spoke at once, and with some feeling, making it clear that she would accept no such assignment. When she was asked to "think it over," she began a spirited attack on the administrator's "undemocratic methods." While no faculty member spoke out in support of her views, it was evident that the group as a whole sided with her.

At this point, the consultant broke in. Ignoring the very personal argument, he asked who was the committee chairman. The college dean named a professor who, in turn, said nothing, gave no sign one way or the other. When the consultant asked her if she had accepted the appointment, her reply was: "I didn't say I would, and I didn't say I wouldn't." This brought the laugh that was needed, and talk became general.

Skipping the chairmanship issue, one committee member and then others supported the outspoken professor. As protests were registered, the administrator became more defensive of his methods. His own excitement led to awkward phrasings, and to details that were irrelevant. He was, in all honesty, doing "the best he knew how to do" to keep the College Study program going. With a question on whether anybody had a better method, he looked at his watch, saw that he was late for an appointment, and left the room.

This time the laughter was truly integrative. Was the chairman going to accept the appointment? She would, but only if the group wanted her to do so, a point on which their response left no doubt. What about a work program for the year? It was a curious thing, unnoted by the faculty, but almost the same projects were worked out after an hour of sweat labor as the dean had put on the board at the start of the meeting.

"Democracy" is a concept that can be stretched in many directions. It can mean, for persons fully adult, just the right to want what they want, to make up their minds as to a course of action. No group worker dare ignore this important fact about people, for it is the basis of their integrity, dignity, and self-feelings. Armed with freely made decisions, backed by the faith that others have in us, we will face onerous tasks with high spirit, in fact, find pleasure in them. This is, in effect, what occurred in the Z-College faculty. Once the intergroup project became their own, they ran it with moderate dispatch and efficiency.

Such incidents as these X-Y-Z cases are exciting moments in a field-work program and, of course, they excite readers. Since their occurrence in large-scale human relations activities can be predicted as inevitable, why are they never reported in project assessments? What canons of good taste or considerations of policy dictate their repression? More to the point of our concern, does this neglect of realities in a field-work picture tend to distort the actual learning process? Is this process all sweetness and light, all moving forward without a hitch toward meaningful goals? On the contrary, we suspect some unwillingness to discuss things that happened, or else the project never dug deep enough to get at people, to disturb them in their everyday routines.

Whatever one may think about the consultant's role at these points of crisis, turning points in these college programs, the behaviors described suggest the reality level at which the College Study sought to function. Of course, mistakes were made, inexcusable errors; yet in fairness it should be said that field work in human relations has few precedents to follow. One must learn as he moves along, the wisest learners profiting by their mistakes.

Over the years we have noted, as many educators have, the visit of big-name people to college campuses. These people are wonderful people—genial, informed, helpful, and everyone feels the lift of their presence. Yet the activities they were paid to appraise and, perhaps, to redirect, might be awful failures, full of hidden jokers. Few of these visitors ever took the time to find out, assuming they knew how to do so. Their aid to a college faculty, and it was very real, took the form of being just *a wonderful person,* a character in every profession that merits more study than has ever come his way. College Study consultants were not "front men" for any program but rather idea men and technique men, the best-trained workers the Study was able to find within its time-cost limitations.

ASPECTS OF COLLEGE LEADERSHIP

From the outset, the Study was interested in local college, school and community leadership, its selection, retention, and improvement. In theory, democracy was not enough. To it we wished to link the know-how found in social science and the good judgment that comes from practical experience, a three-way combination hard to find in one and the same individual.

If, for this account, the leader be defined as the chairman of the general (local) committee on intergroup work, thirty-eight different persons have held this office. This number, while sufficient for study, is smaller than it would have been had each college changed its chairman at the end of each academic year, as a few colleges did.

Who were these leaders? How were they selected? What factors are related to their success or failure? To one college president these questions made little sense. "A leader here," he wrote, "is a person to whom we give a job to do. If he does it well, he is a good leader. We reward him by giving him more work to do." On assumption that a leader's associates would know why he was appointed or elected to office, we have gathered such reactions on every college campus.

REASONS GIVEN FOR THE SELECTION OF COLLEGE COMMITTEE CHAIRMEN

10 chairmen, general interest in teacher-training
7 chairmen, research specialists, study skills
6 chairmen, administrative favorites
5 chairmen, not overly busy, time for the work

3 chairmen, liked by everybody, good coordinators
2 chairmen, strong interest in community affairs
2 chairmen, specialists in intergroup relations
3 chairmen, no logical reason, reason unknown

What inferences can be drawn from a table of this sort? For instance, was leader selection based on conceptions of job fitness or on extraneous, expedient factors? Assuming the former to be true, it is a curious commentary on the state of affairs in intergroup education to note that only two all-college chairmen had had any previous formal training in intergroup relations. Working on the contrary assumption, so-called expedient influences are plain to see. One is the type of administrative favoritism found in every bureaucratic system;[7] the other is a kind of ascendancy by default, the awarding of office, when everyone is busy, to the person who seems to have the least work to do.

To continue with the job fitness idea, it will be recalled that the College Study was a study-action-training project, a viewpoint accepted in all twenty-four college communities. Again, in theory, leader choice could have followed either of two pathways, that of choosing a specialist in study, action, or training, or a generalist having some competency in all three areas of knowledge and skill. The tabulation shows no clear trend on these alternatives. We believe the ten chairmen, each known for his over-all views on teacher education, were as near "generalists" as it was possible to find.

How can one tell, in the college president's words, if a leader "has done his job well?" We were unable to answer this question to our own satisfaction, partly because of the rush of field work. Objective statistics, such as number of local projects, counts of participants, amounts of time spent, final achievements, tell only a part of the story. To be complete, these file records should be related to personal factors, situational demands and opportunities, as well as to a stream of chance occurrences over which no control was possible. Because these complex data cannot now be obtained, it would be pointless to attempt an over-all evaluation of college

[7] See R. Bendix, "Bureaucracy: the Problem and Its Setting," *American Sociological Review,* XII (1947), 493–507; R. C. Merton, "Bureaucratic Structure and Personality," in C. Kluckhohn and H. A. Murray (eds.), *Personality in Nature, Society and Culture* (New York: Knopf, 1948), pp. 282–91.

leaders. From a descriptive standpoint, their principal service functions numbered five.

FUNCTIONS OF OVER-ALL COLLEGE LEADERS

1. To channelize College Study contacts and services to the college community, making all consultant schedules and distributing materials.
2. To take initiative and responsibility in the general coordination of the local program, including contacts with college administrative officers.
3. To stimulate project-group work, hold short workshops or arrange other special events as needed, to report team plans and progress.
4. To publicize the local program on the campus, in the community and elsewhere, including interchange of in-process reports with other colleges.
5. To prepare a year-end report on the work done and plans for the next year, and to attend meetings of all college committee chairmen.

These leader functions, broken down into specifics, have been used in several ways. One use has been to discuss leader tasks in colleges before a leader choice has been made. We have used the list in running over with college chairmen their time expenditures when they have asked for an opinion on their work. If college morale seemed low, or work efforts slacked off, we have checked these leader tasks in a search for causes. Finally, this list has been sent to perhaps a hundred colleges as a possible aid to them in planning their intergroup programs.

College Structure and Participation

Participation in college programs has differed a great deal from place to place, in spite of the College Study goal to include as many persons as possible. A college is a social structure, a going concern when a consultant enters. Its social relations are patterned in ways that have to be discovered, including the kind and amount of work that is regarded as normal. While individuals differ in their own standards, the collective view is common enough so that one may speak of college "atmospheres" as basic sociological variables.

One type of college we are inclined to call a "closed system," a network of human relations into which permanent entree is difficult. Closure may be due to either factions or cliques. Factions are larger than cliques and they grow up along broad divisional lines, for example, liberal arts versus education. Cliques represent interpersonal alignments, for instance, in some colleges along racial lines, by geographic areas, religions, and economic circumstances.[8] The closed college, whatever its nature, is in contrast to the "open college," the democratic interaction of students, teachers, and administrators on a basis of personal interest and worth.

It is difficult to widen participation in a closed college system. In one case, for example, the College Study program fell into the hands of a small but enthusiastic clique. These persons were most likeable, hard-working, and efficient, but they resisted every effort to make the program campus-wide. When they were approached directly on this issue, a subcommittee started an evening seminar on intergroup literature, but their hearts were not in it. The group simply took it for granted that College Study work was in good hands, that all was being done that could be done.

Most colleges in the Study were of the open sort. Participation began with the most interested and, by the usual processes of involvement, came to include from a fourth to a half or more of the total faculty. In many cases, students were assimilated into planning groups and shared power and duties with faculty members. Much the same happened in respect to representatives of the local community, especially the officers of intercultural agencies. All of this was so common that it can be regarded as the normal process of participation in the four years of College Study field work.

Another difference among colleges, while implied, should be made more explicit, *the general attitude toward the environing community*. We have worked in some institutions that sat, indeed, upon a hilltop, in others that have been fearful of community reactions, and in still others that made intergroup work a truly partnership affair with area schools, social agencies, civic offices, and churches. In each instance, a group worker's problems differed, as seen, for instance, in college program publicity.

Program publicity was an item of study in several all-college workshops, with widely variant practices reported. In the com-

[8] See Anonymous, "A Note on Intergroup Conditioning and Conflict among an Interracial Faculty at a Negro College," *Social Forces*, XXVII (1949), 430–33.

munity partnership type of college, there was an active interest in news dissemination through meetings, press releases and interviews, and radio broadcasts. In the fearful school, often wary for just cause, the problem was to keep news out of print, to speak innocuously to the public if at all. One effect of this latter policy was to further the spread of rumor, for rumor arises most often to fill a gap in public information. In several instances, rumors had definite effects on college programs and in a few cases were so serious as to lead to sustained efforts at their control.

Another problem involving structure had to do with the distribution of authority, notably *channels to administration.* Things might be what they seemed on a given campus and again they might not, an important fact because no program can do well unless it has administrative backing. An impression formed from field experience is that far too many lines run to college presidents, a centralization of authority that suggests the need for greater delegation of power and its better organization. Areas in which such changes seemed most needed are four: business affairs, public relations, the academic program, and student personnel services. Clear-cut channels here would help greatly in the conduct of any large-scale change activity.

GROUP MORALE AND LEADERSHIP

By group morale we mean the state of health in which a program functions, the worker feelings of well-being and integrity. While these attitudes are, in theory, measurable, field programs must usually operate on a symptomatic basis. Do people feel good about their work efforts? Do they see the worth of what they are trying to do, its immediate and long-range significance? Is group spirit steadily cumulative, or does it show peaks and troughs, time trends that are unpredictable? What about the faith of participants in their leaders, assuming that a great lot of one's ordinary job activities must be in terms of such faith.

Evidence has suggested to us that a College Study program does not mean exactly the same thing to any two of its participants, that each person sees it in terms of his own perspectives. This means, of course, that involvements differ at any moment of time and over time. As consultants, we have tried to study mood swings, say from unconcern through optimism to pessimism or realism, and to analyze faculty attitudes and behaviors. During the course of campus visits we might talk at length with representative persons, often after some routine business, thus making a kind of "listening post" approach to morale problems.

To be more explicit, our preference has been to initiate an interchange of ideas on a confidential basis. On the second or third visit to a campus, a person may be searched out by campus and community people who need to talk. Some simply hunger for talk; others have ulterior purposes in mind, favors to be done. The visitor is a stranger to the campus, with all that this sociological role implies.[9] Coming from the outside and returning to it, he has no invisible commitments on the campus, no in-group loyalties which might impair his functions as a listener. He can be told things in confidence, routine or gossipy happenings, because he can be depended upon not to violate a trust.

From this sort of intimate interchange a visitor can get the feel of a program as he might not be able to do in its formal expressions. And yet this situation is double-edged. We have seen intergroup work ruined by a consultant's careless use of confidential data, his inadvertent peddling of tales. The point to recognize, possibly, is that consultants are more than "professors away from home." They are no paragons of wisdom and virtue; yet they are presumably trained for their work. Above all, they are able to manage their own strivings and frustrations, to identify with people, and to respect them in whatever humanness they may show.

A question we have pondered many times is how to build and keep a relationship of good faith with people whom one aspires to lead—students in a classroom, colleagues on a job, townspeople whose life is not one's own. We say "lead" because the problem is simple if the task is only to be nice, to make friends, a job at which the "wonderful person" is adept. But *to lead* means something different, to influence people toward changed behaviors, to aid them in their own growth processes. Such changes meet psychological resistances, hence put strains on any interpersonal relationship. We believe that rapport may run thin unless its upkeep is

[9] See Alfred Schuetz, "The Stranger: An Essay in Social Psychology," *American Journal of Sociology*, XLIX (1944), 499–507.

made a valued matter, a personality need of both the leader and the led.

If one knows that he cannot really lead any in-group, that his task is to find a group's own leaders and to lead through them, he will become a student of leader types and actions. First off, much of his learnings from psychological literature will drop away— leader age, sex, height, IQ, and so on, for leadership in group life is a sociological phenomenon, a situational product. "The pattern of strong and competitive personal leadership," writes Myrdal, "which we have exemplified for politics, permeates the entire social structure."[10] It is found, too, in colleges, the big man, strong, smart, successful. He is, typically, a dynamo of human energy, an organizer of group action. He takes pride in the fact that he can do things, that a job given him is a job well done.

One finds this character in college; yet most ivory tower figures are cast in other molds. For example, here is a quiet, self-effacing scholar, say the chairman of the committee that worked on the high school fraternity case cited in this chapter. This man is a mathematics professor who felt that some part of his time and energy should be spent on what he chooses to call "the human problem of being human." His leadership was, primarily, a sense of professional responsibility for people as people, a deep feeling that people could be better, do better, than was usually the case. He had no special knowledge of intergroup relations, in fact knew nothing of the caste-class literature until it was discussed with him. He had, he said, "a deep-down feeling" that the high school status system was unjust, that it unfairly sorted and sifted young people.

Other leader types come to mind, for instance, the technique man, a master in study designing. What we have wondered about mostly in each leader type is whether this individual can get the feels of persons, sense their inner personality make-up, their sensitivities and aspirations. Can he understand their lines of reasoning, whether straight away or in a circle, respect their big or little claims to fame, the essential human dignities on which every man takes an ultimate stand? From this perspective we have been watchful for *the linking leader,* a person able to absorb the aggressions of

[10] Gunnar Myrdal, *et al., An American Dilemma* (New York: Harper & Bros., 1944), p. 718.

other persons, to smooth out ego hurts and unite people in a common cause to which each contributes more than he is able, does more and does better than he had believed possible. We are talking about no superman but the kind of leader found on every campus we have visited, a person not always appreciated by a college at large.

In reflecting on resistances to change, we are led to mention the unreasoned conflict that can be found among participants in a good-will movement. To add that people are people, each living in his private world, each striving for personal goals, does not explain much. To wish that good-willers were considerate of their fellows, had better group-action manners, does not prevent them from showing at times the very behaviors their movement seeks to correct. Of course, one has a right to differ from others in his viewpoints, an obligation to think things through and to stand for principles. But this is not what we are speaking about, a point that group workers fully understand.

Much interpersonal conflict within the College Study has come from ignorance, at times such profound ignorance and so pervasive that it can be called only by its proper name of popular logic.[11] This is folk logic, the assumptive values that pop out on proper stimulus and are seldom made a matter of debate. As a rule, they are taken for granted, with the burden on the other person to show why he elects to be different. Another kind of intragroup conflict involves explicit beliefs, value-judgments that clash head on. A third type of conflict centers on uncoordinated levels of thought. To illustrate, here is a scholar, a specialist on some matter, and taking issue with him on this point is an average knower or less. Each can be quite right within his own assumptions and limitations; yet, like two famous Kansas trains, neither can get by a certain crossing until the other has passed. Search for common grounds in any of these cases is a time-consuming operation.

IMPRESSIONS AND A VERDICT

We have dared to speak frankly about College Study operations, knowing that this may not be considered good form. Field project

[11] For discussion, see Robert K. Merton, "The Sociology of Knowledge," in Georges Gurvitch and Wilbert E. Moore (eds.), *Twentieth Century Sociology* (New York: The Philosophical Library, 1945), pp. 366–405.

after field project in education, some running for years at large costs, get organized, do their work, and write up their contributions, but leave no record whatsoever of their inner strains and stresses. No matter how gracious this type of reporting may be, we are inclined to doubt its general utility to the profession. The chief reason is that the proper study of mankind still is man—what men would like to be, what they are and do, and this includes educators as well as educants. A college faculty in particular ought to see itself in a dual role, a contributor to changes in people but also a consumer of changes in itself. It is in this latter sense that one can speak about the College Study as *in-service teacher education,* a four-year training program in actual intergroup relations.

To say that college faculties and other participants have had to face a self-induced crisis, a prolonged effort under pressure to improve their educational processes, is no exaggeration. To add that these persons have worked hard does slight justice to the facts. We have found no easy way of writing what we would like to say, what Dewey says well in his idea of learning as "suffering and undergoing." Maybe the main point can be put by analogy. Most college study groups are not unlike larger civic organizations, even whole communities. Once a fire has been built under them, the power they can generate is something to behold.

What have college faculties really learned? We have asked this question many times and, in the *College Programs* volume, various committee chairmen have given their own answers. One learning has been a shift in thought from a concern for specific underprivileged persons, or for some one disadvantaged group, to a concern for democracy as the common right of all people. Another learning has begun but it will take time to mature: a tendency to break away from the unreality of an extreme individualistic point of view to a functional sociology of group-centered life. In the third place, much has been learned about the worth of collective effort, the organized teamwork approach to problem-solving. In this connection we would mention, fourthly, a greater familiarity with science, especially as a way of gathering data on which a change program can be based.

In conclusion, we would list the hardest learning of all, the fact that national ideals must take priority over smaller value systems, whether these latter viewpoints deal with race or creed, social class, or alien heritages. Faculties have learned, or relearned, the truth found on every copper cent, *E Pluribus Unum,* by which the nation alone survives. Freedom can be freedom only within order, and nothing can endanger freedom quite as much as the suppression of disorder, whatever its guise. Real order, *unity* instead of uniformity, is the product of resolved conflict, the blending of diverse views into a new outlook.

8. Leader Training in Centers and Workshops

In some colleges, one can hear a familiar debate. Shall inter-group education be the function of the entire college, everybody's business? Or shall it be assigned to a special office, a division or department—for example, to the social studies? Or ought it be given over to a person with professional training and successful experience in the intergroup relations field? Wherever a school system is large enough and concerned enough, the same debate can be heard. In Detroit public schools, responsibility has been lodged in the Division of Community Service in the Superintendent's Office. Much of the Division's routine work centers on group relations.

The issue of specialization is very old in education, arising whenever three general conditions are met. A line of work must be regarded as of basic importance, perhaps foundational to some primary institutional function. This work must require special knowledge and skill, and it must have, therefore, a genuine intellectual content. Where these triadic elements have been recognized to exist, specialization has tended to develop, for instance, in curriculum planning, school administration, and evaluation. A current example is individual guidance, a field steadily winning professional status. It is doubtful if specialization ever develops without debate and resistance; yet in retrospect it always seems to have been inevitable. Moreover, it has seldom replaced a total faculty concern but rather has nurtured it, keeping an institutional staff alert and informed, actively involved in over-all planning.

We cite these facts because special training in intergroup education is today a central issue among many educators. In the past chapter, this problem was studied from an on-the-job viewpoint, the implication being that participants learned by sharing in the ongoing College Study project. Here the focus is on *off-the-job training*, the assembly of teacher-leaders, agency workers, and lay citizens in centers of human relations and in experimental short-term workshops. While regular academic college and university courses still enroll most persons seeking training, we know of no recent and reliable course survey. Partial studies exist to which reference will be made, but the chapter's major interest is in the types of college centers and workshops that aspire to develop regional and national leadership.

CENTERS OF HUMAN RELATIONS: CASE STUDIES

By reliable count,[1] the nation has over four hundred intergroup agencies, conferences, foundations, and the like. Some are small, for example, the Rachel Davis DuBois' Workshop for Cultural Democracy, with an annual budget of less than $10,000. Others are national or international, such as the National Conference of Christians and Jews, or the Anti-Defamation League of B'nai B'rith, with the former having about fifty regional offices and a budget well into seven figures. Some agencies work on all intergroup fronts—race, creed, nationality, and so forth; others, on one front or a few. Some are engaged in multiple services, including efforts to influence legislation, while others, such as the Bureau for Intercultural Education, limit efforts to education.

Impetus for the creation of national "centers of human relations" has come from these agencies, though colleges have of late begun to take more initiative. Most centers have been set up *de novo* by joint college-agency agreement, their basis being an outright grant or a fund-matching arrangement. Other centers have had their origin in the move of an established staff to university auspices, for example, the Taba field project group to the University of Chicago.[2] Small centers, departments, chairs, and the like, may be created by colleges with or without outside assistance.

In every average case a center's upkeep costs are high; thus fund raising is a serious problem if experimental work is to be done. While this problem overarches all others, determining within limits the work that can be undertaken, the very newness of the center idea implies a host of other issues. Brief case studies of representative human relations centers will suggest the concrete nature of their operations.

[1] For annual changes in number of agencies, studies, etc., see the directory and the inventory issued by the American Council on Race Relations, Chicago.
[2] For description, see p. 195–96.

RESEARCH CENTER FOR GROUP DYNAMICS,
UNIVERSITY OF MICHIGAN[3]

The Research Center for Group Dynamics is located at the University of Michigan. It moved there in 1948 from the Massachusetts Institute of Technology, where it had been established by Kurt Lewin. It has lately merged, administratively, with the Survey Research Center, also on the Michigan campus, and the total unit is known as the Institute for Social Research.

At the date of survey (1949), the Center was set up outside of the university departmental structure. Control rested in an executive committee of deans and department heads, responsible to the president's office. The Center had its own budget, administered by the university. Most funds came from outside sources on specific grants, for example, from the Naval Research organization. The university paid for staff teaching and housed the Center.

The Center has three major aims. One is basic research on group structure and functioning. The second is the training of group analysts and leaders, and the third is the diffusion of findings of use in practical group-work programs in industry, community life, social agencies, and education.

In 1949, the Center's staff comprised six senior persons, all members of the university faculty, plus research assistants. Most senior staff members had been trained in social psychology of the Lewin type, and all held dual or triple appointments in the Center and in university departments. About a fifth of staff time was spent in teaching and four-fifths on research.

Courses taught by Center staff members are of two kinds: those within the Center and leading to a doctoral degree in social psychology (group dynamics), and those given as departmental offerings in psychology, sociology, and education. Candidates for the doctorate are required to hold an M.A. degree in psychology or a social science field, and to do a considerable part of their work as interns, that is, field work in agency or other programs. In 1949 the Center had from ten to fifteen majors.

Research, rather than teaching, is basic in Center activities. No project in group study or action is accepted by the staff unless it has "elements of public interest." This rules out many services requested on a fee basis, for example standard market research. While the Center's field projects are varied, they deal mostly with group productivity, skill training in human relations, studies of social communication, conduct of workshops, and consultant work. Book publication has been arranged

[3] This case and others are based on interviews and observations made in 1949 by Dr. Richard H. Williams, associate director of the College Study. Descriptions have been brought up to date in data supplied by center officers, and in some cases through visits by the writer.

with Harper and Brothers, with Ronald Lippitt's *Training in Community Relations* (1949) most recent in the series. The Center takes joint responsibility with Tavistock House in London for publication of the journal *Human Relations*.

Coordinated with the group dynamics Center is the Survey Research Center, an organization equipped to conduct surveys and polls on economic, business, and social problems. It was founded at the university in 1946, with most of its senior staff coming with Rensis Likert from the U.S. Department of Agriculture. In addition to its field studies, this staff gives graduate training in systematic field survey methods. While the two centers coordinate administratively, they are focused on different major goals.

While each center studied has its own points of excellence, we are inclined to accord high rating to the Michigan group. At the University of Iowa, and later at Massachusetts Institute of Technology, Kurt Lewin pioneered experimental group-process work, taking the viewpoint that cooperative action was "an engineering problem" in human relations, that it rested upon technical skills and knowledge. Under the leadership of Dorwin Cartwright and his associates at Ann Arbor, the Lewin viewpoints and methods are being carried on. Work has been greatest in governmental research, in industry and community action, but schools and colleges are making increasing use of these teacher-leader training resources. The Center's staff has lately played a prominent part in introducing group-management methods in state and national educational meetings.

THE COMMITTEE ON EDUCATION, TRAINING AND RESEARCH IN RACE RELATIONS, UNIVERSITY OF CHICAGO

This Committee grew out of, in fact has been parented by, the American Council on Race Relations, located in Chicago. The Council has long been a clearinghouse for action agencies concerned with minority problems, racial and otherwise. For example, it has served as secretariat for the National Association of Intergroup Relations Officials, chiefly officers of mayor's committees, unity councils, and FEPC groups. Feeling the need for university affiliations, especially in the promotion of research, the Council initiated discussions which led to the creation of the university committee.

The Committee on Education, etc., began its work in 1948, under a five-year grant of funds from the American Council on Race Relations.

It is interdepartmental in character, composed of key persons on the University of Chicago faculty, chiefly in sociology, anthropology, and education. All committee members have teaching or other duties, with their salaries paid by the university. Intergroup work is centered in a building which also houses the American Council and the National Opinion Research Center; thus making cooperation a natural and normal matter.

Committee aims are six in number: (1) To make summary digests each year of the intergroup research under way in the nation, including a critical review of the gains made. (2) To publish an annual directory of intergroup research and action agencies, an authoritative source of reference. (3) To channel study data, techniques, personnel, etc., into places of need, a more effective use of technical resources than is being made at present. (4) To initiate "action research" in a few crucial areas, for example, the work of one committee member (Joseph Lohman) in studying and publicizing segregation in Washington. (5) To conduct basic research in certain problem areas, for instance the present effort to measure trends in intergroup tensions. (6) To develop graduate instruction designed to train competent technicians and leaders in the race relations field.

The committee has specified four general areas of graduate study: race and culture, racial and ethnic groups, social psychology of intergroup relations, and racial-cultural adjustments. Degree candidates follow the general university pattern of work, except that their campus and field studies are coordinated through the Race Relations Committee. Most of the studies seek either to build a scientific foundation for policies and programs in interracial relations or else to appraise the effectiveness of new techniques in intergroup work. Mastery of intellectual content is stressed, the committee taking pride in its advanced theoretical courses and field research.

The Chicago group does not call itself a "center," a title taken by another university staff to be described shortly. It is a committee of cooperating professors, each a specialist in his field. With the help of a sizable financial grant, plus the contacts and resources of the American Council on Race Relations, the effort is being made to give research direction to intergroup studies throughout the nation. Emphasis is strongly technical and sociological, with graduate student training on a very high level. The interdepartment committee idea is very old at the University of Chicago, showing one kind of institutional framework on which smaller centers of human relations might pattern.

CENTER FOR HUMAN RELATIONS STUDIES,
SCHOOL OF EDUCATION, NEW YORK UNIVERSITY

The Center for Human Relations Studies is an integral unit in the School of Education, being listed as a curriculum. It is based on the conviction that the study and development of skills in human relations is "the new frontier" in American education. It was established in 1947, at the instigation of the Bureau for Intercultural Education, with headquarters in New York City. For a time, the Bureau and the Center had the same director, but each came to need its own executive head. In general, the Bureau stresses field services; the Center puts emphasis on leader training.

The Center has its own budget, with a fifth or more coming from student fees and the balance provided by the Bureau. Eight professional persons are on the staff, drawn from education, sociology, psychiatry, and other fields. Only one, the director, is full-time in Center work, all others devoting half time or more to university teaching. Per capita instructional costs are about twelve times what the university as a whole spends on each student, so that their reduction without impairment of program is imperative.

Center aims are much the same as those listed by the group dynamics staff in Michigan, with less concern for psychological and sociological "field theory." Center functions comprise leader training in school and community work, the conduct of "action research" studies, diffusion of knowledge, and a very active program of school consultant service. The Center takes pride in its practical approach to group problems and in bringing various academic points of view to bear upon them.

Students are limited at present to fifty per year, all graduates, with many coming from education and social work. Most of them are candidates for a doctoral degree. They are registered in the School of Education and are under general university rules. Few students are full time, many holding regular jobs in local intercultural agencies, child guidance clinics, and the like. Placement, following training, is in such agencies and in colleges and schools.

In day-by-day services, Center staff members give most time to instruction. Their preference is clearly for informal, flexible courses, particularly for seminars and clinics. Students also take courses in the university, and they are expected to give considerable time to field work. Here the "team research" idea (joint projects by students and a professor) is dominant. Projects range over studies of area integration, social legislation, frustration-aggression, and evaluation of group productivity. Staff members serve as consultants to schools on their intercultural problems, address educational meetings, and contribute to popular and professional journals.

A feature stressed by staff members is the careful assessment of student growth. In addition to university requirements, candidates for admission are studied from the angle of their interest in human relations, personality characteristics, and promise as leaders. Anecdotal and other records are kept on graduates, staff appraisals are made in regular conferences, and students are guided in their own self-evaluation. After placement, follow-up studies are planned to see how well the Center prepares its degree people for the leader tasks they are called upon to do.

Here is a type of program, a pattern of leader training, which many school people would regard as especially fitted for a teacher's needs. Studies are less academic than at Ann Arbor, much less than at Chicago, for whatever gains and losses to professional competence this may mean. Staff relations are close and so are student contacts with staff members. Professors represent different university disciplines, with an emphasis on the somewhat individualist mental hygiene approach to the problems of social living. Far more time is spent on school, and school-related, problems than in any other center of this size, a fact that helps teacher-leaders in their change-over from some regular teaching field to intergroup work. Staff plans go much beyond present realities, creating expectations which the Center hopes to realize as its maintenance becomes assured.

CENTER FOR INTERGROUP EDUCATION, UNIVERSITY OF CHICAGO

This Center is a continuation of Dr. Hilda Taba's school project in intergroup relations. It is financed by a grant from the National Conference of Christians and Jews, by university instructional fees, and increasingly by contracts for consultant services to schools. It was established in 1948 as a "research action" program, with a staff of six professional members, mostly a carry-over from the prior field project.

Aside from a large summer workshop, the Center's major activity is the promotion of practicums in various school systems in which staff members serve as leaders. At the time of survey, 399 graduates and undergraduates, predominantly public school teachers, supervisors, and school heads, were enrolled in seven of these courses, for example, at South Bend, Denver, and St. Louis.

Staff members offer two practicums in intergroup relations on the university campus, the major aim being a workable integration of theory and practice. Staff members, as said, conduct an annual summer workshop at the University. A few degree dissertations are under staff direction. The N.C.C.J. sponsoring body has contracted for staff leadership in workshop and other services to local and regional directors.

Staff members have written numerous short articles, bulletins, etc., for school people, drawing on their experiences in the four-year, 72-school project. Course units, bibliographies, handbooks, and the like, are sold at near cost as a school service. Mimeographed materials are distributed by the Center, but publications are issued by the American Council on Education. The current book as we write is entitled *Elementary Curriculum in Intergroup Relations* (1950).

The Center just described is a natural continuation of an extensive work program with schools in every part of the country, a project also financed by the National Conference of Christians and Jews. This school program ran concurrently with the College Study, but the two were separate undertakings. There is no particular theory guiding Center group work, nor do research methods transcend elemental levels. Teaching and service demands on staff time make systematic study difficult. Mimeograph materials are mostly descriptive workshop papers, running strongly to resource and teaching units. Longer publications are set at a popular reading level, and they have proved informative both to teachers and lay persons.

INTERDIVISIONAL PROGRAM IN INTERGROUP RELATIONS. TEACHERS COLLEGE, COLUMBIA UNIVERSITY

This program was started in 1948 on a five-year grant from the National Conference of Christians and Jews. It is under the direction of Dr. Martin P. Chworowsky, assisted by an advisory committee representing the interdivisional areas at Teachers College. Major emphasis is on teacher-leader training, though service and research functions are also stressed.

In general, the program follows plans already in operation for interdivisional majors. Two courses in intergroup relations and group dynamics are given for graduate students, and two in orientation for undergraduates. Fellowships are available for advanced students, making selection possible. Both the Ed.D. and the Ph.D. degrees are to be conferred.

At the time of survey, nineteen advanced students were enrolled, with five on fellowships. All but four were majoring in intergroup relations. Of the majors, six have school or college backgrounds and interests, three are in religious work, three in social work, two in community organization, and one in workers education. Each student's program is fitted to his needs, and all students do some field work.

In addition to his teaching, the coordinator spends time in publicizing intergroup work, in recruiting majors, in assisting N.C.C.J. with staff training, and in school-community services. The major problem is staff shortage, the immediate need being for a full-time professional field worker.

From familiarity with this program, we would guess that it has had to build up slowly, to cut channels with care. We do not imply faculty opposition to intergroup work, for Teachers College at Columbia University has pioneered many new movements in education. Mere recognition of intergroup relations in the course offerings of the college, in publicity and the like, assure this emphasis a consideration on a national basis. And yet, the normal hurdles to be run in program building are very great, a severe test of a director's organizational skill. Where the Teachers College consultant should have full time for on-campus leader training, he must spend many hours in other work. We have observed in College Study programs how hard it is for an able person to resist pressures which lead him to spread himself too thin.

A DEPARTMENT OF HUMAN RELATIONS

The University of Miami, at Coral Gables, Florida, has a department of human relations, the staff consisting of one professor and several assistants. This program was instituted in 1947 as an endowed chair of human relations, so that present departmental status is an indication of its favorable reception. Like other center programs, this one still faces the problem of securing some outside aid for its continued support.

Annual reports give much descriptive data on the problems most colleges might expect to meet in creating a department of human relations—definition of aims, amassing of teaching tools, coordinating with other areas, publicizing work on the campus, rendering services to school and community organizations. Dr. Gordon Lovejoy, who initiated the center program, was selected as an experienced worker in these matters, having held appointments at two universities and published research in professional journals.

Starting with a single core course in human relations, departmental offerings have expanded to an undergraduate major. Courses are fairly academic and sociological, stressing standard theory and methods in intergroup relations, particularly race problems in the South. Plans have been made to confer an M.A. degree, with students taking a variable amount of work in regular university areas.

The department at Miami is in the Liberal Arts College, with its offerings listed as electives in several colleges, including education.

Students come mostly from social science areas, many simply taking a brief "flier" in intergroup work. The setup is, quite frankly, an experimental venture. While the outlook appears promising, the future is not felt to be wholly predictable.

The above case shows a small but important step forward, a development achieved or contemplated by several colleges and universities. Given modest financial aid, a chair or department of human relations can be started. Its maintenance and expansion, however, present complex problems. Some problems are internal, for instance, the creation of an institutional framework within which to function; and some are external, the imminent possibility that something may happen, some tightening of intergroup relations, which will sweep the department out of existence. Risks of this sort are never fully calculable, thus introducing a large chance element into this kind of education.

In reflecting on the matter, it is evident that centers of human relations, departments, chairs, and so forth, are few and far between. While those described have developed since 1947, and various colleges are known to be considering the idea, it would be incautious to claim any general trend in this direction. Large, well-staffed centers are needed for top-level teacher training in human relations; yet cost factors are bound to keep their number down. Most off-the-job education seems destined to come from traditional sources, notably from regular college courses and summer workshops.

College Courses on Intergroup Lines

The only recent national study on courses and teaching materials in intergroup relations is the survey made by Wilson[4] and associates of 266 grade and high school textbooks in history, geography, civics, social problems, and the like, and 21 introductory college texts in psychology and sociology. While we are inclined to think that procedures in this study were highly subjective,[5] its general conclusions have been widely cited. "Textbooks are not

[4] Howard E. Wilson, "Intergroup Relations in Teaching Material," *Educational Record*, XXVIII (1947), 114–21.

[5] In comparison, for example, with the much more limited research by I. L. Child, H. E. Potter, and E. M. Levine, "Children's Textbooks and Personality Development," *Psychological Monographs*, Vol. LX (1946), No. 3.

guilty of planned derogation of groups, but of failure to come to grips with the basic issues in the complex problem of human relations. Much material essential to the understanding of intergroup relations and provocative of better relations is simply not presented to pupils." On the basis of these findings, conferences have been held with publishers of school and college textbooks. In all cases, publishers have proved sympathetic to committee views.

Most college departments of sociology and anthropology give work along intergroup lines, as do many departments of psychology. Courses are largely academic, as discussed in a previous chapter. They specialize in some one area, for instance, race relations, immigration, culture conflict, social attitudes, and personality adjustments.[6] Courses centered on majority-minority relations, or even textbooks of this nature, are still few in number, though the trend is toward an integrated "group interactional" approach.[7] Social psychologists have done better at organizing a rounded group dynamics viewpoint than have sociologists;[8] yet we feel that even a rudimentary interdisciplinary "science of human relations" is little more at present than a challenging idea. Klineberg[9] has made a contribution in assembling scattered studies as they bear on tensions crucial to world peace.

In education, intergroup interests are almost always practical, at times too practical, as we shall argue elsewhere. Having no systematic job analysis data to guide them, educators have tended to base courses on student problems—the happenings in and about school that run counter to student and teacher conceptions of fair play. When educators have applied a group dynamics viewpoint to general change problems, books written by them for college courses in intergroup relations show several omissions. For one

---

[6] For the national pattern of sociology courses, with the trend since 1902, R. Kennedy and R. J. R. Kennedy, "Sociology in American Colleges," *American Sociological Review*, VII (1942), 661–75.

[7] The first textbook so labeled was Donald Young, *American Minority Peoples* (New York: Harper, 1932). Recent texts, each an integrational effort, are by Arnold and Caroline Rose, R. A. Schermerhorn, R. M. MacIver, Alain Locke, F. Brown and J. Roucek.

[8] A notable example is D. Kretch and R. S. Crutchfield, *Theory and Problems of Social Psychology* (New York: McGraw-Hill Book Co., 1948).

[9] Otto Klineberg, *Tensions Affecting International Understanding* (New York: Social Science Research Council, 230 Park Ave., 1950).

thing, writings are seldom theory-oriented. They are light on empirical research data, and they do little more on strategies and tactics than to cite illustrative cases and exhort to ameliorative action. Two textbooks in human relations have been written for use in public schools, each a mental hygiene approach to emotional needs.[10]

From a research standpoint, most courses enrolling teachers are still oriented along traditional lines. Academic thinking is dominant, as perhaps it should be, but not we hope to the obvious neglect of the experiential training needed in group-process methods. Many teacher candidates for higher degrees are deficient in research skills and understandings. A number have had no formal training in statistical methods, others only an elementary course, and still others claim credit for "research" which comprises little except talking in a class about problems common to teachers. Bureaus of educational research, in the colleges we know best, have been slow to clear off busy-work in order to focus on human relations, feeling that the "social" was outside their realm. Exceptions came to mind—for instance, Ohio State University—but over-all impressions do not point to any functional intergroup emphasis in these bureaus as a whole.

Service-type courses are common in colleges of education, the reason being the great value these colleges place on their field contacts. Their practical problem day in and day out is to raise the level of teacher performance in routine phases of the mass education task. That this need not, in fact should not, exclude considerable attention to social learning has been demonstrated in College Study institutions, a point made throughout the present two-volume report.

An Experimental Group Dynamics Workshop

The educational workshop had its origins at Ohio State University in the summer of 1936 when Dr. Ralph Tyler assembled thirty-five teachers from schools in the Progressive Education Association's Eight-Year Study. These schools were experimenting with

---

[10] For example, H. E. Bullis and E. E. O'Malley, *Human Relations in the Classroom* (Wilmington: Delaware State Society for Mental Hygiene, 1947).

curricular revisions, and teachers needed help in designing and assessing innovations. The obvious thing to do was to bring these teachers together, organize staff and resources in terms of their problems, and devise a flexible, democratic group-work plan. This is, in substance, the workshop idea, but in its rapid spread over the nation it has undergone changes. The term, "workshop," may mean today almost any kind of study procedure, including straight lecture courses.

From the outset the appraisal of workshop learnings has been a challenge. In the College Study, most workshop faculties have followed the traditional plan of asking participants to evaluate the workshop, to assess it from the viewpoint of its meeting their own needs. The Eau Claire, Wisconsin, college staff made perhaps the best effort to add objective data to student reactions.[11] Workshop teachers were paired on nine points with teachers in the same schools, giving twenty-two matched pairs. On College Study end-tests, the workshop participants showed significantly more liberal attitudes, an effect felt to be related to their summer experience in small-group problem-solving. Matched teacher pairs were then visited in their own classrooms. They were interviewed, their teaching was observed, and attitude tests were given to their pupils. All evidence supported the hypothesis that the workshop technique is an effective way to teach intercultural education.

Most summer and off-campus (year around) workshops have become fairly routine matters, assumed to be worth their relatively high costs. Costs are due to low teacher-student ratios, individual and small-group conferences, special equipment and assistance. Organizational patterns, too, have become somewhat set, with small and large group meetings the general rule. What we wish to do now is to describe a unique workshop in intergroup relations, an intensive two-week effort under direction of the late Kurt Lewin. This venture was a three-way cooperative project, involving the Ann Arbor group dynamics staff, the Connecticut State Interracial Commission, and the Commission on Community Interrelations of the American Jewish Congress.

[11] For details, see *College Programs in Intergroup Relations*, pp. 199–200.

A GROUP DYNAMICS WORKSHOP[12]

How can ideas be translated into action, the gap bridged between the technical expert and the field practitioner? How can a state interracial commission, or other intercultural agency, aid school and community workers in this field? And above all, can a brief but intensive workshop secure measurable changes in human relational skills, changes that will carry over to the participant's job? These were the major questions to which answers were sought in the New Britain, Connecticut, workshop in the summer of 1946.

Much preplanning entered into this small but significant change experiment. Once its general aims were clarified, staff selection got under way. Three teams were set up and coordinated at preliminary gear-meshing sessions. One team comprised the state commission people, their concern being that a good educational job should be done. Another team consisted of trainers, the staff engaged in the conduct of the workshop. The third team was made up of study-action researchers, specialists charged with in-process and over-all workshop evaluation.

In preplanning, it was decided that the number of participants should be about fifty, with forty-one finally admitted. Effort was made to get key persons, preferably by "community teams," with four teams of two to eight persons actually recruited. These individuals did not at the time regard themselves as teams, for this was to be a workshop product. Other persons were recruited as best they could be, making up the forty-one total. In backgrounds, 44 percent of the participants were educators, 34 percent social agency people, and 22 percent lay persons doing work in intergroup relations. Over a fourth were Negro, and about the same number Jewish. Under two-thirds were Protestant and 15 percent were Catholic.

Recruitment was done by state commission workers in field interviews. At the same time, data were collected on workshop applicants, along with the usual statement of problems, interests, and needs. For various reasons, not all the key persons wanted could attend the workshop, yet it was felt that those who did get away for the two weeks' training were persons with high actual and potential influence in their communities.

Preplanning was done also as to workshop conduct and evaluation, staff agreements that we shall skip in order to look at the ten-day experience through the eyes of a participant. This record is in the form of a 13-page diary, a frank human-interest reaction to daily happenings.

At the first workshop session, this teacher writes that she was made to feel very welcome, that this was to be a really serious attempt to measure workshop learnings. That morning was devoted to a meeting

[12] Based on Ronald Lippitt, *Training in Community Relations* (New York: Harper & Bros., 1949), 286 pp. The book should be read in its entirety.

within a meeting, a role-practice session in which good and bad ways of doing group work were demonstrated. After lunch, participants were divided into two groups. One group took a test, that is, told how they would handle a range of intergroup problem situations. After this, the group changed rooms with the other group and began to list the problems on which they wanted help. On a walk that evening past the main room, the teacher noticed the staff at work, presumably classifying participant problems.

On the second day, the morning was devoted to a training session on how to use the expert, followed by a discussion of a mimeographed summary of first-day problems by "an imposing group of visiting experts." To the diarist's taste, there was too much "sitting and listening," indicating that participants had not yet learned to ask for and receive the help of specialists. More sessions in the afternoon did little to change the situation, and the writer shows some annoyance at the kinds of questions asked by group members. That evening some workshoppers dropped in by accident on the staff meeting and were invited to stay, after which the staff no longer met by itself.

During the third day, things really got going. Beginning on some high-priority questions, the big meeting soon broke into smaller common-interest groups, each with its own schedule of priorities. In the writer's group, the main concern was how to interest people in community issues and problems, leading to role-playing sessions in which ways of working with people were demonstrated. Sessions were followed by critical discussion, lasting over the lunch period. Other problems were tackled in the afternoon, for example, how to work on segregation. A number of these discussions were put on a recording machine for later analysis by the research staff.

Days following this important third day run fairly true to pattern, with participants settling deeper into their work. Discussions centered on "the strategy of planning," as well as on the repeated practice of group-work skills. Of most moment were the rise of tensions within the small groups, the need to resolve conflicts, to integrate divergent viewpoints. "Back-home planning," that is, what to do to change home-town conditions, was begun on the fifth day and carried on to the end of the workshop. Mostly, real-life situations were devised, with participants demonstrating different things to do. The diary concludes with brief summaries of "action plans" as teams and others reported them on the final day.

In the field visit to workshop applicants, interviews were held with two of the person's co-workers on the job. The staff concept of training needs came from this source, as well as from the pre-workshop statements of enrollees. These needs included the ability to work with people, ways of changing attitudes, social and psychological knowledge, use of community resources, and the like. The staff idea, as the diary has disclosed, was to build a program about these needs, to keep it adjustive to new needs as they arose. Much thought was given, therefore, to in-process planning, to basing each new day's work on what had taken place the day before. Staff meetings were often fairly tense affairs, with people taking quite opposite stands. There was no dominance, no authoritarianism; compromises were worked out in free-for-all discussions where the idea that won the most following was judged the best. Group-process observers were used, not only in student meetings, but in staff sessions.

Special interest centers in workshop evaluation, and we want to discuss that in some detail. Statistical data were collected on the workshop process, making logical inferences possible, and on the changes seen in participants on the job and by their co-workers in schools and agencies. Such data differ markedly from the usual how-do-you-feel-about-this-or-that questions asked workshop participants in the customary assessment of so-called learning outcomes.

In time use the average student spent about eighty-six hours in workshop meetings, excluding bull sessions. About thirty-eight hours were in general meetings, the same in small interest groups, eight hours in special meetings, and two hours in test periods. Average individual participations were about 161, with two-thirds credited to students. These varied in number from .6 per hour to 12.0. Trainer leaders were three times more active than their most active students over the full ten days, a finding that could have a number of interpretations.

Quality of participation was studied under headings of suggestions for agenda, coordination of discussion, contribution of ideas, requests for aid, agreement with and praise of others, disagreement and criticism of them. Percent figures on an hourly basis show significant differences in the three study-action groups, some moving forward, some caught in snarls, some friendly, some less so. Half to two-thirds of leader time was spent in starting and coordinating discussion. Other roles included caretaker of group routines, expert in data-giving, demonstrator of techniques, and mediator of conflicts. At times, leaders were on the sidelines, and at other times their absence was used as a test situation.

Time-use studies throw still further light on curricular emphases. While groups varied, a fourth to a third of all the time was spent on the development of personal skills of persuasion, interviewing, and the like. About the same stress was placed on group-leader skills, followed by social action techniques in community education, after which came specific practices in conflict resolution. Other emphases comprised general fact-finding methods, diagnosis of problems, and use of mass media such as radio and press.

In respect to back-home effects, three types of data were secured.

Participants were interviewed, along with their co-workers, six months after the workshop, and the state committee kept a record of contacts with workshoppers over this period. Interviews were an hour or so in length and kept informal, though a schedule was used in order to make pre- and end-comparisons of attitudes and behaviors.

A striking increase in intergroup activities was found in pre- and post-workshop comparisons. For example, in the initial interviews almost half the workshop applicants had listed 0-3 participations, 40 percent 4-7 activities, and 13 percent 8-13. In post-work interviews, percentages for the categories were 0, 29, and 40. The remaining 31 percent of participations fell into a new category, 14-36 intergroup activities. In the interviewer's judgment, "motivations to report activities were as great" in the first interview as in the second, suggesting that these statistics show a true workshop effect.

Time-use studies, as well as verbal comments, confirmed the above effects. Major time expenditures were in conducting intergroup educational activities, making talks on the workshop, stimulating interest in action programs, helping to bring pressure to force changes in discriminating policies and practices, sharing ideas with intercultural agencies, making talks on intergroup relations, and working on committees.

Were these activities new or merely a continuation of old interests? Were they individualistic or team-related? A sample of 158 participations was studied in these terms. About 44 percent were new but in an old setting, that is, school, agency, etc., and 33 percent were new and in a new setting, namely, with the workshop team. Other statistics showed the value of the team idea in selecting and training workshop members, the "reinforcement" to good doing that comes from even a small like minded grouping.

It is interesting to compare workshop effects as reported by participants and observed by their co-workers. Over two-thirds of the former claimed to have a broader view of intergroup problems and their responsibility for working on them, whereas about half their co-workers could testify to this effect. About 57 percent of the workshoppers said they were motivated to greater activity, an effect affirmed by over four-fifths of their co-workers. Over 40 percent reported skill learnings, an observation made by 67 percent of their associates on the job. Over 10 percent asserted changes in their own prejudices, a result indicated by 18 percent of their co-workers. A fifth cited new confidence in their own abilities, a judgment given by 15 percent of their associates.

In addition to skill learning, where else did change take place? No change is indicated in workshopper perceptions of Jewish-Gentile tensions. More sensitivity is revealed as to anti-Negro prejudices and to "old American" treatment of immigrant groups. Most serious present conflicts were felt to be in employment opportunities, general social attitudes, housing discrimination, and schooling, a question not asked in the pre-workshop interview.

More than a third of the participants reported no change in their basic goal of correcting injustices and equalizing opportunities. Half affirmed a definite deepening of their general goal, a greater determination to succeed in change-making. Almost three-fourths felt more hopeful that changes could be made than they had in the pre-workshop period, crediting their new optimism largely to the workshop. In reflecting on "a year from now," 58 percent felt that no changes for the better would occur, 6 pecent that intergroup relations would get worse, and 15 percent "didn't know, or couldn't guess."

In respect to their own work, more than two-thirds felt that it was better supported by school or agency heads than before the workshop, with this change credited to their own efforts, to the receptivity of others as a result of the workshop, and to the team and other supportive relations developed at New Britain. Three-fourths affirmed that they had changed their thinking about strategy and methods, and 71 percent cited their new use of from one to four group-work techniques. Among these new techniques, the sociodrama was outstanding, with three-fourths having experimented with its use.

In talks with some of these workshop participants, almost all spoke with genuine enthusiasm about their experiences. Only two critics, both experienced workshoppers, were found. They believed that the program was slow to shake down, that confusion persisted beyond its normal span, and that research got in the way of learning. We are inclined to discount these reactions; yet the staff itself claims no perfection. Workshop strengths and weaknesses were appraised at length and suggestions made for improving any subsequent experimental venture.

What we have in the Connecticut workshop is a truly experimental approach to leader education in intergroup relations, a program concentrating on study, action, and training. Work was kept at a high technical level, a great deal of role practice was provided, and evaluation went much beyond anything so far done. On these and other points, the New Britain pattern stands in sharp contrast to the usual workshop for teachers, an almost unknown quantity from the standpoint of its objective effects. Of course, it costs money to appraise on-the-job carry-overs, money that cannot go into more scholarships for more teachers; thus, again the question is raised of how funds can best be spent, what returns are of most worth.

Planning a Human Relations Center

Assuming that present interest in human relations will continue, indeed that it will diffuse and deepen, enough data have been covered in this chapter and the one on in-service education to warrant some summary of major problems. Whether a center or field program is large or small,[13] at least eight kinds of issues in teacher-leader education can be anticipated.

A planning group faces first of all the problem of its own *functional orientation*. If the college claims a leader role in its area, its region, or the nation, does this responsibility extend to human relations? Words may prove no adequate answer, no foundation for program-making. What will administration do, on faculty recommendation, to implement action? What limits of freedom for a center's operations will it support? Will it clear the way and assist in fund-raising? Does it envision just another paper-and-pencil committee, or do resources permit some kind of staff setup compatible with the work tasks to be done? Failure to clear on these questions can mean a great loss of time to a planning group, a thought process ending in a committee report that is promptly filed and forgotten.

Once anchorage points have been defined, the next cluster of problems might well center in the *curriculum*. What kinds of human relations work should be undertaken? In our opinion, six types of services should be considered.

TYPES OF CENTER SERVICES IN HUMAN RELATIONS

1. *Teacher education.* Pre- and in-service training in the attitudes, knowledges, skills, and judgments of intergroup education.
2. *Basic research.* Systematic study, often of a multidisciplinary nature, to increase scientific knowledge of human relations.
3. *Service studies.* Fact-finding done for and financed by schools, social agencies, industry, etc., serving the public interest.
4. *Clearinghouse function.* Collection and diffusion of research findings, study forms, teaching materials, and the like.
5. *Consultant service.* Provision of trained workers to assist on-the-job groups in the solution of human relational problems.

---

[13] Again, for lack of space, other patterns are omitted, particularly travel seminars here and abroad. From experience with these projects, we are strongly of the opinion that, under equated conditions, they will yield better and more lasting learnings about people, a hypothesis in need of exact test.

6. *Change induction.* Experimental efforts to guide social action groups in change-making in line with democratic human values.

At this point, basic *organizational issues* will be clamoring for attention, chiefly staff personnel, staff organization, and the center's position in the university structure. Finding specialists in intergroup relations is still very difficult, for university-trained educators in this field are few in number. What happens usually is that staff appointments go to persons educated for other tasks, for example, curriculum revision, educational administration, or research. Expert though these persons may be in a particular field, they lack the social science knowledge implied in the type of curriculum we would like to see evolved. A center swings in the direction of a director's general training, righting itself only after a staff accumulates experience in dealing with school-community problems on a broad human relations front.

By this time, no doubt sooner, a planning group will have faced *the fund-raising problem.* No center of human relations known to us is anywise nearly self-supporting, though some are trending in that way.[14] Most of them have been started by an initial grant from an outside agency, usually an intercultural agency or a general welfare foundation, which may continue to give partial subsidies. All centers pay part of their expenses through instructional fees and the sale of consultant services, and some market their own publications and teaching aids.

One planning group we have in mind felt that its work in human relations could be financed through an intercollege cooperative arrangement in the region it wished to serve; yet this development has failed so far to materialize. We believe centers must depend for some years on two main sources of funds: allocations from college or university budgets, and grants-in-aid from good-will agencies, civic groups, and foundations. Continued large expenditures for research by federal government divisions, such as armed forces units, may provide a third major source of income, depending on a number of variables.

Fund-raising has become a technical matter on which a college

[14] Best example, while not strictly intergroup, is the Prescott Human Growth and Development Center at the University of Maryland, with a total annual budget of about $250,000.

planning group may need help. Judging from the requests we have seen, not all proposals have the brevity and logic that potential donors like. Our impressions are that the latter want straight-forward business propositions, that they respond better to actual plans than to aspirational ideals, that they might well be approached on Plans A, B, C, each in turn a lesser venture, with C the minimum costs at which any kind of program could operate. Fund-matching appeals to intercultural agencies, as docs also an emphasis on practical service functions. Often a grant is staggered in amount, tapering off over a given time period.

Assuming that funds are found, that a center goes into operation, *student recruitment* will take some thought. If M.A., Ed.D., and/or Ph.D. degrees are to be granted, what prerequisites must be met? In addition to university requirements, what special backgrounds such as teaching experience should be specified? Whatever standards are set, they are likely to rule out many persons now in intergroup work, for intercultural agencies, unity councils, mayor's commissions, and so on, are manned by heterogeneous staffs. Even more serious is another issue, the question of whether any kind of recruiting can get very far until more job outlets are found. *Job placement* at professional levels is, we suspect, the ultimate bottleneck in specialized intergroup training, the problem of creating a market demand at rates of pay that will attract competent personnel.

If these impasses are hurdled, good sense demands an *integrated campus training and field work program.* Usually, a center's major training is of a seminar or workshop type, with students also enrolled in departmental courses, say in psychology and sociology. The academic nature of courses may contrast with the informality of the seminar, raising questions in the student's mind. Field work, paid or voluntary, has been hard to integrate with campus training, and its supervision has been very weak. Field studies have been difficult to make, even with full-time graduate students, and data-processing equipment costs more than can be invested in it. Often a statistics laboratory cannot be started, so that a sharing arrangement with other university units is required.

Field service is another item, the usual weakness being that an intergroup staff must take school or other contracts on a purely fund-raising basis in order to keep the main program going. Consultants dash here, dash there, often to the neglect of their on-campus teaching and research, a fault that can scarcely be remedied in a small staff. In larger staffs, a division of labor is possible. Some workers can specialize in campus-leader training, some in field services, some in research, some in publication, and so on. Where these functions must be handled by one or two persons, results show the cross-pulls and lack of depths to which reference was made in the descriptive cases.

To sum up, the kinds of problems listed are serious but not critical. The best evidence of this is that large center and field programs do exist, all set up within recent years. Their growing enrollments and expanding services should be encouraging to any college planning group. While foundations, intercultural or otherwise, seldom solicit business, they spend much time examining proposals made to them. Governmental and international organizations have budgets for social science research, often contracting with a university group for technical services. All things considered, the outlook for professional training in human relations looks extremely favorable.

A Viewpoint toward the Practical

Assuming that both social scientists and educators will be involved in center and field work, the problem of maintaining good communication is very real. In College Study work, gaps have seemed at times unbridgeable. On the one hand, educators may have had little or no basic training in any social science. They do not appreciate the tough-mindedness of scientists, the fact that any science advances through rigorous self-criticism. On the other hand, scientists irritate educators when they speak of good will in quotes or with a sneer, charge teachers with lacking intellectual interest, and propound theories with no functional bearing on the life that people live.

In part, this is a problem of "the practical" and "the theoretical." On occasion, every college in the Study has had to face two questions: *what is the practical, and how can it best be tackled?* From a social science standpoint, some teacher education looks like petty business, a matter of common sense in classroom management, record-keeping, and so on, things that a literate person should pick up on the job with casual training. To label such learnings as practical, to rehash them in course after course when a student might be understanding the society he is preparing to serve, its history, sociology, psychology, and the like, appears to be a mistaken emphasis.

It seems relevant to note that a scientist, faced with a practical problem, may not attack it directly. The great advances in engineering sciences, for example, have come in the main from pure science projects undertaken as intellectual adventures.

Suppose, said a specialist in physical science research,[15] it had been decided in 1840 to improve indoor lighting. Imagine that the government had set up a well-financed commission to work on this very practical problem. There would have been improvements in illumination, to be sure, better lamp designs, better oil fuels, better wicks, so on. But would any member of the commission have spent time waving wires in front of magnets, connecting dissimilar metal plates, in short, doing things which led, before a generation had passed, to our present gigantic electrical industry.

An even better illustration is the atomic bomb. If as late as 1930 the armed services had been asked to improve explosives, it is all but certain that they would have moved along conventional lines. They would not have undertaken, as theoretical physicists were then beginning to do, the construction of elaborate devices for studying atomic disintegration. Indeed, if we recall Ridenour's remarks correctly, high authorities in government and outside could not be convinced for some years that the building of expensive cyclotrons was "practical." One large industrial corporation, with millions of dollars to invest in energy research, decided against a cyclotron just five months before the discovery of nuclear fission!

The point to be made is, we believe, important to the further development of intergroup education. In theory, school and community practices, like other arts, should rest on philosophical and scientific foundations. To say that we have no integrated science of human relations, that change actions in this field are largely

[15] Dr. Louis N. Ridenour, Jr., in an address to the American Educational Research Association at Atlantic City, February 1950.

guesswork, are approximate truths. And yet with all our biases toward practical experience, it seems shortsighted for us in teacher education to maintain aloofness from social science areas, to ignore their actual and potential contributions. The real issue, we believe, is not between theory and practice *but rather between good and bad theory,* for educational practice unguided by social theory does not promise much for the future of intergroup work.

9. Strategy and Tactics in Community Planning

There is before us the circular of a brokerage firm. It tells about the "modern way" to invest, to secure savings, and increase income. Various kinds of risks are analyzed, with suggestions for their control. What strikes us about this brochure is that it represents exactly the viewpoint underlying College Study work. An investment in good will, in civic education and community planning, is indeed *an investment*, a venture of money, energy, and concern. How can it be made to pay out, to yield maximum returns? To answer that no one knows for certain, that some risks still appear incalculable, should not discourage a searching quest. Even to think within a factual framework is a great change from the usual emotionalized appeal to save the world.

It is a curious fact that persons who know most about community organizational work talk and write the least about it. We refer to political bosses, labor mediators, area social workers, fund campaigners, and certain civic club leaders. Either they are too busy to tell how the job is done, or they do not comprehend in an intellectual sense, or they fear that discussion would decrease their effectiveness. Whatever the reason, one will find few authoritative writings on group-process strategies and tactics, a genuine handicap to practical workers in the intergroup field. Carr[1] has done something at the local community level, MacIver[2] and Lewin,[3] particularly Lewin, in general theory. While others could be named, our over-all feeling is that an "investor" must still trust pretty much to luck.

By *strategy* we shall mean the rational assessment of a situation, the making of an anticipatory plan of action, and by *tactics* the

[1] Lowell J. Carr, *Delinquency Control* (New York: Harper & Bros., 1940).
[2] R. M. MacIver, *The More Perfect Union* (New York: Macmillan Co., 1948).
[3] Kurt Lewin, *Resolving Social Conflicts* (New York: Harper & Bros., 1948).

213

execution of the plan, the continuous replanning implicit in every group process. What makes thought difficult is not only the little that is known about either of these concepts but also the fact that both are situational composites, hence, conditioned by unpredictable events. One can cite concrete cases, as past chapters have done, but to generalize at the community level is perhaps premature. However this may be, we want first to describe two urban scenes, one a crisis in race relations and the other a chronic condition of area disunity. Reasoning can then proceed with some reference to these materials, though not confined to them.

INTERRACIAL TENSION IN ST. LOUIS

One event we wish to think about is a near-riot in St. Louis in June 1949. Data are taken mostly from a report by George Schermer, director of the Mayor's Interracial Committee in Detroit, who was employed to study the case and make recommendations. We visited the area after the incident and talked with a number of persons, including school, church, and social agency heads. Not only are such situations tense, a tenseness unknown in routine group-process work, but they are many-sided, thus hard to reconstruct and analyze.

THE FAIRGROUNDS PARK INCIDENT[4]

"On behalf of the St. Louis Council on Human Relations," writes its chairman in a letter to the mayor of the city, "I have the honor to transmit herewith a report entitled 'The Fairgrounds Park Incident,' which has been prepared for the Council by Mr. George Schermer. . . ." The writer then explains that the investigator spent two weeks in gathering his data, that he had the full cooperation of everyone. The letter concludes by pointing up certain recommendations made in the study, expressing the hope that a long-range program of education and civic action can be developed.

In accepting assignment to conduct the St. Louis study, Schermer, an experienced person at such tasks, made it clear that he had no interest in either blaming or saving anyone. His job was fact-finding— the exact nature of the riotous action, its backgrounds, causal factors, and the general outlines of a preventive plan. Assured of Council support on these points, and of police and other cooperation, he began the arduous task of assembling facts. He studied news accounts, made

[4] George Schermer, *The Fairgrounds Park Incident.* A study conducted for the St. Louis Council on Human Relations, St. Louis, Missouri. Dated July 27, 1949. (Mimeographed; 28 pp.)

on-the-spot observations, interviewed a large number of persons, and informed himself as to the past and present state of race relations in the city.

What was the Fairgrounds Park incident? The time was mid-June, the weather warm, with young people turning toward outdoor swimming pools. There were only two of these municipal pools, both reserved for whites. Were Negroes once again to be excluded, as in the past? It did not appear so; yet the situation was confusing. At suburban Webster Groves, a new public pool had just been opened. When Negro residents were refused admission, they threatened civil suit. From this point, the sequence of events is unclear and contradictory.

In the Webster Groves situation, newspaper reporters heard that the Director of Public Welfare had issued an order that Negroes were to be admitted to city outdoor pools. When confirmation of this order was sought, the Director denied saying that "Negroes and whites were to swim together." He said that he had instructed the Commissioner of Parks that "Negroes were to be admitted if they so requested." Reporters told him that they construed this to be an order and they went to see the Mayor. The latter asked the Director to come to his office, at which time the "order" was confirmed.

Sensing the explosive possibility of this order, the Mayor consulted with advisers. It was decided to contact all city newspaper editors and ask that the story be given only routine coverage. In one case, top management could not be reached, though a general promise of "careful handling" had been made. The story was headlined on the front page, opening as follows:

POOLS AND PLAYGROUNDS OPEN TO BOTH RACES

Negroes and whites may hereafter swim together in all the city's nine pools and use the same thirty-five playgrounds, Director of Public Welfare John J. O'Toole announced yesterday. O'Toole thus opened the door to members of both races in an order to Park Commissioner Palmer B. Baumes. The order read, "if Negroes apply for admission to municipal pools, they are not to be refused."

This order was also given lead attention in radio newscasts. So far as could be determined, there was still no consultation with the police department, no anticipation of or preparation for any untoward event.

This brings the story to June 21, when Negro children appeared at the city's two outdoor swimming pools and one wading pool. In all cases except at the Fairgrounds Park center, whites and Negroes used the same pool with no record of violence, name calling, or the like. In one instance, white parents did come to the pool and protest but took no further action.

It was found difficult to reconstruct events at the Fairgrounds Park center. About thirty of the two hundred or so boys and girls lined up for the opening of the pool were Negro. Later, in swimming, the latter tended to use one section of the pool, the whites another, but there were no overt incidents. As time approached for the second shift, white boys began to gather outside the enclosure, awaiting their turn to enter. They called names and made threats. A few white adults joined the crowd, whose behavior had become menacing. Negro swimmers were asked by the pool custodian to remain until after the whites had been let out, after which they were given police escort through the crowd and out of the park.

Police reports show that "some additional officers" had been detailed to the pool on the morning of June 21. They were to "prevent trouble" if it should seem imminent. Following the change of shifts at the pool, police cars in the area began to answer radio calls to investigate street fights of white and Negro children. What they found mostly were groups of early teen-agers in hot arguments, all of whom were dispersed. Some Negro boys informed the police that they had been set upon by white boys and beaten up. As more calls came in, both from children who had been cornered by some gang and by parents, police cars began a patrol of the neighborhood but "saw nothing of a serious nature."

Eye-witness accounts, while not in full accord, show that there were "two or three" policemen at the pool, that Negro swimmers were escorted out of the park, that white children would dart in and strike a Negro child, and that this was not prevented by police action. One white adult in particular made lewd and profane remarks, urging the whites to "run the Negroes out of the park." He is believed to have started several rumors, one being that a large number of Negroes were assembling, that they were coming in to beat up and drive out all the whites.

By this time, riotous action had become general. Bicycles ridden by Negro boys were smashed, the boys fighting back but out-numbered. Small groups of whites appeared, all youngsters, armed with baseball bats, stones, a knife, and the like, and highly excitable. They would gather in tight little knots, talk briefly, then run off to attack some Negro who had been seen, or to escape some Negro group which was said to be coming. The witness making this statement felt that the police were doing a good job at protecting Negro youth but doing nothing to disperse the white crowd which kept growing.

For the rest of the day, reports of scattered fights and attacks came in to the Fifth District Police Station. At the park itself, police continued to protect Negro children and adults from injury, confiscated a knife and some clubs but not the baseball bats. When the pool closed at five o'clock as usual, most of the crowd dispersed. Several hoodlum-type white adults continued to advise the boys on how to handle Negroes—"kill the bastards, bash their heads in."

A reporter states that, about 6:20 P.M., he had word that the Mayor had rescinded the order opening pools to Negroes, but the Fairgrounds Park custodian said that he had not been so informed. When, at 6:49 P.M., the superintendent arrived and was advised of the Mayor's action, he phoned the Commissioner for instructions. The Commissioner said he had heard of no change in policy, that the pool was to be run on a nonsegregated basis.

At this time, there were two hundred or more youth and adults at the pool, waiting ostensibly for it to open. Only a few Negroes were in the crowd, perhaps about twenty, and after repeated taunts and threats of violence, they left the park. As darkness came, the crowd grew more and more excited, some parts fracturing off to go in pursuit of Negroes who had been sighted. Fights were general, in spite of police presence, with an unknown number of Negroes brutally beaten. A call was put in for police reinforcements and ambulances, after which a riot call was made, bringing 150 police officers. A semblance of order was established, though the wrecking of automobiles and destruction of other property, along with outbursts of street fighting, continued until at least 9:30 o'clock that evening.

In all of this disorder, seven persons were arrested—three whites and four Negroes. Three of the latter and one white were charged with inciting to riot but warrants were refused by the prosecuting attorney. Four Negroes and two whites were charged with general peace disturbance but not taken into custody. When they appeared in court, the cases were dismissed. One white was charged with interfering with a police officer, pleaded guilty, and was fined $5.00. At least twelve persons required hospitalization or first aid, with six seriously injured. No estimate of property damage was attempted.

This, then, is the Fairgrounds Park incident, starting with an order from a city recreational official which the mayor much later on rescinded, to the dismay of Negroes. In the Schermer report, several pages are given to *background factors*, the nature of the St. Louis community.

In St. Louis, as in many cities, two large ethnic stocks live, work, learn, worship, etc., within the same community, but on respective sides of a traditional color line. Sometimes this line is plain to see, but often it is like Mark Twain's equator, "invisible but very real." To understand recurrent violence in the city's history, one must grasp the play of forces that are forever putting new strains on the color line.

The great majority of the city's Negro people live in a narrow and congested area running from the river westward, with small scatterings in other parts of town. In 1900 Negroes made up 6.2 percent of the total population, and in 1946, 14.3 percent. Over this period the total population increased 31 percent, the Negro population 234 percent. This figure alone tells a big story, the ever-growing pressure put upon housing, jobs, schooling, recreation, and so on. Incoming Negro workers have taken areas vacated by white families as they moved to better places, but the change-over is seldom complete. Resident whites are concerned to keep old *status quo* restrictions, borderline areas fear invasion, and Negroes demand increasingly their full citizen rights.

The general pattern of segregation is much like that found in other border-state cities. Both races work together in factories, stores, hotels, and restaurants. Certain jobs are for whites, other jobs are for Negroes. Workers pass the time of day, help each other out, joke together, and become friends, but job lines are fairly stable. In some factories, they are beginning to be crossed, and in certain city and government work they do not exist or are breaking down. Mostly, however, the preferred work is for whites, the low-pay jobs for Negroes.

In going to school, children cross pathways but do not mingle. The Missouri Constitution requires separate schools, saying that this law may be changed if the people wish. A bill is before the legislature to permit institutions of higher learning to admit students without regard to race. Catholic schools are open to all students, a rule enforced by the bishop on threat of excommunication.

In some Catholic parishes, Negroes and whites worship together. In Protestant churches, there is almost total segregation, although both races join together in many religious services and in federated councils and committees.

Negroes and whites attend separate movie theaters. In the city's three major parks, on municipal tennis courts and golf courses, there are no official restrictions. In team play and organized athletics, *de facto* segregation exists. Nearly all restaurants outside the major Negro district refuse to serve Negroes, and all hotels are segregated. On street cars and buses, in the municipal auditorium, at the civic opera, in city-run cafeterias, in downtown stores, no restrictions exist. In sum, the color line is present, the walls are there, but where and what they are is a matter for exact study. They shift, too, with time, giving a little, firming up a little, so that every study requires a date line.

As to interracial attitudes, such studies as have been made of race riots in East St. Louis, Chicago, Detroit, and elsewhere, show a mounting tension prior to the outbreak of violence. This is a period of rumor-making, of vague alarms, of incipient street fights and incidents. In the Fairgrounds Park conflict, little data could be found as to the state of feelings, the gradual mounting of hostility. Police reports, a barometer often used, show little increase in assault and robbery cases across racial lines. Only two stench bombings of Negro homes and one arson were recorded on the blotter in the six months prior to the swimming pool affair.

On the day of the outbreak, June 21, whites and Negroes played and swam together in other parts of the city without incidents. Only a few assaults of whites on Negroes or vice versa were reported on the days following the rioting. Three days after the violence, two baseball games were played between Negro and white teams at the Fairgrounds Park, as if by agreement the violence was over and best forgotten. Of course, it is unlikely that any of these players, perhaps few of the thousands of spectators, had any hand in the swimming pool incident. They had heard, no doubt, about the trouble, read about it under front-page headings in the city press.

An attitude survey made by a local planning council in February 1949 showed strong dissatisfaction among Negroes as to jobs, housing, and costs of living. Other tensions were named, including lack of educational and recreational facilities. A third of the respondents felt that whites and Negroes were getting along better than they had been, a third could see no change, and a sixth stated that relations were worse than formerly. A full third reported unpleasant and discriminating contacts with whites.

An Urban League study found that white attitudes toward Negroes were based more upon tradition than knowledge. It pointed out that, while St. Louis was not "a typical southern city," it showed most of the patterns which regulate the two races in the South. The same study also commented on "the lack of aggressive leadership among both liberal Negroes and whites in seeking to combat prejudice and discrimination."

In a final weighing of situational evidence, Schermer came to four general conclusions:

1. St. Louis did not show prior to the June 21 riots, nor has it since experienced, "a high level of interracial tension." On the one day, tension was high, but it subsided as quickly as it had developed.
2. "A large part" of the white community holds little malice toward Negroes as long as the latter accommodate themselves to traditional caste patterns.
3. There is a strong undercurrent of tension and resentment among Negroes, "not so much toward whites as toward caste restrictions which limit Negro opportunities."
4. Negro resentment is not being strongly expressed for lack of aggressive Negro leadership. Hostility can readily strengthen "if the whole city does not take immediate steps to remove the restrictions and discriminations now present."

Put in still broader terms, the city was found to be "psychologically unprepared" to undertake the readjustments which a growing Negro population, changing social and economic conditions, are forcing on the community. It is not a case, as the report states, "of some people wanting to move too fast, but rather of a large majority wanting to move too slowly."

The next point of interest centers about an effort to fix responsibility for recreational segregation, a question pursued with cautious realism. The Commissioner of Parks stated frankly that playgrounds, community centers, indoor and outdoor pools, etc., were segregated, showing a map. Asked as to the basis of determination, that is, white or Negro, he shrugged his shoulders and said that he had "inherited this. It depends on pressures within the locality. We try to work out an arrangement that will please both groups." Asked the same question, the superintendent made much the same answer. "It depends," he said, "upon predominant use." When it was pointed out that "predominant use" was impossible if a playground, say, were segregated, his answer was: "We try to please everybody. That is all."

Questioned further on these matters, both city officials took the stand that neither "had had much trouble" for "pretty well everybody in St. Louis knows the line." Asked if staff meetings were held in the recreation department at which race relations were discussed, the superintendent replied, "No, we never have. We never thought it was necessary." The Commissioner admitted that no survey had ever been made as to the equity of city recreational facilities in terms of population needs. He commented on "the woeful lack of facilities" in the city as a whole.

When the Commissioner was questioned about the large and powerful Municipal Athletic Association, a game-scheduling body, he affirmed that it was a private group. He denied that a member of his department devoted full time to its affairs but admitted that Negroes were excluded by it. Sifting this evidence, Schermer came to the conclusion that the association was "only technically separated" from the Division of Parks and Recreation, hence that the latter in effect "gave official sanction and support to racial segregation of play facilities."

What, now, were the findings in this complex situation? They are reported under six main headings.

1. Why was the order opening swimming pools issued? Because Negroes had challenged segregation. Having no legal basis on which to continue exclusion, the responsible public official opened city pools. There was no conference about this, no planning for it; in sum no preparation was made.

2. What started the rioting? Good evidence indicates that street gangs of young white "toughs" set off the crowd, turning vague fears, unrests, and excitements into mob action and violence. Negroes escaped and/or fought back, rumors spread, with rioting dying out as quickly as it had begun.

3. Did police handle the situation well? They did stop the rioting

in good time, considering that they had not been forewarned and were not present in force when violence began. They had no orders from city administration as to what to do, which ruling to enforce. In criticism, they were caught off guard and unprepared. They permitted the crowd to assemble in a threatening manner, but at the same time protected Negroes from injury.

4. What of hate groups and subversive forces? Both fascist-type and communist groups exist in the city, each trying to make capital out of any critical situation. There is no evidence to show that either led the rioting or tried to incite to riot, although both stand ready to sabotage interracial good-will movements.

5. How did press and radio behave? No study was made of the effects of news on the public. The initial Webster Groves story was improperly handled as between city officials and the press. Press and radio reports of the rioting were not exaggerated or inflammatory. Conferences should be undertaken to develop policies for handling race news.

6. What of public responsibility? The St. Louis community, its people and its leaders, must bear a measure of responsibility for the Fairgrounds Park disturbance. Without a seedbed of hostility, of fear and suspicion, rioting is impossible, so that the need for realistic interracial planning is plainly evident. Planning should deal with immediate change and long-term education in democratic human values.

Recommendations cover more than four pages and need no detailed summary. Approach is through the medium of the functions of government (city) in meeting the needs, and protecting the rights, of all citizens, including recreational activities. It is assumed that government must always be concerned with civic education, with teaching people to understand one another, to work together for the common welfare.

It is suggested that city officials be advised that exclusion of any person from any public facility because of race is contrary to law, that all responsible civic leaders urge public officials to adhere to the law, that city outdoor pools be reopened to swimmers, regardless of race, at such time as deemed feasible, and that equal rights laws be enforced.

Further recommendations are that the mayor take initiative in arranging meetings of civic leaders, municipal officials, news editors, etc., to develop a public relations and educational program for the ending of segregation, both mandatory and customary, and for the securing and protection of civil rights for all people.

In such a complex situation various emphases could be made.

Our concern is not with rioting, a behavior well studied by sociologists,[5] or with St. Louis, a place that seems no better and no worse than a number of other large cities. The Fairgrounds Park case was used to frame a sequence of concrete events, moving from tensions through competition and conflict to recommendations for preventive action. That violence might have occurred had ordinary precautions been taken is plausible; yet the wisdom of opening public outdoor pools to Negroes without any study of area sentiment, any preparation of police or briefing of swimmers, is highly questionable. Where does responsibility for violence really lie? Where—if the question has any real significance—but in city officials, civic leaders, news disseminators, even in educators! It is the hope of group-process workers that unity councils, committees, and the like, can prevent such recurring battles in our society, lift us further from the jungle ethics they suggest.

THE URBAN PLANNING SITUATION

Is there a need, a real need, for urban area planning? The most general answer is found in the ever more chaotic conditions of big-city life, the extremes of living arrangements, the impersonality of human relations, the ceaseless push and haul of conflicting groups. Let us put a piece of this society under the microscope, a residential section of Detroit a few miles from the downtown area.

UNITY-DISUNITY, A CHALLENGE TO PLANNERS

Seven miles north of Detroit's downtown center, starting at Six Mile Road, lies an area known to the city's Council of Social Agencies as the Northern District. Here are 128,000 people. Who are they? What are their modes of life, their current civic problems, area groupings, and aspirations? We cannot, of course, answer in detail.

About 87 percent of area residents are white, 13 percent Negro. Thirty-two nationalities are represented, chiefly new immigrant stocks such as Polish, Italian, and Roumanian. At least 40 percent of area dwellers are foreign-born, and many native-born whites and Negroes are in-migrants, chiefly from the South. Forty percent of all employed persons are low-skilled factory workers, 30 percent in skilled trades, about 20 percent in clerical and business pursuits, and 6 percent in professions. A third of the people are Catholic, including members of

---

[5] For analysis of the 1942 Detroit riots, see Alfred M. Lee and Norman D. Humphrey, *Race Riot* (New York: Dryden, 1943).

one Negro Catholic church. There are seventy-eight Protestant churches, ranging from major creeds to store-front missions.

We have spoken about churches, a conspicuous form of area organization. A more dynamic force in certain civic matters is the so-called "real estate interest," meaning, in part, eleven "home owners' associations" organized to prevent property sale to "undesirables." The area has seven large housing projects, including the "Sojourner Truth" homes where whites and Negroes have had knock-down battles. Party politics is much in evidence, for instance, there is a "Roumanian-Democratic" club. There are nineteen public schools and seven parochial schools, each a complete system up to the high school level. No exact count has been made of the many small clubs—neighborhood centers, leagues, Scouts, and the like.

What of civic life and social behavior? Here the picture is much the same as for other heterogeneous lower-middle to lower class urban segments. One can find many evidences of good will and good works, for example, the concern of adults for youth, the time taken to organize health and recreational services. In some precincts, 7 percent of the males over ten years of age have been arrested. On various other indices of social well-being, area rates are low, yet not as low as found in slum residential sections. They are, some data show, about average for the total city.

Enough has been said to show the nature of this social segment— the bodily nearness of people, their diverse backgrounds, their "uncommon" and contradictory ways of life. Minutes covering initial meetings of an area "community council" (a voluntary association of local service agencies) are a tangled skein of value clashes. The council's formal constitution is beautiful to read, saying all that anyone could wish about unity and brotherhood, a language heard in council meetings. But, on the action level, good works are jammed up. For all council members except a handful, brotherhood cannot be extended across racial lines, even though Negro organizations in the area have pleaded for admission. To state the near certainty that a Negro "community" council will be started, that intercouncil competition is inevitable, has not changed white opinion. To add that exploitive interests, real estate and otherwise, find this situation pat for their uses, has also been ineffective.

UNITY-DISUNITY AND GROUP ACTION

One might judge from the two cases given that there is no peace in our society, that its people live in covert warfare. We have made a great deal of this view in past chapters because the need for more cooperation seems evident; yet the disunity idea must not be carried to extremes. No community could exist without a basic integration, a structure of order, including an accepted way of settling value clashes. Figure 5 attempts to show this basic unity both as a process over a period of time and as a state or condition at a given time.

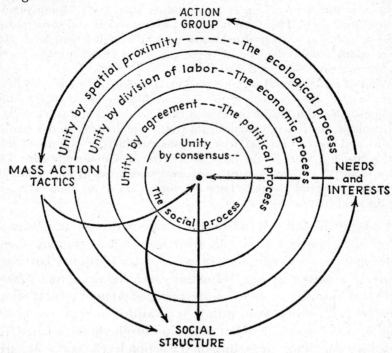

Fig. 5.—A view of community unity as a condition and as a process (*arrows*). From Cook and Cook, *A Sociological Approach to Education* (New York: McGraw-Hill Book Co., 1950), p. 193. Used by permission.

If, in Figure 5, the arrows are followed, it will be seen that civic action has its origins in the impulse of some person, the feeling of need for say a health program for disadvantaged school children. Should this person speak to a friend, who speaks to a friend, and so on, or else address a public meeting, his concern may find instant acceptance. It may move directly to the area in the diagram marked "consensus," then on to some institution for its realization. In these present times, however, and notably in large cities, most civic impulses must travel the outer rim of the circle, gathering support and, at the same time, creating opposition. Mass tactics come into play, organized campaigns, with the public will eventually recorded in the ballots cast for and against the proposal. Since we shall return to this action process presently, further comment here can be deferred.

Unity as a state or condition is seen within the circles, each depicting a type of area cohesion. There is the togetherness of people that comes from general consensus, the "growing alike" by absorption of common core values. This is a unity of custom, not of logic, a sharing of moral norms and emotional involvements. Unity by agreement is what most writers mean by community unity, a deliberate and rational process. This is integration through debate and decision, the rule in a democracy of the majority. Unity by division of labor involves economic processes which need not concern us here, except to venture that they are basic to every social and political order. Much the same seems true of ecological interdependence, the foundational interrelations of organic forms.

In respect to human relations, it is relevant to note that social unity problems differ from, say, a problem of personal health. Everyone, we can assume, wants a sick man to get well, his family, his physician, employer. With community problems, the situation is different. Gains mean losses to some people as they view the matter. Put otherwise, *values cost values,* whether they consist of material goods or status ratings. The ordinary solution is, therefore, a balancing of one side against the other, ending usually in a compromise not fully satisfactory to either side, yet the best bargain that can be driven. Area problem-solving lies, therefore, well within the political process; hence it is a matter of organized group action.

GOAL CONFLICTS AT POLICY LEVEL

Few social planning groups, in our experience, feel the need to think much about unity-disunity problems, to consider the logic of their change efforts. They want, they assert, to increase unity, to further brotherhood, to improve the community, to make life better for people. The need is for action, the quicker the better, and why waste time in talk! Everybody who is anybody will know what ought to be done. The work task is to arouse feelings, to raise funds, and start things happening. At such moments, a logician is a poor prop, a drag upon the group. He seems to say by his attitude, if not in so many words, that he has traveled this road before, that there are problems, that a little more time spent in planning will pay off.

One aspect of this situation involves group dynamics, the interplay of ends and means in collective action. At times, issues are tactical, centering on methods, timing, and the like, a point to which we shall return. At other times, as in the Detroit case and no doubt at St. Louis, debate turns on major goals, the over-all value orientations. Much worse than a sharp debate on tactical problems —and it can be hard to handle—is the situation where group members sit silent, giving no clue to their deepest feelings. If lack of vocal opposition is taken to mean the approval of group policy, this mistake can prove costly to a planning group. We speak with concern on the point because of the extremes to which most group leaders will go in order to avoid basic goal conflicts, deep cleavages which they do not, of course, create, yet may find quite impossible to ignore.

Prime examples of goal conflicts in policy-making can be seen in industrial relations, or rather in labor union objections to management personnel methods. In a concrete case, two out of three girls were needed for Sunday work.[6] All three said they had dates; hence, none wanted to work. Any solution the person in charge might present would, obviously, meet resistance. The problem was put up to the girls. As they talked it over, one girl had a date with girls, which all three agreed was not a real date; hence, this girl said she would work. Another girl had a date with a new man, and the third with the man to whom she was engaged. Again all three agreed that an engaged girl could change her date, thus admitting that the new date should be given priority. The first and third girls went to work, in spite of the fact that the second girl had least seniority and had worked less often on Sunday.

On first glance, this seems an amicable way to handle a bad

[6] From Norman R. F. Maier, "Improving Supervision through Training," in Arthur Kornhauser (ed.), *Psychology of Labor-Management Relations* (Champaign, Ill.: Industrial Relations Institute, 1949), pp. 56–57.

impasse, more sensible than for the boss to point a finger. But a labor-union spokesman, commenting on the case, saw it from quite a different angle.

If the factory were organized, the problem would be handled by asking the girls whether they would be willing to work on Sunday in the first place. There would be no implied assumption that the girls' dates after working hours were any less important than the employer's production problem. If the girls are not willing to work after regular working hours, the employer is expected to seek a different solution to his production problem. This makes the real difference between real democracy, where power is distributed between the employer and the working force, and play-acting democracy, where all problems are solved on the basis of the satisfaction of the employer's achievement of his objectives.[7]

We believe this quote should be studied with care, for it contains the essence of a philosophy in sharp contrast to the way intergroup education is developing in the nation. The real point is how good works can be done, how human needs can be met. This includes, in final analysis, the meaning of democracy itself. Thomas Jefferson once observed that the good health of a democracy does not lie in the "idyllic cooing" of the lion and the lamb, the boss and the worker, even the majority group and the minorities of the nation. It rests in *the mutual distrust of contending groups,* the seesaw bargaining at the conference table, with no group permitting another absolute power. Groups would function together through compromise, preferably through negotiations with all the cards on the table.

While this viewpoint is still uncommon in civic meetings, it is increasing in big cities and spreading fast to intergroup relations. There is nothing conciliatory about it, no assumption that might makes right, that a top power group is good or kind or even intelligent about its actions. There is no evidence that friendly cooperation is a positive value, that it is possible on matters that really count. It is assumed, on the contrary, that there are the haves and have-nots, much as Karl Marx taught, and that the latter will win only what their strength can command. Where this outlook has prevailed in civic action, the campaign for rights has

[7] William Gomberg in *ibid.*, p. 56. Used by permission.

been conducted along labor-union lines.[8] If this viewpoint gains wide following, as now seems likely, the only possible prediction is for bigger and better battles between the ins and outs, each intent on building its own combative efficiency.

We do not state this view in order to argue against it, for the entire volume we hope is a counterargument. The question to be faced is what a unity advocate is to do, how he is to work in basic goal-conflict situations. Certainly Gomberg's "play-acting democracy" must be ruled out, and "power-sharing democracy" ruled in. Make-believe may be valid for little children, but community co-ordination to solve civil rights problems is no child's game. It has—to repeat, a reality about it, a bitter tautness, that anyone accustomed to the atmosphere of college classrooms can readily misjudge.

Assuming the presence of hostile viewpoints, we have seldom found it good policy to by-pass them, to act as if they did not exist. On the contrary, our tendency has been to bring them out, to use our office to see that they get a fair hearing. We call these "risks" which the group must face as it moves forward with its program, listing them if possible on a blackboard. On occasion, as time goes on, the group is asked to review this list, to cross out items which, by full agreement of members, are no longer obstacles to progress. The theory is that these hostilities are repressed fears, that they block integrative thinking, that therapeutic treatment is necessary. As a rule, we do not argue against any risk, bring the force of logic to bear upon it, but rather try to guide the interaction of group members, allowing interpersonal pressures to operate.

Strategies in Good-Will Planning

In past sections we have run ahead of our story, omitting some very practical matters. Broadly viewed, an area-wide attack on discrimination differs little from any other long-run civic campaign. Whether the community is large or small, good-will forces can do little unless they are organized. In most big cities, this has taken the form of a council on human relations, as in St. Louis, or a mayor's committee, intercultural commission, or the like. Each

---

[8] For example, Saul Alinsky, *Reveille for Radicals* (Chicago: University of Chicago Press, 1945).

structure is a situational product, adapted to local mores in ways that only case study could disclose. What we wish to do is to generalize for a score of these councils, the ones encountered in College Study work.

ELEMENTS IN COUNCIL
ORGANIZATION

1. Underlying principles
2. Structural framework
3. Basic objectives
4. Relation to other bodies
5. Action-oriented research
6. Channels of influence
7. Propaganda materials
8. Appraised effects
9. Risk calculations

It has seemed to us that these are basic elements in the councils we have studied, foundational factors in their human relations work. While the list is meant to show sequential order from an organizational viewpoint, councils have had to plan over-all strategy in reference to the whole, to consider each point in relation to others. Risk calculation in particular is the pivot on which much thought must turn, the best guessing possible as to chances of the success of a program.

Councils are, as a rule, the product of a crisis in intergroup relations, for example, the 1942 race riots in Detroit where 31 persons were killed. An aroused citizenry, indignant, ashamed, and confused, wants to make certain that intergroup violence will be stopped, that it will never recur. Councils tend to focus on symptoms, not on causes, on action that is presumed to get quick-term, decisive results. Were it possible to advise such a group before it began to function, what underlying principles of strategy might be stressed?

MacIver[9] has covered this question, discussing points that any council would find useful to consider. Our emphasis would be

---

[9] R. M. MacIver, *The More Perfect Union*, pp. 244–68. For well-argued strategies in anti-Semitic action, see David Riesman, "The Politics of Persecution," *Public Opinion Quarterly*, Spring 1942; "Equality and the Social Structure," *Journal of Legal and Political Sociology*, I, 1942; "Democracy and Defamation," *Columbia Law Review*, XLII (1942), pp. 727–80, 1085–1123.

somewhat different but not enough to develop at length. Of prime
importance is a leadership that will insure council respectability,
adequate funds, and technical efficiency. Minorities should be well
represented, as should all the major governmental, sociocivic, and
educational agencies in the spatial area. Attack should center both
on prejudice and discrimination, for they interact and reinforce
each other. Goals should be stated in terms of public welfare and
equal rights, rather than as an effort to improve the lot of some
disadvantaged group. Care should be taken not to give the impression that interracial or other integration will be forced.

Council action should be begun on as many fronts as possible,
starting with public services to which all citizens are entitled. Unless government itself (jobs, relief, public schools, parks, and playgrounds, and so on) can be fair in its treatment of people, we have
never had much hope for changes elsewhere. Action should be
adapted to the local situation, with initial effort pointed toward
lines of least resistance, inequities most vulnerable to attack. The
idea here is to give council workers the feel of success, and to allay
community fears that a full-scale revolution is in progress. A great
deal of council action will be designed to reach the public through
publicity, but some of it should be in closed sessions with key
persons in positions to facilitate the struggle for equal rights.

From a structural standpoint, a human relations council may
be set up as an arm of city government, as a voluntary civic body,
or as an agency coordinating service. If it is an operational group,
solving problems in its own right, it will likely have a modified
line-and-staff organization, reaching down from a paid executive
secretary and staff, assisted by an advisory council, to various working committees of lay citizens. As a coordinating body, its members will have complete autonomy, simply meeting together to
interrelate their programs. In any case, a central body is needed;
yet the need is equally great for peripheral groupings, for they
can do things that no downtown office can do. This is, we believe,
a weakness in big-city council structure, an inability to see that
not all urban neighborhoods are inert, that even block units in
some parts of a city might be necessary to prevent such incidents
as the swimming-pool trouble in St. Louis.[10]

[10] For theories of neighborhood organization, see *The Neighborhood Unit Plan—
Its Spread and Acceptance* (New York: Russell Sage Foundation, 1947); Walter

Action-oriented research, to take another point in the list, should be envisioned as a continuing council function. One type of study might be a tension barometer, a periodic collection of data such as police calls or the regular reports of lay volunteer workers in various parts of the area. Another type of study would focus on basic sociological trends, for instance vital statistics, population shifts, employment conditions, and housing shortages. In the third place, a council should be prepared to make spot studies where intergroup conflict does break out, keeping a cumulative file of interview data from which general conclusions might be drawn. In all such studies, a council could well coordinate with university research interests and facilities, providing any university with excellent opportunity for student education.

By channels of influence, the sixth item in the list, is meant the communications system in which people live, the dictum of John Dewey that society not only exists *in* communication but *is* communication. Propaganda materials, the purposive transmission of values, are the stimuli which flow over these communication lines —factual data, emotional appeal, official policy, and so forth. One central problem is to determine the various publics which, in interaction, make up the general public on any issue. If these facts were known, council publicity could then be designed and directed to the various kinds and levels of people who should be reached. Civic unity movements, in particular, good-will agencies, are severely criticized on these points,[11] and it is with satisfaction that we note the analytical work done by some national organizations.[12]

TACTICS IN CIVIC PROGRAM BUILDING

If strategy means the theory of planful change, tactics comprise concrete practices. Operational procedures have better pragmatic tests that do broad lines of strategical thinking so that one can

---

Gropius, "Organic Neighborhood Planning," *Housing and Town and Country Planning,* United Nations Bulletin, 2, April 1949, pp. 2–8. We are not inclined to go nearly as far as even these writers have done in their emphasis on "the neighborhood point of view." Further comment can be found on p. 245.

[11] Benedict Glazer, "A Re-Evaluation of the Good-Will Movement," reprinted from *Yearbook* of the Central Conference of American Rabbis, Vol. LII (Philadelphia: Jewish Publication Society, 1917).

[12] A case in point is Samuel H. Flowerman, "Mass Propaganda in the War against Bigotry," *Journal of Abnormal and Social Psychology,* XLII (1947), pp. 429–39.

speak with a little more assurance about them. Consider, to illustrate, a mine-run community case, say, a dispute between Negroes
and whites as to occupancy of a low-cost governmental housing
project. How would an adviser from a unity council assist in settling this issue? To add that "it depends . . . ." is necessary, for
tactics are processual adaptations, varying somewhat with each
successive event.

A good way to start would be to assume that words may not
mean what they seem to mean, that meanings must be extracted.
One will then be watchful for verbal symbols, behavioral gestures,
any kind of obscure sign which will indicate feelings, intent, and
resolve. As group members interact, are there evidences of frustration and aggression, of past battles and deep-seated carry-overs?
Are power alignments indicated, cliques and combinations of
vested interests? How hopeful are these people that the problem
can be solved? At what reality level are thought and action possible? Is group leadership authoritarian or democratic, by member
preference or against it?

Assuming that democratic action is desirable, this fact will set
a number of crucial limitations. The basic feature of democratic
leadership is not to sell an idea, or put it over, or sneak it through.
It is to lodge responsibility for decision-making in the group and,
at the same time, safeguard the discussion process against the
risks that it must run. Leader functions are two: one inviting, the
other guiding. Both are exercised above board and *with unques-
tionable honesty of intent.*

A common dilemma of leadership will help to clarify these
points. With "solutions" to a given problem coming from all quarters, how is one to know which proposal best represents the entire
group? Standard practice is to vote the issue, to decide by majority
rule; yet the procedure may have serious consequences. While
losers are expected to be good sports, they often assume an opposite
role. Their positive motivations may be weakened, their work
output drop off. At worst, a group is divided into pros and antis,
a cleavage that can harden into set opposition. To reduce these
hazards, a leader can work for full agreement in the group. He
can assume the need for more data or for a better sharing of ideas.
He can encourage compromise proposals or appoint a committee to
restudy the issue.

We have spoken of group responsibility for decision-making as if it were an easy thing to achieve, a matter of telling people that they have power to act. In some cases, a group will dodge decision-making, at times in very artful ways. Its members may prefer to argue rather than to think, to let George do it (especially the leader) rather than to work themselves, to call for more and more facts until the issue itself grows stale. As a last resort we have found no better tactic than to face this problem directly with the group. One can say that a new situation has arisen, the problem of how to solve problems from the group's standpoint. Discussion of escapist tendencies, assuming that it comes from inside the group, can diminish this waste of time and effort. If tensionality dictates a less direct approach, the situation is pat for a sociodrama depicting group-member roles, followed by analysis of these behaviors in relation to group aims.

The prime purpose of group action is not, we believe, to meet and socialize, to have fun in therapeutic release, to appease a guilty conscience by going through the motions of democracy. The purpose is civic problem-solving, *the democratic designing of changes in community life*. While good tactics are great timesavers and goal insurers, they are not ends in themselves. They must not be confused with fundamental objectives or used to push past situations where these objectives are not clear. For example, no meeting of minds can occur unless the group atmosphere itself encourages free expression, a climate in which any person can speak without fear or favor. How to maintain this permissiveness is, of course, a tactical problem, and a difficult one at that.

To clarify the situation, there are several things a leader can do. He can inform a meeting, first off, of the limits in which action is possible, the areas where the group has authority, the need of fitting into some larger plan. If the leader briefs the group on specific issues, as he well may do—assuming his prior study—these matters should be put as problems to be solved, not as past actions for which he now needs confirmation. Thirdly, a leader will have facts (or access to them) which other persons do not possess. Instead of using his knowledge to discredit ideas as they are advanced by participants, such data should be given to the group before time is spent on meaningless arguments. To encourage participation, a fourth point, a leader should seldom rule out any idea as irrelevant, but rather ask how it bears on the problem, or if it could be deferred until a certain time. Minority views in particular must be protected—a major function of leadership in any kind of intergroup situation.

If regimentation is to be avoided, if smugness, strictness, and so on are no good, every democratic leader needs ways of keeping a group problem-centered. Some leaders run off into "play-acting democracy" as described by Gomberg; others worry long in indecision or else show marked inconsistency. One corrective is to react to meanings, in preference to terms, to try to figure what a person wants to say, that is, the fears he may be unwilling to put into so many words. Exploratory questions are useful, for example: do you mean so and so, how could that be done, or are there other ideas? Brief summary reviews will refocus attention, as well as show the group that progress is being made. Face-saving devices are important, simple ways of restoring member status and preventing ego hurt. Humor is a tension breaker, provided people can laugh together, or at a leader, rather than at one another.

THE PROBLEM OF RISK CALCULATION

While risk thinking has been implicit in past sections, attention to it will suggest the force of external factors on group strategies and tactics. Consider again the St. Louis case. Assuming the unwisdom of reopening at once the city pools under police guard, the council on human relations would try no doubt to increase interracial cooperation in less controverted phases of community life. While council thought would spread over several areas, much of it would deal with potential opposition to an increasingly vigorous civil rights program. Prime aims would be to reduce existing anti-Negro feelings, keep a countermovement from arising, and strengthen generally city-wide fair-treatment tendencies.

One can see some of the complications implicit in any large-scale action-oriented program by reference to an abstract formula. The formula given below is not meant to be a true algebraic equation but rather a schematic relation of variables. Strength factors, for example, are diminished by weakness factors, not divided by them.

$$\left(\frac{DS}{GC + V + F}\right)_{AG} = \frac{PE_1}{(A, DG)_{GP}},$$

where $_{AG}$ elements indicate the *action group*, such as the St. Louis Council on Human Relations, and $_{GP}$ elements the *general public*, in relation to

$$\left(\frac{DS}{GC + V + F}\right)_{OG} = \frac{PE_2}{(A, DG)_{GP}},$$

with the $_{OG}$ elements representing the *opposition group* at work on the same general public.[13]

To solve the "equation" for PE_1, the *productive effect* of council action, one would have to assess the council's *development strength* as the action program moves through time. This strength would be in theory a composite of factors—involvement of members, use of resources, leader insight, morale conditions, and so on. Whatever this strength was found to be, it would be diminished by three kinds of internal factors. One is marked GC, indicating probable *goal conflicts* among council members. To this predictable weakness in democratic group action a V factor *vacillation* (and deflection) of members has been added, plus an F factor, the normal drain of *fatigue* in any prolonged work effort.

In the $_{GP}$ phase of the formula, the *general public* is assumed to be the prime target of the action group. If its interest can be captured, its support won, the civil rights movement will succeed; people will have perceived the need for better intergroup relations. By definition, the public is uninformed on the issue, uncommitted to an active concern for any minority group in the city. In minimal appraisal, a public must be assessed for A, *apathy*, and DG, *divergent goals*, the latter indicative of its many and varied divisive forces. At the time a council starts action, most publics will contain some sort of opposition group or groups, but these have not been listed in the formula on assumption that they can be circumvented through planful program preparation.

The second half of the equation develops a contrary assumption, the idea that opposition will arise and strengthen to the point where it becomes a decisive force in council calculations. The first

---

[13] Adapted from Lloyd and Elaine Cook, *A Sociological Approach to Education* (New York: McGraw-Hill Book Co., 1950), pp. 421–22. Used by permission.

half of this formula is the same as that explained for council operation, with $_{og}$ denoting the *opposition group* or groups. To solve for PE_2, the procedure would be that followed in respect to PE_1, with the probability of identical group-process behaviors. The idea that anti forces are communistic "hate groups" may or may not be true.[14] Honest, civic-minded people may oppose innovations in interracial or other relations, as is their democratic right.

An aspect of this problem worth comment is the matter of value orientations. Whatever the appeal made, the recurring themes are two, each divisible into two further categories.

I. Utilitarian theme $\begin{cases} \text{Personal, material gain} \\ \text{General public advantage} \end{cases}$

II. Sentimental theme $\begin{cases} \text{Secular ideas, "science shows"} \\ \text{Sacred doctrines and symbols} \end{cases}$

Little by little a literature is building up on the uses made of these values to win public assent, to shape attitudes and to motivate action, with intergroup education standing to profit from these varied researches.[15] Personal gain in our culture is, we suspect, the greatest single motivator of individual action, the material self-interests of the actor. Where these gains can be claimed for the public, or a segment of it, social pressure (or group interaction) increases their force. Sentimental values, in contrast to utilitarian, are seldom couched in individual terms. Whether the appeal is secular or sacred, "do something for children" or the "fatherhood of God, the brotherhood of man," the worth of a cause is reckoned in terms of what people will give to it, not what they hope to gain from it.

It is, perhaps, a telling index of our lack of knowledge, rather than of popular ignorance of science, to admit, first, that the same lines of reasoning or emotional appeal are made by both sides in human rights controversies, and secondly, that no scientist so far as we know has the data to underwrite one prediction (hope, fear, doubt) and refute the other.

The Detroit case is a typical instance. It will be recalled that

[14] For a recent study of "hate groups" in the nation, see Arnold Forster, *A Measure of Freedom* (Garden City, N.Y.: Doubleday & Co., 1950).
[15] For example, Robert K. Merton, *Mass Persuasion* (New York: Harper & Bros., 1946).

Negro representatives were not admitted to the Northern Community Council. While this action was asserted to represent white majority sentiment, it was defended on both utilitarian and sentimental grounds. For example, real estate statistics were quoted by white speakers to prove that rent and sale prices were lowered by Negro settlement in the area: "hence, Negroes should be kept out of the council." Negro spokesmen, on the other hand, cited statistics to prove the exact opposite, namely, "the exploitive costs" of homes to Negro families. To add that both sides made use of identical sacred symbols needs no specific illustration. Every community movement, from the "torch drive" on, uses home, heaven, and patriotic motivations. In human history, people have always been ready to fight for causes they considered worthy, even to die for them, whether or not they understood them.

FUNCTIONS OF THE EDUCATOR

To conclude, let us look again at the point with which we started, the idea of investment. If one puts time into a cause, or money or effort, it appears prudent—as was said—to give thought to the matter, to protect whatever has been invested. Business counts on this concern and so do civic movements. Laws safeguard commercial undertakings much more than they do adventures in good will, one assumption being that good works will result from good intentions.

Here a civic investor faces a considerable problem. Few social action groups can really know the effectiveness of their activities, the exact amount of anything (good will, social change, democracy) their money buys. Moreover, if these organizations had the facts, it is doubtful if they could report them fully to a fund-giving public without endangering its confidence and support. General publics cannot understand the complexities of ameliorative efforts, nor are they conditioned to support experimental ventures. "The case must be made plain to people," said an agency head, "and it must be presented with assurance that the results anticipated will be forthcoming." Being an honest man, a trained professional worker, this speaker felt that all such fund-raising agencies faced a genuine dilemma.

Under such conditions, what is an educator to do? In the first place, some choice of causes is necessary. Which causes are most needful, which ones most promising of desired effects? Secondly, a teacher can inform himself as to the workings of a social action group, its personnel and services, much as any conscientious citizen would do. Were any large number of persons to do this much, the effects on civic organizations would be immediate. For one thing, they could admit to doubt, even to failure, in certain phases of their work, dropping much of the present hocus-pocus on which some are inclined to stand. In view of the little that is known, the very modest contributions of social sciences, *failure to effect significant changes in people can be expected*. What the critic should want to know is how intelligent was the effort, how well was it conceived and executed, and what was learned that could prevent further failure.

It is at the next level that we have, for the most part, conceived the educator's functions. As an active worker in community movements, one can *as educator* make valuable contributions to the betterment of intergroup relations. Assuming interest and training, he can bring technical knowledge to lay people, guide them in theory thinking and study methods. He can take a responsible part in policy-making, helping to clarify values and their implications. He can, in particular, be watchful of minority rights, knowing that change without justice is in effect no lasting change at all.

Summing up, the educator's concerns are two: the job to be done and how to do it, topics discussed in this chapter under titles of "strategy" and "tactics." Admittedly, these terms are distasteful to certain workers in the group relations field. They appear to assume a wisdom which we do not have, and to point toward a "manipulation" of people. They seem to detract from the alleged spontaneity of social action movements, a kind of popular uprising motivated by the noblest of sentiments. To us at least, the general perspective is a little different. The democratic ideal is a moral ideal, a concern for human personality, and this ideal is related to another, co-operative action. To these two, a third should be added, the use of intelligence in problem-solving. It is intelligence that underlies strategy and tactics, the disciplined know-how that comes from science and experience.

Part IV

IN POINT OF EMPHASIS

10. A Viewpoint toward Intergroup Education

In the *College Programs* volume, we spoke about a "confusion corner." At workshop after workshop for college leaders, issues would arise to which there was no ready answer, no viewpoint acceptable to all discussants. At first, in jest, these problems were laid away "for future reference," a procedure that became with time a standard policy. Of course, most questions would be re-argued on occasion, often with success, but mainly participants stood pat on their democratic right to differ. It is to this "stockpile" of value-judgments that we shall turn in concluding the volume, for it shows much of the controversy found at present in intergroup education.

One need not know many colleges, if he knows them well, to sense their different conceptions of role and destiny. Any college large or small is a miniature universe, a microcosm. It can reflect the world about it, its confusions and disorders, its increasing loss of human values, its expedient ways of treating people. Or it can assert a leader function, illuminating social life rather than refracting it, *become a beacon rather than a mirror*. It can, on a microscopic scale, create conditions and diffuse ideals which the macrocosm may come to follow. It is from this latter standpoint that "confusion corner" will be examined, not in detail but in terms of a few issues of general concern to professional education.

THEORIES OF OUR SOCIETY

In point of time, the first item filed away for future reference had to do with the general nature of our society, its structure and processes, changes and stabilities. No college representative, certainly no staff consultant, set out to tell in a few easy lessons what our world was like, how the social order functioned. And yet always, at the outer rim of attention, there were these abstract questions, these implicit assumptions that intruded into discussion.

Presently, midway in the second year, the College Study staff began to consider another problem. Some college programs gave evidence of firm rootage, whereas others skittered about, unanchored. Why was this? In the search for an answer, the importance of a fundamental viewpoint became clear. In colleges where study-action projects were unrelated to some over-all impression of society, some conviction as to an institution's role, *activities did not cohere into a program.* They were simply someone's idea of what should be done and, once done, the doing impulse disappeared. In the other type of college, the one with theory thinking, projects added up into a coherent pattern. Moreover, they seemed to create a dynamic, a vision of distant goals which involved conceptions of what our culture could become.

Of all the theories of society that were peddled in the College Study, the one least liked by educators was the Park and Burgess[1] "social process" point of view. Even Marxian ideas,[2] or the complexities of Parsons'[3] "structure-function" analysis, got a better hearing, although neither oriented any local college program. Reactions were most favorable to Warner's and Myrdal's theories of intergroup relations, for observations seemed to support both.

The Park and Burgess theory, still a very common sociological textbook approach, is in essence a cyclical series of stages through which a specific population such as a minority people tends to pass from initial contact with another culture until final assimilation into it. Competition and conflict are heavily stressed, and cooperation is scarcely mentioned. Aside from the fact that this view is highly schematic,[4] it carries an inevitability which is contrary to a major assumption in education, namely, the possibility of breaking "the cycle," the desirability of social control.

[1] R. E. Park and E. W. Burgess, *Introduction to the Science of Sociology* (Chicago: University of Chicago Press, 1924); also R. E. Park, *Race and Culture* (Glencoe, Ill.: Free Press, 1949). For perhaps the best adaptation, see Emory S. Bogardus, "A Race Relations Cycle," *American Journal of Sociology*, January 1930, pp. 612–17.

[2] Oliver C. Cox, *Caste, Class and Race* (Garden City, N.Y.: Doubleday & Co., 1948).

[3] Talcott Parsons, *Structure of Social Action* (New York: McGraw-Hill Book Co., 1936).

[4] Some ethnic groups do not seem to pass through any predictable cycle, for example, Norwegians in farming areas. See John Useem, "Minority-Group Pattern in Prairie Society," *American Journal of Sociology*, L (1945), 377–85.

The Warner "caste-class" hypothesis has been roundly debated in every college in the Study. Since college groups could turn thumbs down on any dubious time use, this statement in itself indicates the appeal of the theory, its applicability to problems of school and community life.

In the original Yankee City Studies,[5] Warner and his associates sought to discover "an organizing principle," an over-all framework, of American community life. This was found in the caste-class system, an hierarchical status order based mainly, we believe, on the ratings people made of people, that is, reputational factors. Castes are color groupings, with whites in top position and non-whites as subordinates. Social classes are found within castes, and are defined as levels or orders of people who associate with one another as intimates and equals. Classes are "open groups," that is, they show some degree of up and down mobility of persons, whereas castes are "closed groups" in the sense that placement in them is life-long as a rule.

From a teaching standpoint much use has been made of these ideas in education courses.[6] Interest has centered on the study of caste-class studies; the culture of upper, middle, and lower classes; individual behaviors and life chances; upward and downward mobility; caste and class in public schools; and school responsibilities in relation to this social system.

In respect to local community study, field projects have suffered from the general unclarity among sociologists and anthropologists as to how stratification is to be done.[7] Warner's Yankee City procedure has been unclear and, we suspect, subjective, making it impossible to follow with precision. These limitations have been corrected to a degree in the recent publication of an ISC scale,[8] a composite of six items: occupation, amount of income, source of

[5] W. Lloyd Warner and Paul S. Lunt, *The Social Life of a Modern Community,* Yankee City Series, Vol. I (New Haven, Conn.: Yale University Press, 1941). The most recent books by Warner, *et al.,* are *Social Class in America* (Chicago: Science Research Associates, 1949), and *Democracy in Jonesville* (New York: Harper & Bros., 1949).

[6] The favorite volume has been Warner, *et al., Who Shall Be Educated?* (New York: Harper & Bros., 1949).

[7] See H. W. Pfautz and O. D. Duncan, "A Critical Evaluation of Warner's *Work in Community Stratification," American Sociological Review,* XV (1950), 205–15.

[8] Index of Status Characteristics. See Warner *et al., Social Class in America.*

income, house type, dwelling area, and education. Hatt[9] points out that this scale is a step toward objectifying the class concept and making it useful on a national basis. He proposes a still simpler rating method, a two-item score (prestige of occupation, house rental), which he feels is accurate enough for most urban research purposes.

To some College Study committees, the Myrdal[10] viewpoint was more satisfactory than any other. This is essentially a value orientation, and it fits local facts as many teachers have observed them. It has the appeal of simplicity and it puts stress on ameliorative action.

To this Swedish social economist, race relations in our nation are primarily a moral problem. What he seems to say is that we are a democracy but, obviously, we do not practice what we preach about people. One cannot hold a basic conviction and not act upon it without paying a price, the cost often being a bad conscience, perhaps a subconscious guilt complex. One standard escape is to rationalize, to assert for instance that there is no problem of majority-minority relations, that minorities are making out all right. With the costs of ill-will what they are, why, asks Myrdal, have change efforts gone little deeper than "glittering generalities"? The need, he concludes, is for a determined nation-wide effort to end prejudice and discrimination. In this, government would play a leading role and so would public education.

From Myrdal, Warner, and others, College Study educators have tried in several notable cases to establish a foundation for their studies. Our major interests as consultants have been two: to see that educational programs were not built on static data, and to advise against the projection of a rural community viewpoint on modern urban life.

Our present society, however it is structured, is complex, dynamic, and ever in process of becoming. Intergroup relations are, in consequence, changing from year to year, almost from day to

[9] Paul K. Hatt, "Stratification in Mass Society," *American Sociological Review*, XV (1950), 216–22.

[10] Gunnar Myrdal, *et al.*, *An American Dilemma* (New York: Harper & Bros., 1944). For a critical review, Kimball Young, in *American Sociological Review*, IX (1944), 326–30.

day.[11] They are, moreover, increasingly impersonal and efficient, organized and self-seeking, with minorities making more and more use of strategical test cases. For these reasons the basic character of intergroup relations dare not be derived from the semi-static class system as described by Warner. Myrdal's view is dynamic—people in motion, people moving from something toward something. To an extent, the central core of intergroup education can be derived from *the aspirations of disadvantaged people*, their struggle for common democratic rights.

To state the point in another way, our present intergroup situation is not unlike a vast but confused game, a game guided by few rules. The setting of the game, our society at large (perhaps the world), is itself unstable, spinning about from technological change, and each change makes new demands upon the game. Because of mounting pressures, parties to the game are subjected to unceasing strain, increasing player readiness to advance his side at almost any cost. The game is intensely partisan so that, from a player's standpoint, no neutrality is possible. Any person who is not with a given side is judged to be against it. The idea, of course, is to win and to go on winning.

If this analogy is tenable, it would be in error to regard intergroup relations in present urban society as anything like an orderly, enduring system of established human rights. On the contrary, the situation everywhere is decidedly fluid, more so than any structural viewpoint seems to show. Here tomorrow, in this place or that, a new protest movement will arise, a new and determined minority-group action to secure some citizen right, for that is the nature of the times in which we live. An educator in his classroom, like a soldier at his battle station, may understand little of a total campaign. He is dependent upon communiqués, the best ones often being empirical surveys of short- and long-term trends.[12]

The second point, the projection of a primary-group viewpoint onto urban mass society, is well worth more critical thought than

[11] The same point is argued by Herbert Blumer in respect to labor and management relations. See his "Sociological Theory in Industrial Relations," *American Sociological Review*, XII (1947) 271–78.

[12] For example, Charles S. Johnson, *et al.*, *Into the Main Stream* (Durham: University of North Carolina Press, 1947).

can be given to it. In general, our experience in working on school-community problems has taught us skepticism as to the possibility of re-creating in big city environments the kind of community unity found in smaller places. It was, we believe, the homogeneity of rural and small-town people that made their spontaneous neighboring possible. In big cities, spatial nearness should not be thought of as psychological togetherness, for educational levels, tastes, interests, and the like, have become highly heterogeneous. Thus, the imposition of rural forms on urban areas, for example, the old-fashioned town meeting, is doomed to failure because their original meanings have been lost. Put otherwise, the context of community life has changed, calling for new techniques of social area organization.

Individual vs. Collective Action

Another item dropped time and again into "confusion corner" involved individual versus organized group action. From the standpoint of some educators, it seemed enough to focus on specific cases, this underprivileged child, that needy person. "If everyone would do what he felt should be done," said a college representative, "that would be all the program we would need." To the rejoinder that this could only mean "hopeless confusion," the speaker made vigorous denial.

The issue here involves a psychological (or psychiatric) versus a sociological view of human relations, an individual versus a group approach. While we are not at all disposed to argue against the former, it is the latter which we have tried to study and advance. While no one example can provide a safe basis for generalization, the following case has some bearing on the point.

A "RADICAL" RACE LEADER

Once in a southern city, the writer was asked to speak at an Urban League meeting of Negroes and whites, to share the program with a famous Negro leader. The topics assigned were "Why Whites Dislike Negroes" and "Why Negroes Dislike Whites," with the Negro speaker leading off. Not liking the setup, the white speaker decided to base his remarks on what his colleague said, a man with whom he was well acquainted and had worked.

The hall was large and jammed with people, and the chairman had some trouble in getting the meeting started. As his elaborate introduction ended, the writer joined the audience in applause until, to his embarrassment, he was told that he had been introduced. Confused for the moment, his address was even worse than it might have been. He spoke about which white person, under what circumstances, with what effects, and so on. The only virtue of the talk was that it was short, lasting less than its allotted time.

The Negro speaker arose smartly on his introduction, spreading his hands for quiet. He moved to the edge of the platform, master of the situation, staring steadily at the audience. When one could hear a pin drop, he turned and walked in measured pace to the white speaker, seated in a row of honorary guests. With the audience now excited, feeling the drama at hand, he began his oration.

Gesturing at the white man, he spoke in a voice choked with emotion, catching every ear. "You! You, my *friend,* are the oppressor! Your heel is on the necks of my people! You do them out of their birthright! You . . . You . . . ," shifting stance and striking new notes on the master race theme. No person in the audience cared to miss a word and some were urging the speaker on, much as in a religious camp meeting.

It would be hard, as suggested, to overrate the intensity of these moments, or to praise too highly the masterful performance. As point was piled on point, the Negro part of the audience stopped its applause and simply said "Amen, Amen." With the speaker pointing at us, walking back and forth, turning, posturing, but always pointing, it was easy to break into a cold sweat. We began to ponder the ludicrous idea of standing on anybody's neck, the limitations of this common figure of speech.

Fair-play tendencies in American crowds are often something to behold, to remember when people riot and run wild. The chairman had begun to close the meeting when someone shouted: "The white! Let's hear from the white!" Ignoring the request, the chairman started to ask for the benediction but he was drowned out with "Let's hear him! Let him speak! Give him a chance!" Personally, we can say that the white man did not want a chance but, at the chairman's nod, he arose to speak.

"Now," addressing the audience, "I am sure that you will agree that we have seen and heard a wonderful thing, a skilled master of the art of making people think. I do not know what comment to make, what you would like to have me say. Certainly, I have no personal defense to offer. Our times being what they are, any white can be used to symbolize a great evil, and that has been my fate. I have been called an oppressor, an exploiter of Negro people, and I am no doubt part of the social system you dislike. I dislike it also, as does every thoughtful white, and we want to see it changed.

"What I wonder most of all is if you have understood what you have just seen and heard, if you get the big point. Now Mr. Smith and I are not enemies, are we Mr. Smith? (Walking toward the Negro speaker.) We are friends, are we not? We have worked together on Urban League projects, have we not? Do you remember . . . ," the white speaker continued, exchanging memories, with the Negro nodding his head in confirmation. While completely affable, Mr. Smith had begun to feel uncomfortable, to see that his "squeeze" was being reversed.

Turning again to the audience, the speaker continued. "Now, you may indeed be puzzled, but I don't think Mr. Smith's address is hard to explain. You see, my friend is a race leader, a respected leader of opinion in his community and over the nation. He has a good many people to guide, to stimulate, to organize and collect money from. You will misunderstand him unless you see the job he has to do, the work he must do as he sees the interracial situation in this country. This is what he has been doing tonight. . . .

"This is the point, then, that I want you to remember. The battle for common rights, the fight in which we all are engaged, is an organized movement. It is what some social scientists call collective action, the action of group on group, on any number of different fronts. What we have seen, therefore, is a distinguished leader at work, a man who wants you to feel deeply about the wrongs he has named, to remember that no minority can afford to let up in efforts, nor can any self-respecting majority-group member."

Our purpose in this incident is to call attention to a fact stressed over and over, the collective nature of group action in respect to race, to creed and nationality. Interpersonal relations, for example of a teacher to an individual pupil, are important and must never be neglected. And yet overarching them, in fact giving them final meaning, are the ties and bonds of group life, the organized character of the human rights struggle on every local battle front. What this viewpoint argues, if there were time to carry it through, is the obvious need *to make changes in the social system that causes so much individual maladjustment.* Both speakers on the Urban League program were fully agreed on that. Their difference, if there was a difference, involved such factors as timing and method.

This viewpoint should not be read by any teacher as justifying the neglect of any child. On the contrary, it is a call to look outside, to inspect the forces shaping young people, to understand and teach the changes going on in our society. The United States armed services offer such a striking example that recent changes here are worth recording.

In July 1948 the President ordered "equality of treatment and opportunity for all persons" in the armed services. In June 1950 the committee appointed by the President made a report.[13] After World War I, the Navy had banned all Negroes, but later began to recruit them as messmen. Still later, it started to use them in general service ashore and finally put some on ships. At present, by committee data, *nearly half the Navy's Negroes are in general service*, with some in every job classification. Five are trainees at advanced electronics and technician's schools. Only seventeen, however, are serving as officers, and the Marine Corps still maintains separate Negro units.

In the past three years, the Air Force has made an enviable record. Prodded by high authority, no doubt, it broke up the all-Negro 332nd Fighter Wing, and began the general distribution of Negro personnel throughout the service. By January 1950 three-fourths of the Air Force's 25,000 Negroes had been integrated into mixed units. All training schools and all jobs were open to them, and all "racial strength" quotas were abolished. Commanders testified that "racial incidents have diminished rather than increased." At big air bases today, one can see Negroes and whites who sleep in the same barracks, eat at the same mess table, dance at the same service clubs, and swim in the same pools.

On the ground, the picture is not as good. The Army, with by far the most Negroes, has offered marked resistance to nondiscrimination. In World War II it kept most Negroes in transport, quartermaster, and housekeeping duties. Its experience with two Negro combat divisions was reported as not fully satisfactory. In sum, it has clung to segregation, arguing that it had to do so since most of its training bases were in the South. But in June 1950 the President's committee noted "a most heartening change." The Army had begun to mix Negroes into white units and to open jobs and schools without restriction. In April 1950 it lifted the 10 percent quota on Negro enlistments. At Atlanta's Fort McPherson, for instance, Negro and white soldiers share movie theaters, service clubs, and messes. White officers salute Negro officers with less boggling, but living quarters are still separate. "Now and then," said a Negro, "somebody will make a crack at you, but I don't pay them any mind."

[13] Reported in *Time*, June 5, 1950, p. 18.

From these facts it is evident that far-reaching changes toward equality of status and opportunity are under way. Much the same story could be told for other areas of American life, with only here and there some minor, localistic regression. Educators can do much to further these trends. Through their state and national associations, their local area contacts and services, they can pass the news along. They can, in their studies and publications, their classroom teaching and student guidance, focus on intergroup problems, searching out the shape of things, their worth and meaning from a democratic view.

SEGREGATION, COLLEGE QUOTAS, AND REGIONALISM

In these titles are three of the most debated issues in present intergroup education, questions in no sense limited to our "confusion corner." As one travels the country and visits colleges, or attends national educational meetings, these are the things that educators often talk about.

In theory, college doors are open to all students who have the money and ability to secure a higher education. In actual practice, many institutions of higher learning limit or exclude Negroes, Jews, certain immigrant nationalities, and to a lesser extent Catholics and other creedal representatives. To be sure, many of the great universities of the nation—Harvard, University of Chicago, New York University, and so on—place no racial, national, or creedal barriers to student admission.

It should be stressed that discrimination against Negro youth at all school levels differs from that against other minorities. In seventeen states and the District of Columbia, segregation is established by law so that Negroes cannot share the same classrooms with whites. They are to be provided "separate but equal" facilities, which is a myth where the tax dollar, often inadequate for either race, must be divided between the two. The ratio of fund expenditures for whites and Negroes ranges from 3 to 1 in the District of Columbia to as high as 42 to 1 in Kentucky.[14]

Of late the college "quota system," an unpublicized way of re-

---

[14] President's Commission on Higher Education, *Higher Education for American Democracy*, Vol. 2, *Equalizing and Expanding Equal Opportunity* (New York: Harper and Bros., 1948).

striicting student admissions, has come in for a good deal of research study. With space limited, we shall follow Reeves[15] somewhat in his summary of data on "the barriers faced by youth who desire a higher education."

One barrier to young people who want to go to college has been *the serious shortage of educational facilities.* On assumption that the desire to enter college would be much the same the nation over, the Connecticut study focused on the age range of twenty-five to twenty-nine years. In 1940 the percent of persons at these ages who had attended college varied from 8 percent in Alabama to 22 percent in Utah, a finding related to the number of higher educational institutions. The President's Commission found that colleges select students, in terms of academic abilities, discounting other kinds of aptitudes, skills, and interests. The New York State study found the greatest shortage of facilities in general education and technical training. This was true especially for high school students who desired one to two years of college work, and for those wishing graduate professional training.

Limited financial resources keep many young people out of college. On the assumption that parent occupation was related to family income, the President's Commission assembled data to show that the chances are two to three times better that a high school graduate will go to college if his father does professional or managerial (business) work than if he is a farmer or any kind of unskilled laborer. Youth living on farms had about a fourth of the chance of completing college as those living in cities, a finding attributed in large part to low farm incomes. The American Council study showed that three-fourths of the youth whose fathers were professional men or business executives applied for admission to college in 1947, as compared with a fifth of those whose fathers

[15] Floyd W. Reeves, "Barriers to Higher Education," *Phi Delta Kappan,* XXXI (1950), 214–24. Chief sources of data are as follows:

1. *Higher Education for American Democracy.* Report of the President's Commission on Higher Education, Vols. I-III.

2. Four reports from the New York State Temporary Commission on the Need for a State University, Chiefly Floyd W. Reeves, *et al., Matching Needs and Facilities in Higher Education* (Albany: Bureau of Publ., State Educ. Dept., 1948).

3. H. G. Stetler, *College Admission Practices with Respect to Race, Religion, and National Origins of Connecticut High School Graduates* (Hartford, Conn.: State Interracial Commission, 1949).

4. *On Getting into College* (Washington: American Council on Education, 1949).

were farmers or factory workers. By use of income tax returns, the New York State study got at actual family earnings. Where parental incomes were $9,000 per year or higher, youth were more than two and one-half times as likely to attend college as those from homes with incomes of $5,000 or less.

Geographic barriers stand in the way of college-going. In the New York State study, the percentage of youth of college age at colleges was two to three times greater in communities where colleges were located than in places having no college. Three-fourths of all New York State students attended local colleges. In the American Council study, fewer resident young people secured admission to colleges in the northeastern part of the nation than in any other region. For the nation, it was uniformly more difficult to secure admission outside the home state of the applicant than within it, and the same was true for home city.

The precise weight of *racial, creedal, and national backgrounds* has been impossible to determine. The case seems clearer for Negro students than for any other group. While Negroes make up a little more than 10 percent of the nation's population, they constitute only about 3 percent of all college students. The President's Commission reports that 85 percent of Negro college enrollment is in segregated institutions, mostly in the South. This is felt to be due to residence, economic handicaps, distribution (and shortage) of Negro colleges, white college quotas, and exclusions.

In the Connecticut study, application for admission to college was made by 87 percent of all Jewish high school students graduating in the year of the study, 63 percent of the Protestant students, 57 percent of the Catholic, 49 percent of Italian-American students, and 38 percent of Negroes. The American Council study sets the percent of high school students in the nation applying for college admission as follows: Jewish, 68 percent; Protestant, 35; Catholic, 25; with no data on race or nationality.

Many high school students apply to more than one college. In the American Council sample, the average number of applications was 2.2 for Jewish applicants, 1.3 for Protestant applicants, in comparison with 1.4 for all high school student applicants. In the Jewish student sample, a third applied to two colleges, 16 percent to three, and 14 percent to four or more.

To what extent do colleges actually discriminate on a basis of race, creed, and national origins? Of the 207 private nonsectarian institutions reporting in the New York State study, seven stated that student admission was restricted on the grounds of race, 18 on creed, with both reports judged as too low by the researchers to be representative of the state. Over half the 233 college units in the state required data other than an applicant's academic record for admission. These data comprised a photograph, record of extra-curricular activities, alumni connections, and at times race, nationality, and religion, with no college giving evidence that any of these factors had any relation to academic success. Obviously, such requirements permit discrimination if a college so elects. The Connecticut study cited similar data, leading to the general inference that "college admission practices lend themselves to discrimination" in what is probably a large number of colleges and universities throughout the nation.

In respect to graduate professional schools, the President's Commission stressed the need for more trained Negroes. In terms of population ratios, whites have four times as many dentists as Negroes, four times as many social workers, five times as many doctors, 36 times as many lawyers, and 203 times as many engineers. Of the almost 6,000 physicians graduated from the 77 medical colleges in the nation in 1946, only 154 were Negroes, and all but 20 of these were graduates of two Negro medical colleges. Of these 77 medical schools, 20 are in the South and do not admit Negroes. While the remainder are, in theory, open to any qualified student, only a third admit Negroes.

Creed, like race, has been the object of intensive investigation. Among 14 nonsectarian liberal arts colleges in New York State, five accepted about equal ratios of Jewish and non-Jewish applications; five, more than twice as large a proportion of non-Jewish applications; and four, almost four times as many. For the nation, the American Council study shows the following rates of acceptance: for Protestant applicants, 88 percent of the students; Jewish, 87 percent; and Catholic, 81 percent. Both Jewish and Catholic students took second and third choice colleges much more often than did the Protestant applicants.

In summary, all these studies agree well enough to warrant several tentative generalizations. While they show that young people who want to go to college face a number of handicaps, *these handicaps are substantially greater for minority youth.* Many institutions of higher learning, although by no means all, follow admission procedures which lend themselves to discrimination on the basis of race, creed, and nationality. Native white Protestant applicants are given priority, a fact not justified by academic backgrounds or academic success. Negro youth are grossly discriminated against, Jewish young people much less so, with the issue still in doubt as to Catholic students and native-born children of white alien parentage. Research along these lines is still in process, in fact is probably increasing, all of which would appear to be a very healthy sign in American higher education.

We believe that racial segregation in college education is breaking down, the change coming most rapidly in border state areas. It seems evident that this change has been speeded up by United States Supreme Court decisions. In the Gaines case in 1938, for example, the University of Missouri was denied the right to exclude a Negro. It was held that payment of out-of-state tuition did not constitute "equal provisions" for Negroes, a decision that has led a number of southern states to create separate colleges for Negroes, many with most inadequate facilities and with only a handful of students. In June 1950 the Supreme Court ordered the University of Texas to admit Heman Sweatt, a Negro, to its Law School, on the grounds that the law school set up by the state for Negroes was not the equivalent of the university Law School. At the same time, the University of Oklahoma was ordered to stop the segregation of Negro students in classrooms. A Negro student had been admitted to classes but put in a small anteroom.

In 1948 the "Regional Compact" was entered into by fourteen southern states and, in 1949, ratified by seven state legislatures. The ostensible aim was the creation of a few big regional universities by the pooling of financial and other resources, thus ensuring a better-grade graduate education for both white and Negro students. Since the plan provides for segregated education, it has been vigorously opposed by educators who fear the further fixation of "unlike and unequal" education on the South. In a case now pending in Maryland, the highest court will have an opportunity to pass on part of the legislation implementing the Regional Compact. A student of nursing (Negro) was rejected for admission to the graduate school of the university but told that financial provisions would be made for her to study at Meharry Medical College in Tennessee, a Negro institution.[16]

The inclination of educators to face up to the discriminations we have discussed was seen recently at an important conference.[17] Representatives of 36 national and regional organizations in higher education, along with 62 other leaders in education, were in attendance. While debate at times was vigorous, a general statement of policy was unanimously adopted. It urged, in substance, that colleges and universities do everything possible to "eliminate the use of unjustifiable criteria" in student admissions, and it defined at length desirable admission procedures. Conference level of thought is well illustrated in three of its major propositions.

> WHEREAS, It is considered undemocratic, and therefore undesirable in the United States, to deny equal educational opportunity to persons because of a quota or of segregation based on race, creed, color or national origins; and
>
> WHEREAS, It is both uneconomical and undemocratic to attempt to operate so-called "separate but equal" graduate and professional schools for Negroes and whites;
>
> *Be it Resolved* That, beginning now, these unjustifiable practices be discontinued and that students be selected for admission . . . in terms of the common good [to the nation] and evaluation of the applicant as an individual.

EDUCATIONAL LEADERSHIP AND SOCIAL CHANGE

Of all the issues tucked away in "confusion corner," the one with most emotional content involved the question of college leadership in effecting social change. Official college philosophies, as expressed by workshop participants, differed greatly by regions and otherwise, and arguments as to desirable college functions in advancing

---

[16] For detailed discussion of the "quota system," see Arnold Forster, *A Measure of Freedom* (Garden City, N.Y.: Doubleday & Co., 1950), chap. 7, "Cracking the Quota."

[17] Called by the American Council on Education in cooperation with the Anti-Defamation League of B'nai B'rith at Chicago, November 1949. See initial report, *Higher Education and National Affairs*, Bulletin No. 149, American Council on Education, Washington.

human rights waxed very warm. Early in these national meetings, the College Study policy as inferred from staff values and behaviors was called into question. An illustration can be taken from the stenographic record of a workshop for college leaders held at Trenton, New Jersey, in 1946. Someone has stated that, in his opinion, "the College Study staff has no policy in race relations," and the director's (C's) reply brings other views into the discussion.

LISTENING IN ON A WORKSHOP
FOR COLLEGE COMMITTEE CHAIRMEN

MR. C: You may be right, Mr. R, but we have not thought of staff work in exactly that way. What do you think, Mr. M?

MR. M: I think R is wrong. When you visited us last time, we talked about this, remember? We can't go very fast on race in the South, and you said that was ok. You said to do what could be done. Isn't that right?

MR. C: Yes. Do you agree Miss H [same college]?

MISS H: We are conservative at our college, whatever anyone may care to think. And we are going to stay that way.

MR. R: That is just what I mean. Conservative. Afraid to take a chance, and we call ourselves leaders. That is not leadership. I claim the College Study has no policy of honest, aggressive leadership.

MR. W: The U. S. Constitution was not made by cautious people. I have noticed a lack of courage in these discussions. We err too much on the side of caution.

MR. C: Now, Miss H, suppose you have a situation there at your college where one of your committees wants to make studies of Negro-white attitudes. Would that be all right?

MISS H: Yes, we do that right along. Our students do it.

MR. C: What about service projects for Negro children, say starting a play lot for them, supervising their play?

MISS H: We have two of these projects, as my report shows.

MR. W: But can you socialize with them, mix together, treat one another as equals, like we do here?

MISS H: No, I don't know. That might lead to trouble. In our community, white and colored people do not do that.

MR. R: That is just what I mean. You are afraid. . . .

MR. C: I think we all see now, R, what you mean. Let's get a concrete social-action situation and see how far each of us thinks it is possible to go.

MISS L: I am not following this discussion at all. When Dr. C was on our campus, he gave a big push to our intercollege (Negro-

white) visiting program. He found some extra funds for us
to use for travel. . . . Now what about that?

To these leaders of local college programs, College Study policy
seemed confused and inconsistent. Staff procedures varied from
campus to campus, as implicit in the above discussion, a condition
unsatisfactory alike to liberals and conservatives among college
spokesmen. In explanation, staff aims were to assess college conditions, to ask only that study-action committees work up to their
"calculated change potentials." For example, if racial segregation
was at issue in a specific college or community, every effort was
made to help responsible persons end the practice. If it was not at
issue, we have sought to make it an issue, to bring it up for inspection. Failing in this aim, we have gone to work on either side of
the color line, not liking the situation but doing whatever was
possible to advance white and Negro education.

We have brought up the leadership question not to defend
College Study policy, for it may indeed have been in error, but
rather to discuss the larger issue. At any moment of time one can
identify a great number of local and national groups at work to
improve race relations. All these organizations, movements, causes,
and so forth, would appear to fall into a single collective action
continuum. One type of grouping is racial, meaning a one-race
grouping. Another is interracial, for instance the Urban League,
and the third is nonracial, groupings of people where skin color
is of no consequence.

Wherever segregation is in vogue, intergroup education will
trend toward the *one-race form,* whites studying Negroes, Negroes
studying whites, with each seeking to improve the other. While
contacts across the color line can be numerous and friendly, this
will hold only for persons who accept in principle the caste system.
Genuine social relations, spontaneous and intimate, are taboo
because they imply equality of status. Interracial association is
usually steeped in ritual, as a case will show. At this Negro college,
the writer's place at a dining table was marked off by some low
screening. Asking that this be removed, a friend remarked, "Sure,
if you want, but I'd suggest that you grin and bear it. You see, you
are a visitor here. You'll be gone tomorrow but we have to live
here, to get along with whites."

Interracial groups draw members from both sides of the color line, thus creating rather personal problems of adjustment. Some Negroes will laugh at a white man's naïve mistakes, his slips of tongue and the like, whereas others will resent him, charging him with prejudice. "Boy, oh boy, that was a swell job," meaning a bit of work well done, can be deeply offensive to a sensitive Negro even when spoken by a white within a friendly context. With inter-action so intimate and multiform, interracial situations are of course ideal educational experiences, assuming the give-and-take which neophytes need when they first enter into such associations. Group action centers on goals which, if they are realized, will further social integration on a basis of individual reaction and worth.

Nonracial groups also draw members from across color lines, but racial features, past history, and other such factors, are of no functional significance. Artists and scientists illustrate this, as do some labor union members. Professors and students in mixed classes, schoolteachers and their children, may show this form of association to an extent. Interaction is on a basis of personal worth, with this person liked, that person disliked, all because of what he is as a human being. Race, if it does exist in consciousness, is neither a privilege nor a handicap. It is individual personality that counts —brains, talent, initiative, and the like.

The order in which these associational patterns have been discussed would appear to suggest the pathways our society is traveling toward realistic democracy in human affairs. "The appearance of nonracial movements," writes Glick,[18] "is incontrovertible evidence of extensive assimilation of at least some proportion of the different groups [white and Negro] into an emergent unified society." To add that this assimilation is slow, that it goes on by starts and stops, does not detract from its importance in the nation. It is found in the Deep South, as well as elsewhere, and it seems to flourish best in big-city environments.

Each of these three group-oriented movements is, in effect, an orientation toward social change, hence it implies leadership. At least five kinds of leaders can be identified: reactionary, conservative, liberal, radical, and revolutionary. In some ways this series

[18] Based on Clarence E. Glick, "Collective Behavior in Race Relations," *American Sociological Review*, XIII (1948), 287–94.

could be scaled from "right" to "left," but in other ways it is discontinuous, showing difference in kind. No assumption is made that our society is moving in any straight line; yet we believe the past decade would show significant net gains in liberalism.

The *reactionary leader* asks that a group face toward the past, that it strive to re-create earlier conditions. In race relations, this might mean a return to forced labor, or at least a rigorous enforcement of caste dominance and subordination. The *conservative leader* desires to hold a disintegrating color line, to preserve *status quo* values as the best way out of a bad deal. He knows that changes are in process but he does not want them to get out of hand, in fact would prefer to turn the clock a little back. Many good-will groups are of this sort, prominent citizens who deplore intergroup strife and fear intergroup changes. Their language is the rhetoric of liberalism but their hearts are not in it, for the "costs" are reckoned as too great.

The *liberal leader* can be thought of as about midway in a hypothetical scale ranging from the reactionary to the revolutionary. Like the *radical leader,* the liberal is pointed toward ideal public policy, that is, full equality of opportunity, fundamental human rights, and fair treatment of people. Unlike the radical, however, he believes in change as a process, a time-taking process in need of strategical planning. Thus he differs from the radical in timing and in method more than in purpose, although personality variations in leaders would offset the generalization somewhat. The *revolutionist* would resort to physical force, assuming peaceful and orderly processes failed. It is possible that all three of these leader types envision to an extent the ultimate fusion of all Americans into a unified society, implying as this does shifts in the present balances of power. Insofar as each holds a democratic philosophy, social unity would stop short of dead-level uniformity. It would contain freedom, as much freedom as found compatible with the public good, the final test being the "clear and present danger" clause under which the Supreme Court acts to preserve the nation.

What we have outlined in these paragraphs is, of course, the ideology talked over in all-college workshops and on several college campuses. Out of these various alternatives, which leader role in intergroup relations is an educator to play? Here, as indicated earlier, we could find little or no consensus among colleges, the range of choice being from conservative to radical as best these concepts could be spelled out. Choices were felt pretty much to be free, that is, "you like this, I like that, so what," although we can recall some emphasis on "teacher responsibility."

From our standpoint, the concept of *position* needs to be added to the idea of role; otherwise the latter can make little sense. Leader roles in our society have long since been institutionalized, that is, distributed among the primary institutions of every community. Had workshop discussants been labor union spokesmen, businessmen, ministers, etc., their professional role might have differed from that common to educators the nation over. For a CIO official, for example, radicalism is usually a matter of public expectation, as well as a situational demand within the union. For a teacher educator, it is as much ahead of the times as conservatism is behind them.

In expressing preference for the liberal leader role, we have been mindful of the educator's anchorage in the school institution. What kind of an institution is the school (or college) as comparative sociologists see it? Without detailing an answer, it seems obvious that the public school is expected in terms of democratic ideology to educate all the children of all the people, to show favoritism toward none. Moreover, we believe that its prime functions are to clarify issues, not merely reflect the cultural confusions, and *to lead toward the ideals expressed in all great American public documents on the rights and talents of people.* Finally, to lead is to educate, to help people understand and act on understandings, so that an educator can go only as fast as people can go.

Another set of facts has also been kept in mind in formulating this conception of school leadership. The kinds of leaders our society has produced are, we believe, the kinds it needs, and there are jobs for them all. In concluding the *College Programs* volume, it was argued that each type of leader helps other types so that the nation as a whole keeps some sort of basic balance, some necessary connection between change and stability, union and disunity, even conflict and cooperation. If this is true, the practical problem is how to start young people on their preferred leader roles, to "position" them in the social structure where their services can be of most worth.

Retrospect and Outlook

"If men are to remain civilized," said De Tocqueville long ago, "the art of associating together must grow and improve." In retrospect, it is to this art of association that the present volume has been devoted. That living and learning in freedom and decency should be called "intergroup education" is possibly no semantic accident. At any rate, we believe the deepest fissures in our common life, those most threatening to substantive unity, are cleavages between so-called majority and minority people. Our most urgent business, aside from maintaining world peace, is to remove the last semblance of prejudice and discrimination on the basis of race, creed, and nationality, to make free men free.

It was the purpose of the College Study to focus the attention of teacher educators on this aspect of human relations, to assist them in developing study, action, and training programs appropriate to their conception of local needs and opportunities. Results have been assessed in past pages, along with work procedures felt to be transferable to the profession as a whole. Change efforts, rather than study-making, have been central in our thought, plus the implications and extensions found in the growing literature on intergroup education at college and school levels.

What of the immediate future, the years just ahead? Can one foresee, for example, a nation without intergroup conflict, a nation with no form of group intolerance? We doubt it. Such a vision seems as unreal as a world without pain and sorrow, struggle, success, defeat. These processes are universal experiences, normal parts of living, preventable only to a degree. In Madach's *Tragedy of Man*, the devil exposes Adam to the future of mankind, the range of human meanness, tyrannies, and strifes. Discouraged, disillusioned, Adam asks of God: "What is the sense of life if living leads but to frustration?" God's words to Adam are "to struggle and to trust." While the author's meaning is anybody's guess, we believe that frustration without hope ends mental activity; with hope, serenity is possible, or better still from our standpoint a considered effort to master chance, to control life.

For no highly relevant reason, thought goes back to our graduate school days, to a term paper in an anthropology course. It was not much of a paper, or so the professor said, yet it had significance to us. It was a study of folklore and fable, the tales people tell when they follow freely their imagination. And what was found time and again, in the samples taken, was the motif of frustration. To deserve the princess, the hero had to slay the dragon, to conquer the sorcerer, the tyrant or villain, or else he was given some other feat of strength or cunning the like of which no ordinary mortal could hope to do. What this suggested to us was the character of everyday living, the universal presence of barriers, the importance of challenge, the use of intelligence in creative and adjustive under-takings.

The point we would make is not novel to anyone who has thought about teaching, the complex task of influencing learners. We live today in a spectacular culture, a mechanical *Schlaraffen-land* satirized by T. S. Eliot as:

> Here were decent godless people;
> Their only monument the asphalt road
> And a thousand lost golf balls.[19]

We would write no jeremiad about this culture, no lamentation over its chronic insecurity, its waves of scapegoating and hooligan-ism. We would ask simply, as did the Lynds in *Middletown,* why people work so hard, what their daily living is all about? If a teacher cannot answer, if the answer does not specify human values of a democratic nature, one might question that person's right to teach. Of course, methods are important, and so is judgment in their application, but these are the means of living, not its basic ends.

Americans are great technicians, handy people with machines. But we are dreamers, too, dreaming since our origins a startling dream. We dream of a day when all people will be treated like people, that is, in terms of personal worth, when fair play, good will, and cooperation will have great value because they will be viewed as the essentials of decent living, *the goals of our society as a whole.* This is the aim of intergroup education, in fact, of all education in human relations, and it is in this faith that educators work. One does not need success to keep this faith alive, as pleasant as success can be. He needs only to know in his heart that he is on the right road, that his destinies lie somewhere ahead.

[19] T. S. Eliot, *Collected Poems,* p. 190. (New York: Harcourt, Brace, 1936.) Used by permission.

APPENDIXES

APPENDIX A

Some Resource Agencies of Aid to Educators

1. American Association for Adult Education, 60 East Forty-second St., New York City.
2. American Association on Indian Affairs, 381 Fourth Ave., New York City.
3. American Civil Liberties Union, 31 Union Square, New York City.
4. American Council on Race Relations, 32 West Randolph St., Chicago, Ill.
5. American Friends Service Committee, 20 South Twelfth St., Philadelphia, Pa.
6. American Jewish Committee, 386 Fourth Ave., New York City.
7. American Jewish Congress, 212 West Fiftieth St., New York City.
8. American Library Association, 520 N. Michigan Ave., Chicago, Ill.
9. Anti-Defamation League, B'nai B'rith, 212 Fifth Ave., New York.
10. Bureau for Intercultural Education, 157 West Thirteenth St., New York City.
11. Commission on Community Interrelations, American Jewish Congress, 212 West Fiftieth St., New York City.
12. Commission on Interracial Cooperation, 710 Standard Bldg., Atlanta, Ga.
13. Department of Race Relations, National Council of the Churches of Christ in the United States of America, 297 Fourth Ave., New York City.
14. Department of State, Office of International Information and Cultural Affairs, Washington, D.C.
15. Institute of Ethnic Affairs, 1719 K St., N.W., Washington, D.C.
16. International Council of Religious Education, 203 North Wabash Ave., Chicago, Ill.
17. Jesuit Educational Association, 221 N. Grand Blvd., St. Louis, Mo.
18. National Association for the Advancement of Colored People, 69 Fifth Ave., New York City.
19. National Catholic Educational Association, 1785 Massachusetts Ave., N.W., Washington, D.C.
20. National Conference of Christians and Jews, 381 Fourth Ave., New York City.
21. National Urban League, 1133 Broadway, New York City.
22. Southern Regional Council, 63 Auburn Ave., N.E., Atlanta, Ga.
23. U.S. Office of Education, Washington 25, D.C.

APPENDIX B

A Minimal Bibliography on Intergroup Relations

ADORNO, T. W., *et al. The Authoritarian Personality.* New York: Harper & Bros., 1950. 990 pp.

One of five "Studies in Prejudice" sponsored by the American Jewish Committee, with other volumes in preparation. An exhaustive study of the personality traits of the authoritarian type of person. Scale data, clinical interviews, projective testing.

BERNARD, JESSIE. *American Community Behavior.* New York: Dryden Press, 1949. 688 pp.

Competition, conflict, and social planning in our present-day society, with stress on economics, politics, religion, race, and nationality. Effects on personality and society.

BETTELHEIM, BRUNO, and JANOWITZ, MORRIS. *Dynamics of Prejudice.* New York: Harper & Bros., 1950. 227 pp.

Another of the "Studies in Prejudice" sponsored by the American Jewish Committee. A psychoanalytical study of the prejudices, anxieties, and tensions of war veterans, with broad implications.

CHILD, IRWIN L. *Italian or American: The Second Generation in Conflict.* New Haven: Yale University Press, 1943. 208 pp.

A sociological (or situational) approach to problems of culture conflict among second-generation immigrant children, with analysis of three common adjustment patterns.

COLLIER, JOHN. *The Indians of the Americas.* New York: Norton, 1947. 191 pp.

General survey, historical to present times, with emphasis on changes made in U. S. Indian policy.

COOK, LLOYD ALLEN (ed.). *College Programs in Intergroup Relations.* Washington: American Council on Education, 1950. 365 pp.

Volume I in a two-volume report on the College Study in Intergroup Relations, 1945–49. Descriptions by 24 college committee chairmen of intergroup programs in their colleges, schools, and communities. Introduction and conclusion by editor.

COOK, LLOYD, and COOK, ELAINE. *A Sociological Approach to Education.* New York: McGraw-Hill Book Co., 1950. 514 pp.

Patterns of American community life and school services, with the central focus on human relations and group-process education.

DAVIS, ALLISON, and DOLLARD, JOHN. *Children of Bondage.* Washington: American Council on Education, 1940. 299 pp.

Personality development of Negro adolescents within the southern framework of caste and class. Teachable case materials.

266

FORSTER, ARNOLD. *A Measure of Freedom.* Doubleday & Co., 1950. 256 pp.

> Broadly based survey, with major attention to anti-Semitism. Factual, critical, and competent.

GRAEBER, I., and BRITT, S. H. *Jews in a Gentile World.* New York: Macmillan Co., 1942.

> A standard, scholarly analysis of Jewish life and culture, and Jewish-Gentile relations, by selected authorities.

HOLLINGSHEAD, A. B. *Elmtown's Youth.* New York: Wiley & Sons, 1949. 480 pp.

> The best analysis to date of the role of social class in a small-town public school, including pupil-to-pupil and teacher-pupil relations.

KLINEBERG, OTTO. *Tensions Affecting International Understanding: A Survey of Research.* New York: Social Science Research Council, 230 Park Ave., 1950. 238 pp.

> An integrative survey of social and psychological research on international tensions relating to world peace.

LEWIN, KURT. *Resolving Social Conflicts.* New York: Harper & Bros., 1948. 230 pp.

> A collection of papers, edited by his wife after Dr. Lewin's untimely death, defining his experimental social-psychological approach to intergroup problems. Emphasis is on anti-Semitism.

LIPPITT, RONALD. *Training in Community Relations.* New York: Harper & Bros., 1949. 286 pp.

> Analysis of an experimental workshop in intergroup relations for school people, agency representatives, and state officials. Intensive skill training, with objective evaluations.

LOWENTHAL, LEO, and GUTERMAN, N. *Prophets of Deceit.* New York: Harper & Bros., 1950. 164 pp.

> Third of the "Studies in Prejudice" sponsored by the American Jewish Committee. A psychological analysis of the techniques of agitators in translating vague hates, hopes, and fears into dynamic anti-Semitic beliefs and actions.

MacIVER, R. M. *The More Perfect Union.* New York: Macmillan Co., 1948. 311 pp.

> Nature of prejudice; a general study of strategy and tactics.

MYRDAL, GUNNAR, *et al. An American Dilemma.* New York: Harper & Bros., 1944. 1483 pp.

> Analysis of Negro-white relations, current and historical, in terms of the nation's democratic ideals, with proposals for improvement.

On Getting into College. A Study Made for the Committee on Discriminations in College Admissions. Washington: American Council on Education, 1949. 99 pp.

> Lucid, interpretative summary of a statistical study of barriers to college admission, with stress on race.

ROSE, ARNOLD, and ROSE, CAROLINE. *America Divided.* New York: Knopf, 1948. 342 pp.

> Outspoken survey of racial, religious, and national minorities in the United States.

RUNES, D. D. (ed.). *The Hebrew Impact on Western Civilization.* New York: Philosophical Library, 15 E. 40th St., 1950.

Eighteen chapters by distinguished scholars on Jewish contributions to Western culture, current and historical.

SCHERMERHORN, R. A. *These Our People.* Boston, D. C. Heath, 1949. 635 pp.

General survey of ethnic minorities, the new immigration, the Jewish community, adjustment problems and programs.

WARNER, W. LLOYD, and LUNT, PAUL S. *The Social Life of a Modern Community.* New Haven, Conn.: Yale University Press, 1941. 460 pp.

Initial volume in the famous "Yankee City Series." Major findings of the Newburyport (Mass.) study, and theoretical basis of the modern "caste-class" approach to intergroup relations.

WARNER, W. LLOYD, and ASSOCIATES. *Democracy in Jonesville.* New York: Harper & Bros., 1949. 313 pp.

A general interpretation, based on a small American city, of social class in the nation. Best statement to date of this much discussed viewpoint.

WARNER, W. LLOYD, et al. *Social Class in America.* Chicago: Science Research Associates, 1949. 274 pp.

A theory of social class in the nation, including methods of stratifying an individual or a population.

WILLIAMS, MELVIN J., *Catholic Social Thought.* New York: Ronald Press, 1950. 567 pp.

Contributions of Catholic sociologists and others to social theory; trends in Catholic social thought; applications to current social problems.

WILLIAMS, ROBIN. *The Reduction of Intergroup Tensions.* New York: Social Science Research Council, 230 Park Ave., 1947. 153 pp.

Theoretical analysis of intergroup tensions; critical study of tension-reduction programs; some general principles of ameliorative action.

INDEX

Academic education, as college course orientation, 200
  conclusions from change projects, 86–88
  course revisions in, 90–96
  critique of, 98–103
  and faculty coordination in supervised teaching, 96–97
  learning outcomes wanted in, 96–98
Acculturation, of children, 32–34
  and social roles, 34–35
Action research, 82
  as conflict resolution, 148–51
  and status research, 146–48
Adorno, T. W., et al., 38
Allport, Gordon W., and Kramer, B. M., 25, 46
American Council on Education, 255
American Council on Race Relations, 193
Angell, Robert C., 13, 154

Caste-class system, 12, 30, 243-44
Changing learners in education
  (See Education in human relations)
College leadership, 20 21
College morale and leadership, 183–86
  structure and participation, 181–83
College Programs volume, 4, 87, 116, 160, 201, 241, 260
College quota system, 250–55
College students, social action, 142–44
College Study findings, anecdotal study, 53–54
  autobiographical papers, 58–62
  community study, 76–77
  formal tests, 62–69
  group description and sociography, 77–79
  inter-test correlations, 73–74
  projective test, 69–73
  school surveys, 54–58
College Study in Intergroup Relations, aims of, 7, 257
  college programs, 9
  colleges included in, 8
  frame of reference, 10–11
  morale and leadership, 183–86
  nature of study data, 52 ff.
  organization of, 157–61
  pre-planning in, 161–63
  reality level of work, 170 ff.
  selection of colleges, criteria, 0
  staff members, 9–10, 162

(See Consultant's role)
  test forms used in, 62 ff.
Community, audit study, 136–38
  changes in, 153
  and good-will agencies, 141–42
  plan of study, 145–46
  problem clinic, 139–141
  and society, 241–46
  study-action methods, 151–52
  study data, 76–77
Community education, and group action, 223–25
  nature of, 144 ff.
  school cases of, 132–38
  strategy and tactics in, 213 ff.
  study-action methods of, 151–52
  tactics in program building, 231–34
  teacher training projects in, 138–44
  urban planning situation and, 222–23
  viewpoints toward, 153–54, 227–28
Cook, Lloyd and Elaine, 4, 6, 8, 73, 109, 123, 145, 168, 224, 235
Cooperation, social, 18, 154
Consultant's role in human relations education, 119–20, 178–79, 232–34, 247–48
Creed, nature of, 15, 16
  intercreedal understanding, 115–16
  (See Religions)

Davis, Allison, and Dollard, John, 34
Democracy, changes in, 118–19
  as change making, 233
  in human relations, 178
  and social science, 179
Dewey, John, 19, 144, 231
Discrimination, and college quotas, 250–55
  and prejudice, 17–18
  and school teachers, 88
  and U. S. armed forces, 249–50
Dollard, Charles, 98
Dublin, Louis I., 28
Du Bois, W. E. B., 51

Education in human relations, academic and group process, 88–90
  conclusions from change projects in, 86–88
  general approaches to, 81
  pre- and end-test comparisons, 85–86
  as re-education, 81
  resistance to change in, 186

THE AMERICAN COUNCIL ON EDUCATION

ARTHUR S. ADAMS, *President*

The American Council on Education is a *council* of national educational associations; organizations having related interests; approved universities, colleges, teachers colleges, junior colleges, and technological schools; state departments of education; public and private school systems; selected private secondary schools; and selected educational departments of business and industrial companies. It is a center of cooperation and coordination whose influence has been apparent in the shaping of American educational policies as well as in the formulation of American educational practices during the past thirty-three years. Many leaders in American education and public life serve on the commissions and committees through which the Council operates.

COUNCIL ON COOPERATION IN TEACHER EDUCATION

The Council on Cooperation in Teacher Education is a council of twenty national educational organizations cooperating actively in studies, experimental programs, conferences, clinics, and other projects for the improvement of teacher education. Its membership is given on the page facing the title-page of this book.